To Mary
with fond,
good wishes,

Goro

winter 1985

DISTANT DANCES

SONO OSATO

DISTANT
DANCES

ALFRED A. KNOPF ✦ NEW YORK 1980

Library of Congress Cataloging in Publication Data
Osato, Sono [date]
Distant dances.
1.   Osato, Sono [date]
2.   Dances—United States—Biography.
I.   Title.
GV1785.O6A33   1980   792.8'092'4   [B]
ISBN 0-394-50891-2   79-3487

Manufactured in the United States of America
First Edition

To
Victor,
Niko,
and
Tony

Tradition cannot be contrived or learned. In its absence one has, at the best, not history but progress—the mechanical movement of a clock hand, not the sacred succession of interlinked events.

—Osip Mandelstam

ILLUSTRATIONS

Illustrations

Acknowledgments

I would like to thank these people: Genevieve Young; Robert Levine; Peggy Tsukahira; Genevieve Oswald, curator, and the staff of the Dance Collection, the New York Public Library at Lincoln Center; Paul Meyers, curator of the Theatre Collection, the New York Public Library; the late German Sevastianov; Irina Baronova; Paul H. D. Findlay, Royal Opera House, Covent Garden; Margaret L. Nickleson, Archive Department, and B. J. Skidelsky, Archive Office, Royal Opera House, Covent Garden; Rear Admiral P. N. Buckley, CB.DSO, Naval Historical Branch, Ministry of Defense, London; Roger Debut, Chef de Protocol, Ministre des Anciens Combattants, Paris; Madame Louise Alcan, Secrétaire Général de "L'Amicale des Déportés d'Auschwitz et les Camps de Hte. Silésie"; and Peter Rossi of the French Line.

Very special thanks to Elaine Markson, my agent, who believed in me, and to Andrew M. Wentink, whose understanding help, in large measure, has made this book possible. And finally, much gratitude to Robert Gottlieb, my passionate, ballet-loving editor at Knopf, and to his staff, including Neal Jones, who oversaw the editorial production, and Margaret Wagner, who designed the book.

P R E F A C E

For many years, twenty-five or so, my husband has been urging me
to write of my dancing experiences. I always laughed and said, "I
can't write!" But somewhere, deep inside me, I was tempted to, not
so much to speak about myself, but because I feel so strongly that a
very important part of modern ballet history has not been really ac-
counted for. I speak of the nineteen thirties, the years between the
demise of the Diaghilev ballet and the births of two great American
ballet companies, Lucia Chase's American Ballet Theatre and George
Balanchine's and Lincoln Kirstein's New York City Ballet.

Ballet was scarcely talked about in those days, except by those
faithful balletomanes who went to performances, and there was very
little written about it. Grammar is not my forte, but I have quite a good
memory, and so these are my loving recollections of the people and
events of my youth. I had the very good fortune to have a patient,
skilled, and determined editor, Andrew M. Wentink, who helped me
put these memories into their present form.

New York City, 1980

DISTANT DANCES

think I am one of the few American dancers who ever saw the Diaghilev ballet at the peak of its glory.

Before that day in 1928, I had never seen a ballet before. But when my mother took me from the warm sunlight into the darkness of the large, elegant theatre, my heart pounded so that I could hardly breathe. My anticipation was so overpowering that my senses barely registered the elegance surrounding me. All that I knew of ballet was the memory of having seen a photograph of Anna Pavlova posed on her toes in front of a large wicker trunk. She was smiling; draped over her shoulders was a shawl that reached her tutu. Her striking image was the only link I had to what was about to appear on that stage in Monte Carlo.

Although there were three ballets on the program, I remember only one—*Cléopâtre*. The curtain rose and I was drawn into an awesome Egyptian setting. Four huge columns lined the rear of the stage, and half-naked stone figures loomed on either side. Slim, dark-skinned dancers in vivid costumes danced in groups and pairs until an extraordinary cortege made its entrance.

Four black men bore a casket of gold and ebony high on their shoulders. Making their way through the crowd of dancers, they finally placed their litter in the center of the stage. From the darkness of the casket they brought out a mummy. Several young women approached the motionless, upright figure and slowly unwound the many veils that encased the mysterious figure. At last the Queen of Egypt was revealed.

Near the end of the ballet, the leading male dancer began to walk towards Cleopatra, trembling so that even the muscles of his bare feet quivered. His enormous dark eyes never left her face as she handed him a goblet and commanded him to drink. He took the golden cup; as he drank, his body suddenly stiffened and, in a spasm, he arched backwards and fell to the floor. Very slowly, surrounding dancers covered the inert body with a large cloth. I thought he was dead. The final sight of his beloved, grieving prostrate over him, totally convinced me. I was dumbstruck. As we left the theatre, I told my mother I wanted to be a dancer.

There had never been any performers in our family. I was born August 29, 1919, in Omaha, Nebraska, the first child of an Irish–French Canadian mother and a Japanese father.

Shoji Osato, my father, was born in Akita, a town in the northern part of Honshu; he was the second of three sons whose mother died when he was ten years old. While still in his teens, he converted from Buddhism to Methodism. Soon afterwards he decided to make a career of photography. At nineteen, with little money and only a word or two of English, he came alone to the United States. Shortly after his arrival in California, he found work picking strawberries on a farm for twenty-five cents a day. Later, he and a friend had the idea of starting a library for the growing number of Japanese immigrants settling in California. In order to raise enough money to realize their dream, they took whatever odd jobs they could find.

To save money, Father and his friend rented a single room with one bed, and alternated day and night shifts as dishwashers in a small restaurant. This routine and the plans for their library were shattered by the San Francisco earthquake of 1906. Father gave all his savings to his friend to help him find his family, lost somewhere in the devastated city. For the next ten years, Father's love for photography developed into a profession. After working from coast to coast, he finally settled in Omaha, where he opened his own studio.

Mother's family, dating back to 1027, had produced many military men. Through the generations, her ancestors had emigrated first from Spain to France and then to Ireland. By 1781, a part of the Irish branch of the family had settled in Canada near Quebec. My grandfather, Francis W. Fitzpatrick, an architect, had been one of the engineers of the Canadian Pacific Railroad. He met Agnes Lanctot, a young French-Canadian girl; soon after their marriage, they moved to Washington, D.C. There my grandfather opened an office, leaving to my grandmother the chief responsibility of raising eight children, of whom my mother, Frances, was the youngest.

Mother was an exceptionally beautiful child with soft, brown hair, delicate features, lovely brown eyes, and a tiny gap between her two front teeth which, rather than blemishing her looks, gave her an even more irresistible charm. At fifteen, her beauty and personality so captivated the prominent theatrical producer Daniel Frohman that he offered her a stage career. Though liberal in most of her views, my grandmother wouldn't hear of her youngest daughter going on the stage. She turned him down by saying, "Mr. Frohman, you've obviously never been a mother!"

Although Mother's will to become an actress was not strong enough to change Grandmother Fitzpatrick's mind, she was a true nonconformist. Rather than wear clothes chosen by her mother, she designed her own. She smoked in public and she wore her hair bobbed, which, in 1917, was considered daringly modern. She was fascinated by everything Japanese and at eighteen decorated the Oriental Room of the Blackstone Hotel in Omaha, which her father had designed.

Visiting the hotel one evening close to the end of World War I, she saw the movie actor Sessue Hayakawa, accompanied by his wife, Tsuru, who was dressed in a kimono. With them at the dinner table was Shoji Osato. Mother found the small group fascinating. When the *Omaha Bee* sent Osato to photograph Miss Fitzpatrick for its society page a few days later, they were completely taken with each other and fell in love on the spot.

Nebraska barred marriages between Japanese and Americans, so Shoji and Frances were secretly married in Red Oak, Iowa. When news of the wedding reached Omaha, the town was scandalized. Some citizens wrote angry letters to my grandfather, demanding to know how he could allow his daughter to marry an Oriental. Prejudice nearly ruined my father's business and my parents' social life, but the Fitzpatricks stood by the young couple.

Under such conditions Mother's romantic notions about life with a Japanese husband must have disintegrated. Soon after I was born she left Father and me for Hollywood, where she hoped to succeed as a costume designer for films. Things did not work out as she had planned, and she returned to Omaha. In October 1920, fourteen months after my birth, my sister Teru was born.

In 1923 we all sailed for Japan to visit Father's family. After a month Father took Teru to Tokyo for a visit, while Mother and I stayed in Yokohama in the foreigners' residential section, a group of Western-style houses built high on the bluffs overlooking the Bay of Tokyo.

The most vivid memory of my early childhood is the moment when the great Kanto earthquake struck. At two minutes before noon, September 1, 1923, I was on the second floor of the house, sitting on the edge of the bathtub, watching Mother wash her hair. Just as she bent over to rinse it, the house began to tremble. The trembling increased and an ominous silence pervaded the air as the birds suddenly stopped singing. Then came a tremendous quake. The air was filled with terrible, tumultuous noises. The walls and the ceilings cracked, and the house began to collapse.

Mother threw herself over me, screaming "Cover your head! Cover your head!" Cowering together, doubled over almost in a ball, we were surrounded by the falling and crashing of furniture, pipes, and sections of walls. Minutes later we were half-buried in heaps of rubble but managed to crawl out and onto some picket fences that the Yokohama firemen were tearing from the ground to use as bridges across the deep fissures the quake had slashed into the earth. Fire was everywhere. It was lunchtime, and live hibachi coals, scattered by the tremors, ignited the wood-and-paper houses, spreading flames throughout the city. Mother grabbed me, and stumbling through wailing crowds and total disorder, we inched our way towards the bay. Much of the time she carried me on her back.

Twenty hours later we staggered onto the grounds of one of Yokohama's country clubs, and from there a British sailor led us to the waterfront. Oil from cracked storage tanks poured into the drainage canals of the city and flowed, blazing, into the waters of Tokyo Bay. Thousands of dazed people waited on the shore to be evacuated. Atmospheric chaos, dangerous, suctionlike air pockets, swirled around us. Suddenly the wind shifted into calm, allowing lifeboats to ferry us to safety on one of the many foreign ships anchored in the bay. Mother and I climbed aboard the *Empress of Canada*, which sailed for Kobe as soon as it was filled to capacity. We never did meet our Japanese family.

The quake struck Tokyo three seconds after hitting Yokohama. Leaving Teru in the care of friends, Father started walking the seventeen miles that separate the two cities. He found our names on a list of survivors posted on a crumbling building and for five days searched for us in the smoldering ruins of Yokohama. Finding no trace of us there, he walked on to Kobe. When he got there, Father was assured by the American consul that we had sailed for the States.

Somehow, Father managed to keep his sanity during this ordeal and was later decorated for heroism. My aunt told me afterwards that the heat of the earth penetrated Father's shoes during his long search, destroying the soles and burning the bottom of his feet. Thousands suffered far more pain, and over 140,000 people died.

On the ship I prayed every night for Father and Teru. Mother helped care for the injured passengers. Twenty-one days later, in donated clothes, Mother and I landed in Seattle. After a few weeks we went to Evanston, Illinois, where my grandparents now lived. My Aunt Corinne spent many nights walking the streets with Mother, who was left an insomniac by the traumatic shock of the catastrophe. Awhile later the Red Cross notified us that Father and Teru were safe and on their way home, but several months passed before we were all reunited. Father started work in Evanston and life gradually returned to normal.

My brother Tim was born on New Year's Day, 1925. Soon afterwards we moved to Chicago, where Father hoped to find more work. It was when we moved to Chicago that I began to become aware of my parents' personalities. Father was a quiet and reserved man whose influence on our upbringing was not as much in evidence as Mother's. He seldom answered my questions about his childhood and never discussed his family. He did tell me that he had disliked school. I never found out the reasons behind his strange habit of leaving the room if the subjects of religion or death were brought up. Because of his strong Japanese accent in English, he was short on words, but he was forceful in action. A quick slap or a spanking told us all he had to say about unacceptable behavior. Father was mysterious and unknowable to me, and it is difficult to describe the love a child has for such an inscrutable man.

Mother never laid a hand on us. She disciplined us with words, finding it very hard to be physical. She didn't caress; she didn't kiss. She explained everything in great detail and was very sure of all her opinions. She loved to reminisce about her childhood and her large, talk-loving family. I loved to hear her stories about family picnics and pony rides and the family servants she still called "darkies." Best of all were her stories about the dances she went to, accompanied by not one, but two, escorts.

The creativity and talent of both my parents compensated for their having little money. Our railroad flat in Chicago was dark and not a child's idea of pleasant, but it was warm and attractive. Among Father's Japanese treasures were a beautiful silver paper screen, with pale green water lilies painted on it, several bronze vases, and an ancient suit of Japanese armor. The armor stood on a pole in the dimly lit hallway, and it so frightened me that I would skip and whistle every time I passed by it. These few exotic objects gave our very ordinary rooms a unique, though somber, character. Every supper was by candlelight, and Mother made beautiful centerpieces out of flowers and a few dried leaves and berries. She still designed and made her own clothes and ours, and for a long time my favorite blouse was one she had made from an old sheet and trimmed with Mexican embroidery.

Though I was only six, I was aware that we had little money, despite the fact that Mother and Father never discussed money in front of us. Our friends had cars and radios, which we considered luxuries far beyond our means. Sometimes our clothes were secondhand—Aunt Corinne tutored well-to-do children in Winnetka and Lake Forest, and sometimes brought us their unwanted clothing in what we called "the poorbox." For me the poorbox was exciting because I could wonder, just a little, about what kind of children had worn these clothes. We also made a game of "Will it fit?" It was like winning a prize if it did. A real thrill was finding a blouse or dress with a label saying "Blum's" or "Marshall Field." The item I cherished most was a suit knitted in several shades of green—not particularly attractive, really, but it fit well. I called it my "spinach suit," and it was one of those things that a child becomes inexplicably attached to.

Our family life was quiet and without incident until late in the spring of 1927, when Mother made an announcement: we were going to France, the land of her maternal ancestors. She didn't say why we were going or for how long. Thrilled with the chance to take a long trip with her, I wondered only in passing about the curious fact that Father wouldn't be going with us.

We left soon afterwards, and the voyage on the small S.S. *Roussillon* was to be the first of many I would eventually make on the French Line. Tim was still too young to walk steadily, so Mother held him by a strap harness when we strolled the deck. He was a fine sailor, though, and ate everything Mother fed him, while Teru and I were nauseated for most of the ten-day voyage. But seasickness was a small price to pay for the joy of traveling with Mother, whom I adored without reservation.

Only twenty-nine at the time, Mother arrived alone in Bordeaux with a toddler and two small girls in tow. With complete self-assurance, she bypassed the usual travel bureaus, following instead the advice of a butcher who assured her that it would be nice and cheap to live in Cap Ferret on the Bay of Arcachon. Cap Ferret was not even a town; it was a hamlet where mail was delivered once a day by a little steamboat. The postal station, unused to foreign visitors, had our trunks left in the sand by the front door of the small villa Mother rented there.

Our villa was close to the water, and on the little gate hung a sign reading "Tou Ski Fo," a pun for "tout ce qu'il faut." And it *was* all that we needed. It had a dining room in the basement and a small "salon" on the first floor. Mother and Tim slept in a little room off the salon, and Teru and I had a tiny bedroom upstairs, with bamboo wallpaper that, with only a little childhood imagination, could be transformed into an exotic forest. For protection Mother kept a large pair of scissors on the table next to her bed. At night we were lulled to sleep by the sound of pine branches swaying in the wind, a world away from the street noises of Chicago.

For a short time after our arrival, Teru and I strolled down the beaches and rolled in the sand dunes in total freedom until, one day, Mother told us we had to go to school. I had never liked school and was an eight-year-old bundle of grudging, nervous apprehension when Mother took us to the little school in Cap Ferret. It was here that I first experienced the sensation of being an "outsider." Teru and I knew absolutely no French, and our Oriental faces and Buster Brown haircuts made us even more conspicuous. Our French classmates openly stared at us and giggled. Their behavior made me very self-conscious and ill at ease, and I spoke only to Teru, who became so nervous in class that, one day, she wet the bench in silence rather than raise her hand and state her need. I could only try to comfort my little sister as she wept.

But on nice days, when our classes met in an open courtyard, we giggled right along with our classmates at our teacher, who often breast-fed her infant while picking her nose. That sight never failed to amaze us, and we would rush home to tell Mother, "She did it *again!*"

Mother always gave the appearance of being cheerful, but one day she startled me. We were picnicking in the dunes and she was reading the newspaper. Noticing tears in her eyes, I stopped playing and asked her why she was crying. "Children," she answered, "a very young man named Charles Lindbergh has flown all alone across the ocean." Too young to understand the significance of the Lindbergh flight, I was chiefly concerned with my mother's reaction. I stared at her, wondering how the act of a stranger so removed from our immediate lives could move her to tears.

As the summer of 1927 approached, Mother made new plans. Without hesitation she picked us up and moved south to St. Jean de Luz in the Basque country, which Mother had heard about from a friend. The blissful blue skies and the Bay of Arcachon were replaced by rainy days and nights spent scratching at fleas.

"Monsieur, you must change those infested mattresses," demanded my outraged mother. "My children are covered with welts."

"Madame," replied the landlord with typical French hauteur, "I keep a clean house. You and your children must have brought the fleas with you from the North."

I was more than compensated for suffering the dismal weather and fleabites when I fell in love for the first time. Buddy was your typical American boy, a little blond god with very, very blue eyes, nine years old and *terribly* religious. In the garden of the Hôtel de Golf, the largest hotel of the town, I sat transfixed not only with his beauty but with the passion of his sermons. A bath towel hanging down his back, he held some of his most reverential services for drowned kittens we found while bathing in the ocean. After he had delivered his eulogies, we dutiful members of his congregation placed the animals in discarded shoeboxes, then solemnly marched in single file, with complete propriety, to the graves in a funeral ground of Buddy's choosing.

That summer most of the days were spent swimming and sunning ourselves among the striped tents on the beach. The most interesting tent to me belonged to Feodor Chaliapin and his family; I first heard the Russian language here. Splashing with the Chaliapin children in the water, I was instantly drawn to the strange rhythms and expansive sounds of my playmates' speech. I never saw the famous basso himself, but Mother did—she met him at a party and later told me that he was very charming and had flirted openly with her in a rose garden.

One night Mother and some of her friends took Teru and me to a festival in the town square. Crowds of Basques, dressed in their colorful traditional costumes and espadrilles, were all dancing the lively, syncopated fandango. As I sat watching the couples, I noticed that their arms were always held high in the air, open and rounded. Carried away by the excitement, I finally jumped up and joined the dancers. I quickly picked up the basic steps by watching a nearby couple and, when someone handed me a pair of castanets, I clacked right along with the best of them. Swept away by the rousing Basque spirit, I felt wonderfully natural while dancing, following the music easily, tossing my head, stamping my feet, and springing off the ground. The celebration ended when a figure dressed like a large bull, sparks spewing from its horned mask, charged into the crowd. I jumped back with delighted fright as it lunged close to me.

"Sono," called Mother. "Come now. It's time for bed." Reluctantly I obeyed; I could have gone on all night. As we left the square and started for home, sounds of exploding firecrackers merged with the exhilarating music.

Something important had happened to me. This was the first time I had joined into the spirit of communal happiness and freedom. I had not only followed unfamiliar steps but, without constraint or inhibition, had shared a feeling of unrestrained personal expression. Unlike my struggles to understand the formalities of classroom learning, my response to the irrepressible urge to move was quick and total. As I lay awake in bed that night, I felt that dancing was something I could do naturally, something that made me feel totally satisfied with myself without fear or self-consciousness.

Regretfully I left Buddy, who was very busy with God anyway, and St. Jean de Luz, when Mother, eager to see more of France, decided to move on again. This time we traveled with an American family in a chauffeur-driven car, heading for the Côte d'Azur. Our destination for the winter of 1927 was Menton, a town lying between Monte Carlo and the Italian border. When we arrived, the air was heavy with the scent of mimosas.

After searching for a while, Mother found a small villa overlooking a large vineyard in Gorbio, just above Menton. Surrounding the villa was a garden filled with flowering bushes and a few palm trees, and pink roses entwined the window shutters so thickly that they could never be closed. A low balustrade encircled the garden, and there were several statues of women that I found especially romantic and beautiful for their missing arms and broken noses.

My happy hours playing in the garden were cut short when Mother sent us back to school in the autumn. I hated the new school as much as the one in Cap Ferret. Again Teru and I were the only foreigners, and there was no breast-feeding now to relieve the long hours spent struggling with the complexities of French grammar. Although I was slowly learning to speak the language, I was still far from fluent, and when the teacher called me to the platform in front of the large classroom to recite what I had studied the previous night, everything would fly out of my head. Very often I would stand there not speaking at all in fear and embarrassment. I preferred daydreaming to boring lessons about Charlemagne and the Crusades; often I sat at my bench, hypnotized by the sun dancing on the Mediterranean.

After school I was free to dawdle on the way home. On the way I always stopped to watch the village women of Gorbio doing their laundry. They worked in bare feet with their black dresses hitched up about their waists. Leaning on large, flat rocks, they would soak their linens, beat them against the hard, natural surface, then hold them again in the fast-moving stream as the current carried off the soap bubbles. They chatted among themselves, and sometimes a woman would sing a love song. They looked completely happy.

The beauty and serenity that surrounded me were painful reminders of my own unhappiness. The difference in Mother's attitude towards me and my brother was becoming increasingly clear. It seemed that she never liked to hold or caress me, but with Tim she was openly affectionate in every way. Most of her references to me were to ridicule either my looks or my habits, although in a gay tone of voice. Her blithe mockery was all the more devastating for being unprovoked, but I felt instinctively that showing her my pain would make me even weaker in her eyes. So to protect myself, I withdrew and struggled to keep my face a mask, revealing nothing. Crying, shouting, petulance, running from the room, would only add to her inventory of my faults, whereas what I wanted was some of the praise she gave to Teru and Tim for their beauty, charm, and brightness. The four of us were like a tiny island adrift in an ocean of strangers, with only each other to turn to for comfort. Yet I began to be as lonely at home as I was at school. I became moody and silent. Mother now compared Teru's "Susie Sunshine" to my sullenness, which was my disguise for unacknowledged jealousy.

Seeing the Diaghilev ballet that spring swept me out of my gloom. The moment we returned home from Monte Carlo, I rushed about trying to recapture what I had seen. "We need a throne," I shouted to Teru, and she dragged Mother's chaise longue from her bedroom into the middle of the garden.

"We need jewels!" After rummaging in some drawers, we found some Christmas ribbon, which I wound around my fingers.

"Remember, there were slaves," we cried. Teru grabbed a palm frond and fanned me most willingly as I re-created the spectacle. For more atmosphere, we rushed to carry the Gramophone and any record we could find into the garden. In our version the illusion of Egypt was inspired by a Chopin étude. Everything was perfect until the "orchestra" faltered as the heat of the sun softened the wax record. Back went the couch into Mother's room, back went the Gramophone onto its shelf, and our fantasy drifted away as we were called to supper.

But as I lay in bed at night, flashes of color and music echoed in my mind. I kept seeing the dark slave reaching for the goblet. How bravely he faced his queen, how stoically he accepted his death (I probably was trying to identify with his courage). Nobody spoke, yet his body conveyed everything I needed to know. I wanted to be on that stage in that theatre, dancing with those people.

We moved again—this time to Annecy, a town high in the French Alps. With her usual knack Mother located a tiny apartment atop a large stone house. It was set in an enclosed area called Clos Nemours, which, in the fourteenth century, had been the jousting grounds of the Dukes of Nemours, whose château remained intact across the square. From our two little balconies we could see all of Annecy and the surrounding countryside spread out below. On the grounds remained a small, ruined stone tower, accented only by one narrow stained-glass window. In this place, centuries before, ladies had waited for their knights to return from battle. This little tower became my favorite secret place, and I spent my free time dancing in the dramatic setting. Sometimes I pretended to be a lady of the château—holding an invisible train, I would dance on the stones and curtsy to my imaginary knight. At other times I was Joan of Arc, leading my army into battle, arms held high. My music was the wind and the rustle of lizards darting among thick ivy. I was confident in my imagination that each step was the right one for my medieval surroundings. Dancing momentarily extinguished my loneliness.

Mother enrolled us in yet another school, this time Annecy's lycée for girls. It was a very large school, but Teru and I were so distinct from the rest that the very first day, to our delight, our classmates renamed us Thérèse and Solange. Being given French names by total strangers was our first sign of acceptance.

My teacher, Mademoiselle Davignon, was a thin, middle-aged woman, who wore her hair in a topknot. A pince-nez perched at the end of her very narrow nose exaggerated the features of her face into a caricature. One day, looking up from her desk, Mademoiselle saw me unbuttoning the collar of my blouse to show some insect bites on my neck. "Quelle horreur!" she gasped. Throwing up her hands, she rushed to my bench, grabbed me by the ear, and hauled me off to the principal's office. As I sat there, outraged by the unjust accusation of indecent behavior, the scandalized principal telephoned Mother. When she arrived, I was ordered to stand before the three women and swear that I would never unbutton any part of my clothing again. Mortified, I spoke the words they demanded, but silent rage stormed inside.

Other than the severe discipline, my main memory of Annecy's lycée is lunchtime in a big hall. Placed in front of every girl was a plate of *boeuf* "something-or-other"—which to me looked and tasted like leather floating in pale brown juice. The chore of having to eat that lunch was offset by *le goûté*—fresh white bread and chocolate—served every afternoon at four o'clock.

I fell in love again. This time, his name was Pierrot. A strong, red-cheeked, dark-haired fourteen-year-old, he lived between the château and a mysterious house with shutters tightly closed night and day. *"C'est un bordel,"* whispered my playmates. Running out of pretexts for meeting Pierrot "by chance," I finally went to visit his mother. As I sipped my glass of milk, we discussed how I liked Annecy. For no apparent reason she started telling me about her husband, who had been killed in the last year of World War I. Soon breaking down completely, she threw herself on the bed, sobbing, *"Je déteste Dieu."* I hate God! I had never seen such overwhelming despair except for the grief in *Cléopâtre*. Completely stunned at a grown-up cursing God, I silently backed out of the house. Following this scene I spent many of my hours alone trying to untangle my confusion about despair, lost love, and God.

My religious knowledge was almost nonexistent. As a child Mother had gone to a Catholic school. Father, born a Buddhist, was now a Christian. We had never been baptized at all. Our state of religious limbo so shocked Céline, a young Catholic girl who helped around the house, that she begged Mother to allow her to save our souls. Feeling that nothing could be gained or lost, Mother agreed to Céline's pleas to convert us, but said that Tim was too young.

Christmas was the day chosen for our salvation. That morning we dressed in the dark and walked, as dawn appeared, through deep snow to a large church in the center of town. The early service had already begun. Hundreds of candles shimmered in the darkness of the church, revealing a vast congregation kneeling on prie-dieus, heads bowed, rosaries in hand. Clutching the hands of our "savior," Teru and I tiptoed solemnly down the center aisle. Gradually all the heads turned in our direction, until it seemed to me that hundreds of eyes were staring at us out of the darkness. I was amazed that pious grown-ups could ever be diverted from prayer, and I was convinced that our Oriental faces distracted them far more than our small presence. Then and there I decided that my soul must remain my own. Though deeply moved by the Latin hymns and the life-sized Christ child lying in real hay, I gave up wanting to be devout.

So, unsaved, I continued life as usual, still puzzling over Life, as children do. Mother was cheerful and lively and created fun for us all. She took us ice-skating on bright winter days and, when the fierce wind from the Alps kept us indoors, she'd applaud our home theatricals.

Strolling home one day, Mother told me, with her usual enthusiasm, that she had a lover. Without a trace of embarrassment, she explained that he was Henri, the neighbor's son just home from military service and several years younger than herself. I don't remember any confession of love on her part, but the fact of his infatuation with her seemed to please her. With devastating candor she described nocturnal escapades, beginning with Henri's climbing three stories to her balcony and going so far as to enumerate physical details.

I would have preferred a beating. "Why is she telling me this?" I wondered. "What does it mean?" For an instant, part of me was flattered by her choosing to confide in me and share her grown-up secret. But a larger part was shocked and enraged. All that I immediately understood was that she had betrayed Father. Refusing to reveal any emotion, I remained perfectly silent, staring down at the path. Mother talked cheerfully for a while longer about Henri and then went on without pause to another subject. Fortunately she didn't seem terribly interested in my reaction.

Mother's compulsive honesty caused me to develop a wall of silence as a defense against her words. In trying to emphasize the appearance of strength, I began to dress myself like a boy, except, of course, when I was at school. I started to lie to Mother. I lied about what I did. I lied about where I went. I lied about whom I saw.

"Why are you late?" Mother would ask.

"I was kept after school," was my calm reply.

"You know that's not the truth," she'd retort. "Céline saw you waiting on customers at the patisserie this afternoon."

After a month or so, Mother found such exchanges intolerable. One day, she calmly informed me that she would break me of the habit for good. "Come here," she ordered.

I stood before her, not knowing what was coming, but determined to bear the punishment.

"What I'm about to do will hurt me more than it will you." (I found that hard to believe.) "Stick out your tongue," she commanded next.

I did. Quickly, she lit a match and held it for a moment under my tongue. I neither cried nor ran away, and I never lied to her again. But in that moment the great love I had always felt for her was irreparably damaged.

Dancing was my solace. Summer came and it blossomed when I found a partner, an audience, and an accompanist all at once in the person of Mother's new friend, the elderly composer Albert Bertelin. Years before he had been a pupil of Jules Massenet and now, during the winter, he taught theory and composition at the Schola Cantorum in Paris. Walking by the lake one afternoon, Mother had met him and they had fallen into conversation about their mutual love for music. Almost immediately he had invited us to join him in cheering a bedridden friend.

As we entered an elegant but dark apartment, Bertelin was already playing for his friend, an invalid antique dealer. Tall and thin, with a pointed grey beard, Bertelin was the picture of refinement seated at the grand piano. I remember that even on the hottest days, he would wear a formal black suit and stiff collar. Mother stood beside his chair and sang songs by Fauré and Chausson. A tenderness and vulnerability totally unfamiliar to me showed through the sadness and longing in her voice. Even for a child, the contrast to her outer brightness was strangely disturbing, and I was too uncomfortable to watch. Music must have been a vital part of her being, for it released depths of her nature that she normally concealed.

"Sono, why don't you dance?" she would ask after a while. Bertelin would improvise at the piano, and I would respond by jumping to my feet and following his music as closely as I could. Totally unselfconscious, I played a game with the music, matching every change in rhythm with my dancing.

The praise of the grown-ups that followed our improvisations made it a real joy for me to perform. I had never danced for anyone but myself, but now I was being watched and taken seriously. They actually liked what I loved to do! Their admiration made me feel pretty, while at home I had only felt cloddish and even ugly.

Our lovely musical afternoons came to a close with the added treat of tea and sweet cakes. Walking home at dusk, I wandered dreamily beside Mother, who was more subdued than usual. Making that invalid man smile gave me a sense of value: dancing not only made me happy, it also brought happiness to someone else. The security of feeling that I could do something well made me feel less lonely. Dancing meant more to me than ever.

In the spring of 1929, at Easter, Mother, at the urging of some American friends, decided to join them in Paris. So she made us some new clothes, packed up the household, and we were off for a short visit. We stayed at the Hôtel Castille in the Rue Cambon. Exploring the neighborhood, we found the House of Chanel down the street and the arcades of the Rue de Rivoli nearby. I loved the luxuriousness of the hotel—pink eiderdowns on the brass beds, café au lait and croissants brought to our room on a tray by a man in striped trousers, and a silent electric clock that I used to stare at in wonder.

From the moment we set foot in France, Mother had kept an account of our expenses. I remember watching her every night, making lists in a little tan notebook, particularly during our sojourn in Paris. Father sent us money every month, and each letter from Chicago reminded me of how far away he was and how he was missing all our fun. I wondered if he was lonely but was far too preoccupied with our endless adventures to dwell on him.

On nice days we went sightseeing in the morning. Afternoons, dressed in our new clothes, we walked with Mother along the Champs-Elysées, rolling our hoops down the wide promenades. We often joined the crowds of children gathered at the Rond Point to watch the guignol shows. In a mixture of fear and delight, Teru and I squealed and cringed along with other children as the puppets, their voices screeching, violently whacked each other over the head.

All the sights were wonderful, but the highlight of our stay in Paris was a benefit concert to which our friend Bertelin invited us. Once again my heart palpitated as we entered a large theatre, this time the red-brick edifice that was the Trocadéro (the present site of the Palais de Chaillot). All that I remember of the concert was a little girl about my own age. With long black hair falling to her waist and enormous black eyes, she was the most beautiful girl I had ever seen. What made her not only beautiful but mysterious to me was that she danced on her toes. As she waltzed alone onstage, first offering the single rose she held to the audience, then pulling it back, I noticed that the music for her dance seemed vaguely familiar.

"Albert," I whispered, plucking at his sleeve. "I think I know that music."

"I'm glad you remember, Sono," he whispered back. "I call it *Danse Lente* and I wrote it for you after one of our improvisations in Annecy."

This beautiful child onstage, dancing to *my* music, was Tamara Toumanova. I wanted nothing more than to dance myself, and my happiness would be complete.

Easter vacation over, we returned to Annecy and our routine of horrid lunches, delicious *goûtés*, family picnics, my handsome Pierrot, and medieval fantasies.

One day in the fall of 1929, Mother announced, without explanation, that we had to go home. Amidst our packed trunks and suitcases, I stood alarmed and confused by the sight of Mother weeping as she went from room to room on our last day. Back in Chicago I noticed grim grown-up faces all around me. I didn't know what the stock market was, but something that had happened to it made everyone frightened, and some had even killed themselves.

I was very happy to see Father after two years and thought Mother would be too. Unable to understand the difficulties between them, I wanted them to be happy together after their long separation. But as time passed, I sensed that, although they never argued or got angry at each other, something was missing. Mother never called Father "dear," or "sweetheart," or even Shoji. Speaking to us, she referred to him as "Osato" or "your father." He seemed as remote as ever. Their behavior was always calm and polite, but I never saw them kiss or touch or give any of the signs of affection that a child notices. I remember seeing Father relaxed and quite gregarious when his Japanese friends came to play cards and drink, but when they left the house, he became silent again, retreating into his darkroom.

The somberness of life in our little apartment went unrelieved on the outside. Walking to school every day, I passed breadlines of downhearted men of all ages, waiting for a cup of soup. Others stood on street corners selling apples. The sight of many of them without socks, and with safety pins holding their coats together, made the meaning of poverty very real to me. The gleaming muscles of Cleopatra's slave, the happy hours of dancing to Bertelin's music in Annecy, and Toumanova's exquisite beauty all belonged to another world. The gaiety of life in France receded from reality into memory.

My relationship with Mother continued to be strained. It was hard keeping up with her alternating barbs of painful sarcasm and acts of generosity. She often made me sulk, but she could thrill me as well by exposing me to what she knew I loved most. Once she took me to the Auditorium Theatre to see the great Spanish dancer La Argentina. All alone onstage, Argentina, with feet stamping beneath a cascade of ruffles flowing from the base of her arched spine, generated an audience-gripping electricity. An incredible range of sounds poured from her castanets. They purred like muted whispers, then fired off a staccato volley in unison with her rapidly tapping heels. Framed in smooth black hair, her oval face seemed grave and a little sad until a dazzling smile set it aglow.

After the concert we went through the stage door hoping to meet her. In a bathrobe Argentina sat at her dressing table. She was much smaller and thinner than she appeared onstage, and streams of sweat ran through her thick makeup and down her neck. I could not believe that this subdued, exhausted woman was the same tireless, vibrant dancer I had seen only minutes before. As I stared, Mother spoke to the only other person in the room. Sitting demurely in a chair next to Argentina's dressing table was a tiny blonde woman whose feet, I remember, didn't even touch the floor. She introduced herself as Mrs. Adolph Bolm. Mother mentioned that I loved to dance.

"Oh, you like dancing!" she said. "Come to my husband's Christmas party at studio."

No one had to coax *me* onto the floor at that party. Bolm's son Olaf grabbed me by the hand, and we polkaed wildly around the room. Having the time of my life, I was oblivious to Mother talking to the Bolms at one end of the studio. Later that night she told me what they had talked about.

"It's all arranged," she said. "I had a long talk with Mr. Bolm and he has agreed to accept you as a student." I was ecstatic! I threw my arms around her in gratitude. A few weeks later, early in 1930, I reentered Bolm's studio for my first ballet class.

Nothing I had ever seen or done prepared me for the absolute discipline of the ballet class or the complex vocabulary of movement demanded of me. Bolm was a stocky but handsome middle-aged man with graying hair. He was dressed in soft shoes, bright purple stockings, knickers, and a starched white shirt. He demonstrated steps far more than he spoke. He had such a thick Russian accent that I could hardly understand the French names for the steps he showed. None of those French words he used had the same meanings I had learned for them in France. I thought *battement* meant beating, but in ballet it means a kind of a kick.

At the time, I was so bewildered by Bolm's instructions that I couldn't think of him as a "real" dancer like La Argentina. I later learned that on the opening night of the Ballets Russes in Paris, twenty-one years earlier, Bolm, as the Chief Warrior in Fokine's Polovetsian Dances from *Prince Igor*, drove the audience into such a frenzy that they tore out part of the orchestra railing.

Improvising had come naturally to me, but now I had to learn to mold my body to a particular form. Feet had to be placed facing in opposite directions in fifth position, straining to "turn out" the legs from the hip. I had to round my elbows and avoid broken, drooping wrists and stiffened fingers. After years of hanging my head in front of Mother, I now had to raise it and look serenely forward.

The newest member of the class, I felt terribly self-conscious about my ignorance. I was desperate to catch up and learn as quickly as possible what the other students already knew. I soon discovered that the best way to do so was to watch. My eyes learned faster than my ears. I adjusted my body to what I saw but still felt miles behind the others. There were no shortcuts, and the class had no time to stop and wait for me. Inspired by memories of Toumanova and the Russian ballet, I struggled along as unobtrusively as I could.

Everything seemed to conspire against me. The bus I took after school from the North Side of Chicago down to the studio in the Loop invariably made me late for class. Pounding up the stairs to the dressing room in a rage, I could hear the music beginning the class. Even then my problems were not over. Mother had turned a ruffled purple nightgown of her own into my practice dress, because a plain black or pink tunic would never have satisfied her. As a result, I was constantly trapped in the dressing room, frantically trying to shove my arms through a welter of confusing straps, while the piano played for pliés.

The memory of those first classes is colored by a feeling of terrible desperation. I wanted to be on time and to look like everyone else. More important, I wanted to learn all the steps right away, regardless of whether I understood what they were about or not.

Bolm left for San Francisco two years later. Berenice Holmes, one of his students, took over the class. She was a blonde beauty with perfectly arched feet and a lovely classical technique. Not knowing that she had danced for years with Bolm's Ballet Intime and Chicago Allied Arts, creating the role of Polyhymnia in Bolm's version of *Apollon Musagète*, I often wondered why she was a teacher rather than a ballerina in some company. But I was grateful for her classes and inspired by her beautiful body. She was extremely patient and always took the time to be explicit, particularly about the correct placement of the arms and shoulders. She demonstrated comically how they should *not* look, and then how they *should* look, which was certainly a faster way to learn than listening to lengthy explanations.

Thanks to a scholarship Berenice gave me, I was taking several classes a week with her by 1932. Slowly the alien movements became easier. I began to love Berenice and, as I devoted myself to emulating her, my self-consciousness slipped away. I had less trouble with my arms and head than with my feet. Berenice singled me out for individual corrections in class and worked tirelessly with me on my worst problems. She had a special gift for teaching. She uttered the French terms with an almost musical precision and demonstrated as full out as any performer. She spoke without sarcasm, and I treasured her direct words and interest. I began to make real progress and spent more and more long hours at the studio. During my summer vacation, I took two classes a day.

On rare occasions I would practice at home, proudly showing Teru the five basic positions of the feet and some exercises from class. She reacted by laughing and would imitate me grotesquely. I got so angry that I stopped dancing for her and kept my ballet strictly to myself. Dancing was no joke. It was the most important thing in my life. At the studio I was treated like an adult. Sharing the intimacy of after-class conversation and a sandwich in her dressing room, Berenice showed me the same respect that she gave her close friend Ludmilla

Speranzeva, a character dancer who had performed in Balieff's *Chauve-Souris* and who was now the teacher of a modern dance class given at Bolm's studio.

My "debut" was scary and exciting. As part of our school recital at the Pabst Theatre in Milwaukee, Berenice had choreographed a solo for me called *The Little Shepherd* to music from Debussy's *Children's Corner Suite*. Warmed up and eager to begin, I couldn't resist parting the curtains for a peek at the audience. Berenice pulled me away. "That's *not* the way professionals act," she told me. "Don't you realize that if you can see the audience, they can probably see you as well? They must never be able to see you backstage. It destroys the illusion."

I didn't mind her gentle scolding and loved her for even hinting that I might be a professional. A few moments later I felt for the first time the mounting nervousness that becomes stage fright. I forgot not only that I was a professional, but the steps of the dance as well. The music played and my mind went blank. I improvised as best I could until I found my place in the music again, finishing my dance in the proper pose, curled up on the floor as if drifting off to sleep.

The studio became my life. I became more outgoing and talkative as my twelfth and thirteenth birthdays passed, largely because of the self-confidence Berenice instilled in me. Outside the studio I talked only with casual acquaintances. Teru's lighthearted mockery and the climate of tension between my parents kept me aloof at home, but I used to have long, serious conversations with a blind man who sold apples on the street near our house. He told me sadly that before the Depression, he had been a well-paid musician. I confided to him that my dream was to be a dancer.

School was intolerable because it had nothing to do with dancing. When my teacher called upon me to review last night's homework, I would stand petrified, consoling myself inside with the incantation, "In five years it won't matter. In five years I won't be here. In five years I'll be someplace else." I was bored and lonely among my classmates (one of whom was the daughter of a gangster), and I preferred playing hooky. I spent some days in a bookstore on Michigan Avenue, chattering nonstop to the owner or whoever would stop long enough to listen, as I thumbed through the books on the display table. For one period of nearly two weeks, I'd wave goodbye to Mother every morning, and instead of going north, I'd take the trolley south into the Loop. There I'd spend most of my day at the movies. The school eventually notified Mother that I was missing from class, and I had to go back to school, but the haunting image of Greta Garbo in *Streets of Sorrow* kept rising from the pages of my schoolwork for months.

The brightest spots in my life were the performances for which Mother bought us gallery tickets. She sought out the most extraordinary dancers of the day. One night we saw Uday Shankar and his exotic troupe from India. Another night she took us to see that passionate gypsy Vicente Escudero. I remember being frightened, but fascinated, by the macabre portrait of a madman danced by Harald Kreutzberg. Dressed in white pajamas, he moved spasmodically, his shaved head held at a stilted angle, staring at a flower, and let out a long agonized scream in the middle of the dance that made me gasp. I was really puzzled by Mary Wigman. At one point she sat on the stage, picked up her foot by the ankle, hit it against the floor with a thud, and spun once around on her buttocks! Her meaning was completely lost to me and I nearly laughed out loud. The German girls in her company, with their short-cropped hair and stocky bodies, seemed very ungraceful. By comparison, the ballet dancer's body, with its long line and smoothly muscled limbs, became even more appealing. Mother made sure that I understood that Wigman was revolutionary, and I could see that Kreutzberg was dramatically expressive, but my sights were set on ballet alone.

One cold night in February 1934, the phone rang as we sat at dinner. Her voice filled with excitement, Berenice told me to bring my toe shoes and practice clothes to the Auditorium Theatre, where Colonel Wassily de Basil's Ballet Russe de Monte Carlo was appearing. She said I had to get down there immediately, because it was the last night of the engagement and she and Ludmilla had arranged for me to audition for the company! I shrieked, dropped the phone, and ran around the room in circles, completely hysterical. "Settle down, settle down," Mother urged. She calmly helped me gather my clothes and we set out for the theatre.

Before the curtain rose on the first ballet, I sat sounding out the Russian names in the program syllable by syllable. "Tamara Toumanova." That name I remembered. But I nearly tied my tongue in knots trying to pronounce "Leon Woizikovsky" and "Tatiana Riabouchinska." Sitting high in the gallery for my second look at the Russian ballet, I was mesmerized by the tiny figures below, bathed in blue light. In billowing white tulle the dancers moved in perfect unison through Fokine's *Les Sylphides* with such silent poetry that I held my breath.

I was too nervous and excited to notice the rest of the performance; all I could think was, "I'm going backstage! I'm going to see them in real life! I'll be right there onstage with them!"

Backstage was total chaos. Stagehands yelled back and forth as they lowered scenery from cavernous flies towards the maze of wicker costume trunks onstage. Men in henna-brown makeup of Polovetsian warriors, with fierce, slanting eyebrows, packed their cosmetics cases on top of the trunks. Ballet fans, programs and pens in hand, milled around looking for their favorites. I was surrounded by snatches of talk and shouted directions in Russian, French, and English.

Somewhere in all this commotion, one dancer, still and cool as a mannequin, stood out dramatically. She wore high heels, a chic black suit, and a small black hat. I knew by her pale beauty and regal bearing that she must be a ballerina. I had to tear my eyes from the sight of her as a disembodied hand dragged me away to change clothes for my audition. I was led to a cleared space at the rear of the stage, away from the confusion.

With a casual wave of his hand, a tall, gaunt man in full evening clothes and round eyeglasses motioned me to begin dancing. I pulled myself together and, after a pause, started to dance part of a little dance Berenice had choreographed for our class. I danced as much as I could remember and then stopped after only a minute or two. The man spoke briefly to Mother, then turned without another glance at me and walked away. I rushed to Mother and demanded, "What did he say?"

"He doesn't speak much English," she said matter-of-factly. "He told me in French, 'We'll take her for three years. Go home and reflect.'"

I stood rooted to the floor. What that man had told Mother hit me like a bolt of lightning. He wanted me. I had a chance to become a dancer! I could go with the Russians and dance! Suddenly, my fantasies had become a reality.

For the next two months I lived in a daze, barely conscious of eating or sleeping. I drifted along, thinking only of my new life. The tall, pale man who had chosen me, untrained as I was, was the director of the Ballet Russe de Monte Carlo, Colonel W. de Basil. He had invited me to join the company in April, after they returned east to Philadelphia from their West Coast engagement.

Concerned about sending me off at my age with no one to look after me, Mother and Father would say, "You'll be gone for months. Where will you live? Who will take care of you? How can you manage alone? You're not even fifteen!" Their questions were rhetorical—not really aimed at me. Long after I had gone to bed each night, I heard their voices rise and fall, judging, weighing, assessing every angle of a problem that I wouldn't even admit existed.

Mother came up with a possible alternative to my going so far for so long. "Instead of going with the ballet," she suggested, "why not study with George Balanchine at the new school he's just opened in New York?"

"Go to *school*?" I cried in dismay. "The only school I want is the Russian ballet. If I don't go with them now, I'll never get the chance again."

"But we don't know anyone in that company," Mother said. "And I can't leave home to chaperone you myself. Who will take care of you? You're simply too young."

"If you *don't* let me go," I wailed, "I'll run away." I saw myself trudging along the road to Philadelphia, with a hobo stick over my shoulder and my toe shoes dangling behind me.

My adolescent threats had nothing to do, I'm sure, with the decision Mother and Father finally made. I think it was crucial to Mother that she allow me the chance to pursue my own life as she had never been free to do. They must have reasoned that the Colonel knew what he was doing in selecting me. He was a businessman, not a sympathetic friend. If he had been sufficiently convinced of my ability to accept me on a permanent basis in less than five minutes, why should my parents think they knew any better? There was, perhaps, also the reason that, despite the way she spoke to me or judged me to my face, Mother must have privately believed in me more than I thought she did.

To mollify Mother, I later auditioned for Mr. Balanchine in New York. Standing at the barre I told myself that this audition was as much a pretense as my solemn oath before the school principal in Annecy. Going through the motions Balanchine indicated, I was repeating joyfully to myself inside, "I'm going with the Russians! I'm going with the Russians!"

The morning I left home, Father posed me near a window and took my picture, straining to smile without showing his concern. Grandmother Fitzpatrick bought the bus tickets to Philadelphia for Mother and me. The bus pulled away from the platform and Father grew smaller and smaller in the distance. I sat beside Mother in tears, torn between the grip of familial bonds and my determination to seize my one chance.

When we reached the Hotel Sylvania in Philadelphia, we found the entire company rehearsing *Swan Lake* in one of the large public rooms off the lobby. Pulling me from Mother's side, one of the girls took me to a corner and began showing me some steps. I didn't even have time to be surprised. "What's this?" I asked, stumbling a bit in my street shoes as I followed the steps.

"Is coda, Act Two," was the terse reply. "Understand?"

"Sure," I said, without the faintest idea what a coda was.

"In line here. Look, others. Now—go!" She gave me a little shove and I ballonnéed out between two dancing strangers.

I had no time to be shy or nervous. I had to catch up, had to learn the steps, had to remember every word and every movement I was shown. It was like the first day of Bolm's class all over again, only *this* time, it was the real thing—the Ballet Russe!

As our line moved forward, a thin man in ordinary dark trousers and a white shirt sat facing us, his body tensed like a coiled spring as he concentrated on the rehearsal. The minute I saw his enormous black eyes, I was positive he had been the Slave I saw die in *Cléopâtre*. He showed no surprise at seeing a "swan" ballonné by in a brown wool dress and oxford shoes.

We were excused from rehearsal and shooed off the floor by a tall, balding man with a paunch, while several older, obviously more important dancers began to rehearse. I paid no attention to where Mother was, but slipped into a straight chair at the side of the room from which I could examine the people around me.

The women appeared to range in age from about sixteen to their late twenties, and the older ones among them, some of whom smoked and wore heavy beaded mascara, looked incredibly sophisticated. The younger girls wore no makeup. Their hair was pinned neatly in pigtails or chignons and they wore short black tunics to the tops of their thighs and black woolen tights. A few, like me, were dressed in street clothes. On average, the men seemed slightly older than the women, from their late teens through their thirties, and some were even getting bald. Their behavior around the women seemed totally uninhibited. They were all virile, dynamic, and very flirtatious. Everyone spoke Russian mixed with French.

At rehearsal a few days later, I had my first brush with the Russian males' candor. Two of the older men sauntered over to my chair during a break. Without a word they planted themselves squarely in front of me and looked me over from head to toe. Their eyes finally focused on my breasts. They stood there and stared, making unintelligible comments in Russian to each other out of the sides of their mouths. I was mortified, but I tried to appear nonchalant. I folded my arms across my chest, hunched forward in my seat, and fixed my eyes on the floor. With their view hindered, they lost interest in me and strolled away as cockily as they had come.

As the days passed, I saw that that sort of behavior was typical of the Russians. I was the first Japanese to join the Ballet Russe and also the youngest member of the company. The women were as curious about me as the men, and I was no less curious about them, so we all spent a lot of time staring at each other. Mother had always taught us that staring was rude, and I had felt the misery of being the object of staring eyes many times in France, but there was really nothing rude or hostile about the undisguised curiosity of the Russians. In fact I found their unabashed interest rather refreshing. Their casual friendliness soon put me completely at ease.

During the stay in Philadelphia and the week in New York that followed, I spent most of my time observing. I would stand in the wings every night to watch performances, and I attended every rehearsal. Since the Russians' English was so limited, I couldn't join in their conversations very much, but by just being around and watching everything that went on around me, I began to feel like part of the company.

Formal arrangements for my future with the company were being made. The colonel suggested that I take a Russian name. I refused. "Sono is like Sonia," I said respectfully but firmly, "and Osato looks just right next to Obidenna's name." He must have been rather surprised at the vehement reaction of a "little girl," and, just as surprising to me, he let the subject drop. My name remained my own.

My spirits soared when I got my first weekly paycheck for twenty-five dollars and my own passport. I was slightly miffed that on the passport I was classified as a student rather than a dancer, because of the child-labor laws, but it was a small price to pay for the independence of earning my own living. Sailing for Europe with the Russians would release me from the ties of my childhood more completely than I had ever imagined. I didn't know it at the time, but Mother had finally arranged for two guardians to "watch out" for me—Jan Hoyer and his wife, Nathalie Branitska, two of the older dancers, who had been in Diaghilev's company. Even if I had known at the time that I was going to be "taken care of," I doubt if it would have dimmed my eagerness to sail. I was ready to go even if I had to cross the Atlantic in a shoebox.

Mother and I stayed at the Wellington Hotel on West Fifty-fifth Street during the New York engagement. We shared the same bed, and the last nights we spent there, I lay awake listening to Mother trying to muffle her crying in her pillow. I wanted to put my arms around her and comfort her, but the years of reticence bound them to my sides. I was sad to be leaving her, too, but the happiness I saw for myself in my new life dominated even grief.

On April 21, 1934, Mother returned to Chicago and I sailed for France with the Ballet Russe de Monte Carlo.

B allet Russe de Monte Carlo. How grand those five words sounded to me, and what an illustrious group of dancers performed under that title! Like all past and present ballet companies, ours was structured in a definite hierarchy. As I entered the corps de ballet, I studied the ranks of talent and experience that loomed above me. "Cleopatra's slave" led all the others.

The incomparable Leonide Massine was our leading male artist and also maître de ballet. After years as Diaghilev's protégé and choreographer, Massine now had the responsibility of rehearsing de Basil's company for performance, and of keeping the Balanchine and Fokine ballets, as well as his own, in top condition. He also danced every night. He was noticeably thinner and paler the day we sailed for Europe than on the first day I had seen him at the Hotel Sylvania.

His closest contemporary was Lubov Tchernicheva, the wife of Serge Grigoriev, our regisseur. She was quite tall—five foot six, I would guess—and imperious in her bearing. Admiring her flawless complexion, patrician features, and brandy-colored eyes, I could easily believe the rumor that King Alphonso of Spain, a patron of Diaghilev's, had been one of her most ardent "admirers." Trained at the Maryinsky in St. Petersburg, Tchernicheva had joined Diaghilev's company in 1912 and remained with it until his death seventeen years later. She no longer danced on pointe but appeared in the leading roles of Schéhérazade and, later, Thamar. She was also our teacher, and company class, which she taught every morning at nine o'clock, kept up our high technical standards.

Alexandra Danilova, a much younger alumna of the Maryinsky, was our reigning ballerina. Chic and immaculate, whether at the barre or on shipboard, she was the elegant dancer I had noticed backstage just before I had auditioned. To me, "Choura" was the personification of style. Her taut line, magnificent legs, and finesse left an indelible mark on her roles in *Swan Lake, Les Sylphides,* and *La Boutique Fantasque.* Just the shaking of her petticoats as she entered as the Street Dancer in *Le Beau Danube* was enough to prompt a wave of thunderous applause from any audience. A sense of humor, sharp at times, masked her fatigue and sore muscles, but she made no attempt to hide her pique at the plottings of the mothers of her costars. There had been no stage mothers at the Maryinsky, and Choura had no patience with intrigue.

The dark, compact Polish dancer Leon Woizikovsky was not as handsome as Massine, but he had inimitable dynamism and charm. He had been one of Diaghilev's prized character artists, and he adored dancing as much as he did women, drinking, and gambling. His memory was phenomenal. In a revival of a ballet, whenever there was any doubt about a step or the tempo, the solution was always, "Just ask Leon. He knows."

Tamara, Tatiana, and Irina were our teen-aged ballerinas, distinctively individual and each chaperoned by one or both parents. Tamara Toumanova was still one of the most beautiful girls I had ever seen. Her large, glowing black eyes were typical of the people of Georgian Russia, and her perfect features were framed by coal-black hair that lay like ravens' wings on her olive cheeks. In 1928, Diaghilev had spotted her dancing in a Russian cabaret in Paris, where Tamara, aged nine, was performing to support her family. Without makeup offstage, she looked soft, sweet, and fifteen, but onstage she became intensely dramatic. She attacked rather than approached motion, yet the upper part of her body and particularly her arms moved with fluidity and grace. She was a superb technician and concluded a series of fouettés with five pirouettes before stopping dead still on pointe with such precision that she never ceased to amaze dancers and audiences alike.

The featherweight, bounding Tatiana Riabouchinska looked as ethereal as a Botticelli nymph. With platinum hair, gaunt cheeks, and golden eyes, tiny Tania seemed too frail for her profession. But within her bones lay a reserve of enormous strength and stamina, enabling her to jump and move with lightning speed. The air was her natural element. In it, her movements seemed effortless and her comfort so complete that she never panted and hardly ever perspired. Her dancing radiated a tenderness or childlike gaiety. Her interpretation of the Prelude in *Les Sylphides* was windborne. Tania's mother chaperoned her teen-aged daughter, as did Tamara's and Irina's parents. But for me, Mamitchka Riabouchinska's romantic past made her special. A year after I joined the company, we were touring America and, as we sat on the train, Mamitchka told me her Tolstoyan story.

An officer noticed a beautiful girl skating one day on the frozen Neva and instantly fell in love with her. Mamitchka was very poor and had only one skate. The officer not only offered her another skate but proposed marriage as well. She married him and entered into Moscow society, where her beauty captivated all who saw her, including the Tsar's private banker, Riabouchinsky. Riabouchinsky swore he would kill himself if Mamitchka did not become his. He wounded himself, Mamitchka divorced the officer and married Riabouchinsky, and Tania was the second child of their impassioned union.

The third ballerina was Irina Baronova, just fifteen years and one month old when we sailed. She was fair and blue-eyed and had a radiant smile. Her voice was unusually low and musical, and her sense of humor was bawdier than Choura's. She had quickly picked up some American slang words, along with some naughtier ones, and "Okee-dokee" was her favorite expression. Her arms and hands were very long, her waist tiny, her breasts full; her body already had a womanly voluptuousness. She danced flowingly, giving as much importance to the small steps that connected larger ones as she did to a final grand pose. At fifteen she was already a remarkable actress, each portrayal of her different roles skillfully thought out. Her interpretation of Odette in *Swan Lake* was regal but retained a human warmth. In *Le Beau Danube*, dancing a secondary role for a short time, she was a true soubrette, earthy and comical, with just a hint of arrogance making the part a real delight, for she also possessed an irrepressible sexuality.

Another young dancer was the dark and temperamental David Lichine, son of a Cossack mother and a Jewish father. He had been an expert soccer player before joining Ida Rubinstein's company in 1928 and never became a classical dancer in the strictest sense. He was not "turned out," his feet were not beautifully arched, but he exuded an animal vitality and was exceedingly virile. The first time I saw him, Lichine was standing outside his dressing room at the St. James Theatre in New York, yelling, *"Qui a du coton?"* I couldn't understand why he would need cotton for a performance. "Is for legs ven he vear tights," explained one of my older Russian friends. It seems that he glued the cotton to his calves so they would have the contours Lichine thought attractive. He brought this same kind of attention to detail to his dancing, infusing it with startling theatricality and sharpness of attack.

The seventeen-year-old André Eglevsky was also a premier danseur and the breadwinner of his family. His magnificent, strong body moved like a panther's, and his beautifully arched feet landed onstage without a sound. His gray-haired mother never took her eyes off him, either in class or in performance. He tossed off pirouettes as easily as I tied the ribbons of my pointe shoes.

The other male soloists were Roman Jasinsky and Yurek Shabelevsky, both blond, beautiful, and modest young Poles. Of the two, Jasinsky possessed the more classical line. His body was more delicate than Eglevsky's. He resembled the statue of Mercury. Shabelevsky was shorter and more muscular. His powerful thighs gave him the strength to perform grueling Russian character dances with real energy and ease.

There were sisters in the company. The first pair were Nina Verchinina and Olga Morosova, who were born in Moscow and raised in Shanghai after the Revolution. A stunning blonde, with slanting blue eyes, Nina was considered the intellectual of the company; she was always reading, and her dance training had included the Rudolf von Laban method of movement as well as ballet. Her sister Olga was pert and pretty, with reddish hair and an upturned nose. She was not as interested in reading as Nina but preferred to talk. She danced with animated grace but always a beat before the music.

The other sisters were Tamara Sidorenko, later Grigorieva, and Galina Razoumova, who also differed in looks and temperament. Tamara was thin and about five foot seven, which was considered tall in those days. She had green eyes and a dimple in her cheek, and she danced with an authority that stemmed, no doubt, from an awareness of her own exceptional beauty. Her sister Galina's body was rounder. She had light brown hair and her eyes were even bluer than Baronova's. Her feet were the loveliest in the company, curving like pigeon breasts, yet deceptively strong. They were the hallmark of the powerful technique she had acquired from the teaching of Olga Preobrajenska, one of the generation of great Maryinsky ballerinas that included Egorova and Kchessinska.

There were five English dancers in the company. Betty Cuff had become Vera Nelidova; the colonel had renamed Prudence Hyman, Polina Strogova; and Lisa Serova had been Elizabeth Ruxton. Edna Tresahar was the fourth English girl. The only Englishman was Algeranoff. "Algie," as we all called him, had been in Pavlova's company and spoke Russian fluently, but I never knew his real name.

The backbone of the company was the group of older, experienced dancers who had been with Diaghilev: Tatiana Chamié, Nathalie Branitska, Galina Chabelska, Lara Obidenna, and the Polish men Marian Ladré and Jan Hoyer. The character dancer Edouard Borovansky had come from Czechoslovakia via Pavlova's company.

But, though she stayed only a year or so, the true glamour girl of the company was Nina Tarakanova. I was fascinated by stories of her mysterious ancestor, a Russian princess who had died in a tower and was eaten by rats, but I was *amazed* by her popularity with young men no matter where we danced. Even on one-night stands, she somehow managed to develop a social life, and every night as we left the theatre, young men would rush backstage, imploring us, "Where is Nina Tarakanova?"

I was too seasick on the S.S. *Champlain* to do more than lie in my bunk and try to remember all the difficult new names in my life. My roommate, whom I don't even remember because I was so ill, stayed in our cabin only long enough to change clothes before scooting off through tourist class, where we were, to first class, via the kitchen. The leading dancers, with the exception of Danilova, paid extra out of their salaries for first-class cabins, while our tourist accommodations came out of the company budget.

I was so afraid to eat, for fear of losing it all, that I lay in bed, too weak to move. Near the end of the voyage, Hoyer carried me to a deck chair and bundled me up in blankets. There I lay, watching those energetic dancers playing shuffleboard and deck tennis. At eleven in the morning and four in the afternoon, stewards on the decks passed out either crackers and bouillon or tea and cakes. Without losing a moment from their games, the dancers would wolf down as much as they could, while I sat wondering how they could eat and play when I couldn't even walk. But after a while, my mind drifted away to thoughts of the honor I had received so soon after joining the company.

Shortly before sailing, we had presented the first ballet based on an American subject in our strictly Russian repertoire. Archibald Mac-Leish, who had won the Pulitzer Prize for poetry in 1933, came to Massine with a libretto. *Union Pacific* was the result of their collaboration. Albert Johnson, another American, designed the sets, and Irene Sharaff did the costumes.

The ballet depicted the furious race between the Irish and Chinese laborers, competing from opposite directions at top speed to be the first to complete their stretch of track to the proposed midpoint of the new American railroad. To evoke the historical atmosphere, Nicolas Nabokov worked a lively arrangement of railroad and cowboy songs of the 1860's into his score. Baronova danced Lady Gay, a Western courtesan; Lichine was her Chinese lover, supervisor of the Oriental workers; and Eglevsky danced the leader of the Irish team who competed for Lady Gay's favors. Appropriately, Massine cast Toumanova as a Mexican beauty. She was partnered by Woizikovsky and Shabelevsky as Mexican peons.

Most important—to me, that is—Massine, the bartender, cast me as his assistant, a Chinese barboy. I did everything I could to make my simple actions clear. In a scene that took place in a big tent, I wiggled through the crowd of rival laborers and bargirls, carrying a tray high in one hand and, after dancing a few simple steps, served drinks to all my customers. Later in the scene, when a fight broke out, I whacked some of them over the head with a bottle. "Make hit real," Massine instructed me, "but don't hurt dancers."

The jumble of choreography seemed clear enough to me, even with everyone in practice clothes, but Toumanova's dance remained a mystery. Every day I watched her practice small, intricate steps in a tiny circle, and every day I wondered what she was doing. Since no one had any time to explain anything that wasn't pertinent to the moment, I didn't understand her solo until the day of dress rehearsal. When she started to dance on pointe inside the rim of a huge straw hat, every step made sense.

DANCES

Irene Sharaff dressed me in a high-collared red-and-white tunic, mauve trousers, and a little round hat. The trousers had significance only to me. In Annecy I had worn pants as my armor, the symbol of strength. Now I saw them as the first sign of my acceptance into the world of the Russian ballet.

During the rehearsal period for *Union Pacific*, I was wondering how Massine was going to show the laying of the rails. The answer came the day after I read my name on the call sheet one night: *"Répétition à dix heures—Union Pacific, 3ème scène."* All the women, I among them, were to be waiting in the wings, dressed in long-sleeved brown jumpsuits and matching cloth helmets. The Chinese and Irish laborers carried us, stiff as boards, two by two, from the wings, laid us head to toe until our inert bodies formed the tracks. Later on, during the long tours, the mothers stood by sometimes to serve as replacements. Fully costumed, they too stood ready in the wings. Lifting them with extra care the men would whisper, *"Nu,* Mamitchka, *pai dom*—let's go!" At those times the men lugged on the rails with grins as bright as the footlights.

Massine went to great lengths to capture the authentic period flavor. In New Orleans he learned the cakewalk from an old black man. After absorbing the essence of the dance, he created a wonderful solo for himself. As the Barman he wore bright red highbutton shoes, a large apron over black-and-white checked trousers, a red wig, and thick white makeup with an enormous moustache and thick eyebrows. His dancing blended the wonderful precision of the old American steps with the breadth of his Russian emotion and never failed to bring down the house. Sometimes, he just *had* to repeat the dance, it was so good. During the applause and whistles, Massine sauntered back to the bar where I was busy cleaning my glasses and tray. Breathing heavily as he leaned on the bar, he would look straight at me and wink.

A wink was totally out of keeping with his offstage manner, which was polite but aloof. Smiling back at his nearly unrecognizable sweating face, I couldn't believe that he and I were sharing the same stage. I was overwhelmed by the joy of being singled out for a solo role so soon by a great man I thought had never even noticed me.

Union Pacific was the distinct hit of the 1934 spring season in New York. My dream of dancing with the Russians came true even before we left America, and I felt that my little solo was a good omen for the future.

By the last evening on the ship, I was sick of being sick. I wanted to be part of the fun that my seldom-seen roommate was enjoying. I got out of my berth, stood on very shaky legs, and put on a lovely evening dress that Mother had made for me. After slapping on some makeup to cover my wan, green face, I wobbled through the kitchen and up to the Grand Ballroom.

"Der you are, Sonitchka," the dancers greeted me warmly, "You look sterrible—drink champagnski, quick!" I grabbed a glass, gulped some down, and within minutes was waltzing away. Whirling across the floor with Shabelevsky, I felt my strength return. Only two months earlier I had been agonizing over schoolwork in Chicago. Now, giddy with wine, I felt like the sun dancing on the Mediterranean outside the schoolroom in Menton. I was fourteen, free at last, and sailing to a new life.

We sighted England the next morning. I stood alone on an upper deck watching the low shape rising from the dark sea as screeching seagulls circled the ship. The following morning we docked at Le Havre. I was guided past our mountains of cheap trunks and suitcases and through the long ordeal of customs. All the Russians were traveling on Nansen passports, identification cards for displaced persons that had been introduced by the League of Nations in 1922. These passports unfolded like small accordions, and each one was closely scrutinized by the customs officials, a process that kept us aboard ship long after all the other passengers were gone. At that time I simply couldn't understand why I was passed by with a glance and a stamp, while Danilova, Toumanova, Baronova, Riabouchinska, and all those great artists were examined suspiciously. The answer was the dark-red American passport I carried.

The train ride to Paris reminded me of Mother, Teru, and Tim, and I was suddenly very homesick. But the feeling passed. Jan Hoyer and his wife, Nathalie Branitska, found us rooms in a small hotel in Pigalle, quite near the Casino de Paris. An old brass bed nearly filled my small room, and lurid orange zebras galloped across the purple wallpaper.

"Natasha, *qu'est-ce que c'est, ça?*" I asked, pointing to a strange object resembling a porcelain bedpan standing near the sink in my room.

"*C'est un bidet,*" Branitska answered. The word meant as much to me as "coda" originally did. So I used it to soak my underwear.

That spring we were engaged for a short season at the Théâtre des Champs-Elysées, which was far from Pigalle. Rising very early to be on time for nine o'clock company class onstage, I had to take two buses to reach my stop at the Rond Point. Chestnut trees and lilacs were in bloom, and their fragrance mingled with the delicious smells of coffee from the cafés that dotted the long route to the theatre. Despite the heady blend of sensations, I entered the theatre and dressed, at last, in proper black practice clothes—the dancers' uniform which, since the shortages of World War I, had replaced the diaphanous pastel tunics the Diaghilev dancers had customarily worn.

Watching me at the barre, one might have thought I was exactly like all the other dancers. But I was painfully aware of how far their techniques surpassed my own. Hoping to make myself, if not invisible, then as inconspicuous as possible when we left the barre, I would sneak into the back line of the class, where the men practiced, instead of taking my place among the girls.

My difficulties increased as the class progressed. The barre work presented no problems; neither did the opening exercises in the center of the room, nor the adagio exercises, for which I had both feeling and ability. But as the tempo picked up for the jumping and beats, I fell further and further behind. For the last half hour, the women changed into pointe shoes to practice. Unlike the rest of them, I had been dancing on pointe for only a year and a half. My feet and ankles were still not very strong, and I had barely mastered the entrechat six, a vertical jump during which the legs crisscross each other several times in the air.

The other girls had been on pointe for years and consequently had developed the strength and control needed to perform both beats and pirouettes confidently. The strongest technicians in the company were the girls who had been pupils of Olga Preobrajenska—they turned like tops, and could execute four or five pirouettes as easily as I raised my arms. As I struggled with the difficult fouetté, a pirouette in which the dancer is propelled into turns by a whipping motion of the free leg, they calmly whipped off sixty-four of them. The girls who had studied with another great teacher, Lubov Egorova, competed laughingly with the Preobrajenska students as the class ended, often performing their fouettés with their arms folded behind their backs or resting on their heads.

I had never seen such feats performed with such ease and grew more self-conscious the more I watched. But only Mme. Tchernicheva commented on my problems. "Don't sit on leg. Pull more up," she would say. And I would try again. While friendly rivalry was as much a part of our life as the rosin box, each dancer competed seriously only with herself. The class was a constant reminder of the absolute ideal which we were striving to attain. Though unskilled, my own efforts were the same as everyone's. Each of us was concerned with her own progress, and I was grateful that the other girls focused attention on themselves and not on me.

After class one day, Eglevsky led me to the prompter's box on the side of the stage to watch the rehearsal of an orchestra scheduled to give a concert in the Théâtre des Champs-Elysées after our short season there. We settled ourselves in the small place and I peered through the grille at the conductor. "Why does he sing so loudly?" I asked André. "He's not even on key. And look at his left hand. Why is he vibrating his fingers on his chest?"

"It's Toscanini," André whispered in French. "He was a cellist. When he wants a *fortissimo*, he makes his chest a cello and shows it there instead of pointing with the baton."

I looked back through the grille, with a little more understanding, at this musical legend, and I could feel, even from our secluded vantage point, the intense energy that infused his every look and gesture.

Before we left Paris, another man, many years older than myself, tried to captivate me. My guardian, Jan Hoyer, appeared without warning one night in my little hotel room. I chatted with him for a while; suddenly he grabbed me and kissed me hard, full on the mouth. The taste of wine and tobacco on his wet lips was revolting. I was terrified by his panting and the wild look in his eyes and, trembling, pushed him away. He backed off and quickly left the room. Afraid that he would try it again, I resolved that I would leave his care and live by myself once we reached Monte Carlo after our Paris season.

Shimmering in the May sun, Monte Carlo was my talisman. There, as a spectator, I had first seen ballet. Now, six years later, I had crossed America and the Atlantic to become part of the Diaghilev heritage as a dancer. I don't remember our performances, but dancing in rehearsal was more thrilling than any applause. My feet touched the very studio floor on which Nijinsky, Karsavina, and Fokine had once danced.

I paid little attention to the troublesome details of "real life." Having decided to leave the care of Hoyer and Branitska was one thing, but knowing where to go by myself was another. I was too shy to ask another girl to be my roommate, so, mindless of cost, I moved into the same elegant hotel where Danilova was staying.

I revered the great ballerina who, on many occasions, had shown concern for me. Our friendship developed gradually at the hotel. I was increasingly embarrassed by my technical flaws and, foolishly, would skip the morning class, which was optional, arriving at the theatre only in time for the daily ten o'clock rehearsal.

Many of those mornings, I knocked softly on Choura's door after breakfast and sat with her as she prepared herself for the day. At the theatre I saw the public ballerina, true to the Diaghilev tradition, dressed impeccably in pastel-colored tunics with matching headbands. She wore hand-knitted leg warmers over her pink tights and some-times pinned a small diamond brooch on her tunic. In the warm morning sunlight that filled her old-fashioned room, filled with the fra-grance of mimosas, I leaned my elbows on her dressing table and watched the private ritual of a glamorous woman making herself up for the day.

In lace-trimmed underclothes, smelling deliciously of face powder and Coty's L'Aimant, she dabbed touches of green eye shadow above her beautiful greenish eyes. Delicately, she spat on her mascara and fringed her eyelashes in black. I loved her the way I had loved Bere-nice, for no condescension marred the intimacy of our conversations. Choura treated me as a friend and I treasured those hours in her company.

When my hotel bill was handed to me on the last day of our stay, I was appalled by the amount, thinking my only extravagance had been an occasional bottle of Perrier water. I simply couldn't pay the bill and, still stunned, went to explain to de Basil. "I'm very sorry, Vassily Grigorievitch," I began, "but I will not be able to leave Monte Carlo with you. I will have to stay here and wash dishes until I can pay off my hotel bill."

He smiled at me and said, "Don't vorry, I pay."

Leaving him, I felt weak with relief. I had a new maxim for my future life: Never live in the same hotel where a ballerina stays. But, more important, I learned that I never need fear the colonel again. For one who seemed so severe, he had remarkable sensitivity for problems that were not his immediate concern.

We made the long, tiring train trip to Barcelona, sitting on hard, wooden upright seats in third-class cars crowded with Spaniards who traveled not just with suitcases, but with vegetables, chickens, and children as well. I particularly remember Barcelona at sunset. The city lay under a soft, mauve sky, the warm air filled with an aromatic blend of fish, olive oil, and pine trees. The sounds of splashing fountains and mournful Spanish songs filtered through the tall shutters at my pension, where every morning a little girl brought me a pitcher of water and a basin for my bath.

Something within me responded to Barcelona's aura of warm, drowsy sensuality. Although I couldn't express why in words, I began to feel at home, and I relaxed into our new schedule, altered to suit the slow pace of the city. A siesta now followed our morning class and rehearsals. At four o'clock, when the afternoons grew cool, we resumed rehearsals until seven. Performances were at ten, and since I danced in only a few ballets and was still used to nine o'clock bedtime, I had difficulty staying awake.

But the prospect of a late supper with my new friends always gave me a second wind. After the performances, some of the older dancers would take me from the Teatro Liceo through the old, winding streets near the Ramblas to a nondescript restaurant called Los Caracoles, which they told me had been discovered by Pavlova. Inside, garlands of onions hung from the ceiling and dozens of chickens rotated on spits in a huge blue-and-white-tiled fireplace. After trying a few dishes on the menu, I discovered *langostas*, cool spiny lobster dipped in freshly made mayonnaise which, with chunks of rough brown bread, became such a favorite that I never ate anything else. I was rather timid about drinking alcohol until the dashing Woizikovsky urged, "Try! Try! Is good for you!" I had my first taste of the local white wine, Manzanilla. Long past midnight, I strolled back to the pension as the others sang bits of Russian love songs. I can still see some of the men dancing a few tipsy mazurka steps through the silent streets of sleeping Barcelona.

After the long hours of silence onstage or in class, relaxed meals like those at Los Caracoles loosened everyone's tongue. The conversations often turned to the subject of sex, especially the girls' virginity or loss of it.

"Vat you think," someone would say, "does she sleep with him?"

"How should I know, *dushka?*" would come the reply. "I don't hold candle!"

These conversations gave me an idea of the differing attitudes of the men in the company towards the girls. Some were reserved, some "normal," and some truly lecherous. The most boisterous ones were disdainfully called *moujiks*, peasants, by the older women.

I was often embarrassed by the matter-of-fact attitude towards sex in the Russians' conversation, but my curiosity was naturally aroused, and after a while I found their candor quite engaging and started to realize that my carefully cultivated inhibitions were pointless in their company. "What's wrong with what they're saying?" I began to ask myself. "They're just saying what they think. It's not hurting anyone." Soon I was eager to join in.

But on the subject of sex, I certainly had nothing to add to what they already knew! My sexual knowledge consisted solely of Mother's description of human procreation, delivered several years earlier in our kitchen in Menton, during a hailstorm. Tim was two and not interested, while Teru found the whole idea hysterically funny. I was confused by the idea of "the daddy's seeds planted in the mother's stomach" (for those days a far more advanced theory than storks dropping babies down chimneys), and I imagined large weeds with babies sprouting from them like buds. When I was eleven, I was kissed through a window screen by a boy from Boys' Latin School in Chicago. My idea of a passionate kiss was pressing your tightly pursed lips violently against someone else's, until the Hoyer episode scared that notion out of me forever. The more I thought about the subject, the more bewildering I found it.

Mother's explicit truth-telling extended as far as the revelation about her lover and "planting the seeds." Father never said a single word about sex, except two warnings imprinted in my mind just before leaving Chicago. "If a man touches you," he said, "I'll kill him." And then, "Don't get married. It spoils everything." Putting those two thoughts together, even a fourteen-year-old girl knew she had no option but to forget the whole thing!

Of all the men in the company, I felt most at ease with André Eglevsky. André was only seventeen and seemed as naïve as I was. Unlike Lichine—a volatile, temperamental man—André was a calm, level-headed young boy with a healthy, boyish sense of humor. During rehearsal breaks, we would climb together to the roof of the Teatro Liceo for ten minutes or so of sun bathing. All of Barcelona was spread beneath us, and we lay, motionless in the sun, breathing in the fresh air after hours of being cooped up in a dark theatre. André's mother kept a sharp eye on him, and never looked pleased to see us together. Despite Mme. Eglevsky's disapproving glances, my attraction to his gorgeous, virile physique and my fascination with his powerful, feline grace and superb technique developed into a terrific crush.

André's great forte was pirouettes, and from a single preparation he could do twelve turns, increasing or decreasing his speed by altering the position of his arms, which he extended away from or brought closer to his chest. He could also do entrechat dix, which no one else could. "Why can't I turn more than twice?" I would ask him.

"Come, I show you," André said, and when there was time, he would coach me in a corner of the studio. He would turn five times slowly and finish in a tight fifth position. Then I would try, but even after his thoughtful, patient instructions, two pirouettes were all that resulted.

In class I still felt embarrassed. The mirror was a ruthless critic, and my mistakes were instantly visible to me. Though it was "dancing," and necessary to improve my technique, "class" was still a word with fearful implications to me. I suppose the agony of the classroom, any classroom, was still with me. However, when class ended and rehearsal began, my self-consciousness fell away. I concentrated so deeply on grasping the style and the steps of a new ballet that in a matter of moments, I felt totally free, like a new person, though dressed in the same clothes in the same setting.

There never was enough time for analytical discussions about the "why" or "how" of the movements we rehearsed and practiced. Sometimes Massine or Grigoriev said, "Slower" or "Go more front." The "what" we had to do, the choreography, was our spokesman and text. Most often the phrase was "Icho rass, encore," shorthand communication that we understood immediately. Everyone knew his place, his position among the others, and the tempo and movement called for. Words merely pointed out the discrepancies between what we were doing and what we should be doing.

We watched each other, we listened to the music, we danced, and we sweated. We did nothing else for eight hours every day. For those hours we didn't miss conversation or gossip or any other activity. I always loved the silence of rehearsal and wondered for years why I found it so profoundly moving. Now I know that the mystery of the silence is that the eloquence of beautiful bodies in motion, or any elegant gesture, is swifter and truer than any verbal communication I have ever witnessed.

After several intense, fast-paced rehearsals, I was ready to make my debut in *Les Sylphides*. For some reason I was assigned a dressing room by myself, tucked away in some corner of the theatre, far from the stage. Alone in my isolated room I made up with great care, my mind shifting nervously between the hasty rehearsals and the vision of serenity that the ballet had conjured in my mind since I had first seen it. At last I was ready. As minutes went by, and more minutes, my nervousness increased. I could hear nothing. I dashed out of my room and ran through several corridors until, from high in the fly gallery, I looked down at the stage, three stories below, and saw white figures moving in a blue light. I had missed the curtain! Aghast, I stood in the dark, with tears streaming down my face. Then I raced down the stairs to the stage. Someone in the wings said, "Wait!" When several dancers danced in unison near the wing, I was told "Go!" I found my place among them and continued on, hoping that my abrupt entrance hadn't been noticed by the audience. After *Les Sylphides*, Grischa, who assisted Grigoriev, told me that I must always be alert to his calls of "half hour," "fifteen minutes," and "onstage!" which he yelled out in both Russian and French.

The first day in Philadelphia I had learned that the tall, balding man who dismissed the corps de ballet rehearsal at the Hotel Sylvania was the regisseur, Serge Grigoriev, and that backstage his word was law. He too had been trained at the Imperial School in St. Petersburg and then at the Maryinsky Theatre as a dancer-mime. Later he became the regisseur of the Diaghilev company for its entire life, from its first performance in Paris in 1909 to its final one in London in 1929, when, on July 26, Diaghilev came backstage to wish his dancers a

*My father took
these photographs
of me and of me
with my sister, Teru*

With my mother and with my father

*Our living room
in Omaha*

*My brother,
Tim*

*My mother
in Omaha*

*In costume
in Menton, France,
1928*

*Chicago,
1929*

1934   1934

1936

1945

happy holiday. On August 19 came the terrible news that Diaghilev had died in Venice.

Holding the same title in our company, Grigoriev had the responsibility of running each performance. He also directed many rehearsals, paid us our salaries, and fined us for unexcused tardiness. He was always strict, sober, and proficient, whether adjusting light cues or doling out discipline. I felt that this last task demanded tact, since he had to control fifty-two dancers, mainly volatile Russians and Poles, and the mothers, who were ferociously protective of their children. He handled it all, and we all knew that a rebuke from Grigoriev demanded obedience and respect.

Shortly after my inauspicious debut in *Les Sylphides*, our Barcelona season ended. Late in May we left Spain for a two-month season at London's Royal Opera House at Covent Garden.

My first view of the Opera House was a great disappointment. Its name led me to expect a palatial building rising grandly in the midst of a large park. Instead I found it among a maze of alleys crammed with vegetable, fruit, and fish stalls. Rumbling carts and agile Cockneys balancing towers of baskets on their heads jostled past the stage door. But the theatre was large, if not very grand from the outside, and, after my secluded cell of a room in Barcelona, I was relieved to be sharing the corps de ballet dressing room in the basement. It was a large, dark hall, quite near the orchestra pit, made pleasant each night as we prepared ourselves by the obligatto of all the musical instruments tuning up. Over the sounds of the deep, bellowing tubas came the piercing trumpet solos from *Petrouchka*.

Unlike Paris, London was a very warm city, filled with friendly, lively people. On my way to the theatre each morning, I was cheered by a Cockney fishmonger who was never too busy to greet me with a hearty " 'Ello, Miss!" Smoking his pipe, Mr. Jackson, keeper of the stage door, sternly screened all visitors, but always welcomed the performers warmly.

The attendance of our audience verged on outright devotion. Before the premiere of a new ballet, a crowd would queue up overnight on the sidewalk behind the theatre. Equipped for their vigil with folding stools, Thermos bottles, and blankets, they patiently waited through the night until morning came, when they besieged the box office for gallery seats. The rich devotees sent enormous bouquets on such nights. The flowers were piled backstage where we would invariably stop to examine them as we hurried between our dressing rooms and the stage.

"Ooohh! Choura got more than Irina tonight!"

"Yes, but look at the *size* of these roses! They're for Irina."

While the gallery rained choruses of bravos on their favorite dancers, the flowers were formally presented onstage during the curtain calls, when the ballerinas' feet often disappeared in the profusion of blossoms. The ballerina would pick a single flower from the bunches in her arms, as the ovation continued, and bestow it on her partner with a special smile that said, "Thank you for supporting me so well." In return he would kiss her hand as the curtain fell.

This tender ritual was a great favorite of mine. I believe it originated spontaneously at an Imperial performance many years ago in Russia, and was universally adopted because it proved to be so effective. To this day the romantic exchange of wordless gratitude moves me as deeply as it did the nights I watched from the wings at Covent Garden.

Whatever bouquets couldn't fit into the stars' dressing rooms were distributed to members of the corps de ballet and to a steadfast group of admiring balletomanes, the firemen of the theatre. Throughout the season, the whole backstage area was fragrant with the scent of lilies.

The generous London audience expressed their appreciation with lavish supper parties to which not only the stars but the entire company were invited. I'm sure our hosts were amazed at the way we drank gallons of champagne and devoured the hot and cold food served at their buffet dinners. We waltzed happily, among men with military decorations and ladies with elegant gowns and sumptuous jewels, until early in the morning.

But London was not all flowers and champagne suppers. The schedule of classes and performances never let up. In between class and the stage, we were being rehearsed by Massine for a revival of the 1919 version of his ballet *Les Contes Russes*. The problem of resurrecting the ballet after its long absence from the repertory was difficult, even though the former Diaghilev dancers added their recollections to Massine's own. Head cocked intently, remembering the Liadov music, they would start to dance.

"*Nyet*, arms not up here . . . later . . . next phrase," one would comment.

Massine would look, and then murmur, "*Da*, you are right."

He showed no anxiety during the tedious process. His quiet manner indicated that the ballet would be ready on schedule, though I couldn't see how. We could have been a group of archaeologists patiently piecing together the fragments of a mosaic.

Entering the rehearsal room one morning, I spotted a small woman in street clothes, standing near Massine. "Who's that?" I asked.

"Is vife of Stanislas Idzikowski, from Diaghilev," Branitska explained. "Has phenomenal memory."

The little woman stood as if in a trance, listening to the music. Then she slowly lifted her arms on either side of her head and began moving them, her body and feet all at once. The rhythmical pattern she repeated was so involved, like patting your head and rubbing your stomach simultaneously, that it took me several rehearsals to grasp the movements for just a single bar of music. The dance she taught us, stored in her mind and body for over fifteen years, revealed Massine's penchant for unusually syncopated arm gestures. He seemed drawn to geometric motions with the hands held flat. Contrasting these with the limpid, asymmetrical curves of the arms and necks in Fokine's *Les Sylphides*, and both of them with the steps of *Swan Lake*, my mind became a hodgepodge of conflicting styles. But sorting all the movements out, I learned, is an integral part of a dancer's life.

I made friends in the dressing room with one of the English girls, Prudence Hyman, who had danced with Marie Rambert's company. A few years older than I, Prudence took the time to help me in rehearsals and also helped me to find my way around London. After the performance we would run together for the late bus to Chelsea, where she had found me a room in a boarding house for "single ladies." She insisted that I should not make the trip alone, although I was still having trouble staying awake until the last ballet. Many nights, waiting for Prudence, I would curl up on the rolled backdrops stored backstage and fall asleep to the lilting waltzes of *Le Beau Danube*.

When time permitted, we went together to the ballet. Prudence was naturally eager to see her old friends, and took me with her to the Ballet Club, where she had danced before joining us. Founded in 1931 by Marie Rambert, who had assisted Nijinsky with the original staging of *Le Sacre du Printemps*, the Ballet Club danced at the matchbox-sized Mercury Theatre in Notting Hill Gate. When the curtains parted on that minuscule stage, I was introduced to British ballet.

I saw the petite Alicia Markova dancing a cakewalk on pointe with great humor, the delectable grace of Pearl Argyle, and the voluptuous Diana Gould, now Mrs. Yehudi Menuhin. Hugh Laing, as handsome as Valentino, impressed me most of all in a performance of Frederick Ashton's *The Lady of Shalott*. Both the execution and subject matter of Ashton's work seemed miniature by contrast to our lavish repertory and Russian style, but they were no less evocative. I was truly impressed and moved by the English dancers, not only because of their fine technique but because they were such extraordinary actors as well.

By this time, several of the Russians were helping me to adapt in various ways. André suggested that I take a class with the great teacher Nicholas Legat, who had been a principal dancer at the Maryinsky and one of the first to notice Nijinsky's exceptional talent. Taking Eglevsky's advice, I went to Colet Gardens one morning and entered Legat's large studio nervously. Danilova, Massine, and Eglevsky were there already. As I took my place at the barre, I noticed André smile and nod approvingly at me. After the barre, the others took their places at the front of the room for the center exercises. As usual, I edged my way to the back of the studio.

Legat was a short, round man, sixty-five years old, who conducted the entire class from the piano. He was the only teacher I ever saw accompany his own lesson. Swiveling around on his stool to face us, he sang the music and simultaneously moved only his hands, flicking them rapidly in front of each other and off to the side in small gestures, indicating the particular steps and combinations he wanted next. Then, without a word, he spun back to the keyboard and launched back into the music.

All the dancers moved immediately on his first chords and sailed into a series of steps his hand signals had shown. I stayed glued to the floor, totally confused. I watched the others and tried my best to follow along, but the sign language frustrated me so much that after one class, I foolishly never returned to Legat's studio. He was dead three years later.

Legat's class was not my only surprise in London. Arriving late at my Chelsea boarding house one night, I was dumbfounded to discover I had a guest waiting in my tiny maid's room under the eaves on the top floor. There was David Lichine, sprawled on my narrow bed. Aware of his reputation as a leading Don Juan, notorious in the company for his relentless pursuit of women, I asked him what he wanted and how he had gotten into my room. He sat up, coolly evading both questions.

"You know, Sono, you are very young."

I nodded.

"But I think you have talent," he continued, coming nearer to me. "And if you vork very, very hard, you can *be* something."

With that, he began to caress me. The moment of pleasure I had felt at his praise turned to fear, and I burst into tears. My sniveling and shaking cooled his ardor and, after superficial attempts to soothe me, he left the room, tiptoeing down the corridor as stealthily as he had come. To this day I have no idea how he got past the two spinster landladies. But Lichine was amazing in his ability to bypass obstacles where a woman was concerned.

Lichine's visit both excited and alarmed me. I was flattered that this leading dancer, a connoisseur of sophisticated women, should find me attractive, but I was terribly frightened by his advances. Too embarrassed to say a word to anybody about the incident, I confided in no one. I knew I was surrounded by sexual activity in the company, but the Lichine episode thrust it directly into my own life. Now I had to worry about sex as well as pirouettes.

August was the time of the company's annual holiday, and everyone began to talk about the coming month. In the dressing room I was surrounded by dancers talking to each other about their plans.

"Oh! I can't vait to get to Côte d'Azur," many said. "I vill sleep whole month!"

I wanted to sleep, too, but I had no idea where I was going to do it. Prudence asked me what my plans were, and when I said I didn't have any, she invited me to vacation with her in Scotland—she was going to visit a colonel and his family who lived outside the town of Inverness. We took a train and arrived the following morning at what looked like a stone fortress. After greeting me with great cordiality at the door of his grand home, the colonel took me aside.

"Prudence tells me you are fourteen years old," he whispered. Then, in an even lower voice, he said, "Please don't tell my eldest daughter. She's fifteen and eats in the nursery with my younger children."

I looked over to the tall girl who was still wearing her hair in long corkscrew curls and felt sorry for her. I looked back at my host and whispered, "I promise."

Personally, I felt like a child out of school. I reveled in the thought of no more fouettés to practice or Russian to decipher for a whole month. The weather was very cold, and although we slept in large, unheated rooms, we nestled under thick eiderdowns and rose wonderfully late for huge breakfasts. In the dining room, which overlooked a garden, there was a heating table. Hot water under copper pans kept eggs, bacon, ham, and herrings and tomatoes piping hot for hours. I filled my plate and smothered freshly baked scones with homemade jam. After these sumptuous breakfasts we would play, and before we knew it, it was time for lunch. Quite often we drove to Loch Ness for picnics. Lying in the fields of heather on its banks, we relaxed completely and filled our lungs with the cold, invigorating air. Sitting upright without any warning, Prudence would blurt out, "Look! I see something!" All heads would turn, our eyes fixed on the loch, each hoping to be the first to catch sight of the legendary monster rising from the deep water. Not until it was time to leave did our hopes desert us. After another large and delicious evening meal, we would sit by the fire in the living room, where our hosts told us Scottish folk tales. Then, in hushed tones, the colonel described the ghost who haunted his house.

"He was a bra-a-ave maahn, killed in battle," the colonel told us, "ahnd hees resstless soul wahlks the hoose aht midnight!"

Attempting to appear blasé, I would say goodnight with a drawnout, stifled yawn, then, once out of sight of the adults, run to my room, jump into bed, pull the eiderdown over my head, and fall asleep long before I heard any footsteps. I never saw the ghost, not even on my fifteenth birthday, which we all celebrated in that old stone house.

Early in September, Prudence and I went back to London and then joined the company in Southampton, where we boarded the *Champlain* and sailed for New York. The month's holiday had given me time to reflect. Only five months after leaving home, I already felt like a new person. I was financially independent and professionally aware. My technique was getting stronger, and I actually had a little self-confidence. I felt less and less plain and sullen. I felt as if I was growing up.

We stopped briefly in New York before sailing again, this time on a small ship, the *Orizaba*, for the company's first visit to Mexico City. We were to appear as part of the inaugural season of the Palacio de Bellas Artes which, on September 29, would open to the public for the first time (the groundbreaking had been in 1900!).

As we sailed into southern waters, the weather became terribly hot and muggy. I spent most of my time sunbathing and swimming, but many dancers practiced each day, holding on to the ship's rail as they did their barre early in the morning.

The listlessness that pervaded the company was alleviated only by the energy it took us to scrutinize the seventeen-year-old who had just joined us as a leading dancer. While dancing in Europe with Serge Lifar and Anton Dolin, her name had been Brigitta Hartwig. Russianized to fit in with us, she was now Vera Zorina.

Summer was over and Zorina was the color of gold. Long, lithe legs, intensely blue eyes, and soft blonde hair falling to her shoulders à la Garbo made her a dazzling beauty. She was the first girl I ever saw who didn't wear a brassiere. The men surrounded her, like flies around honey, barely able to hide their lust. The women, particularly the ballerinas, eyed her more cautiously from a distance. I was struck by her composure. Despite our relentless inspection she remained poised and cheerful throughout the whole trip.

I had first seen Brigitta, as we still called her, in class on the stage at Covent Garden just before the end of our London season. Dressed all in black, with a boyish black shirt tucked in at her tightly cinched waist, she wore a red workman's bandanna on her head. With her broad shoulders and slim hips, she might have had an almost androgynous Nordic beauty, were it not for her voluptuous breasts. For a girl her age, Zorina was remarkably sophisticated. At Dolin's studio in London one day, I was shocked to hear her call him by the familiar "Pat." She was truly the most glamorous member of the company. At seventeen, only two years older than me, she was already a woman of the world, well-acquainted with the art of feminine allure. I asked her once why she slept naked in a large terry-cloth towel with a glistening liquid spread over her golden skin.

"That's glycerin, Sono. It keeps your skin soft and smooth."

"Oh," I said, standing there in my cotton underwear.

At the end of the eight-day voyage, we traveled from Veracruz to the higher altitude and thinner air of Mexico City. We were told that horses brought to that city for polo matches were given a ten-day training period to allow their systems to adjust to the altitude. We were given four days.

Every step was torture, and we gasped for air after only a few jumps. Baronova fainted in class. Simply running across the stage required our full strength, and anything more demanding seemed impossible. As if the strain of dancing at 7400 feet were not enough, we all suffered from debilitating diarrhea, and we began to doubt that we could give any performances at all, let alone good ones.

To get away from the problems of performing, Prudence, Brigitta, and I, now roommates, made plans to go sightseeing outside the city on our Sunday off. We were roaming the countryside when we heard the galloping of horses and saw a band of cowboys riding towards us through the cactus. Their clothes and sombreros were covered with a rainbow of embroidery, and silver spurs glittered on their boots. Coming up beside us, they made gestures that clearly meant that they wanted us to go for a ride with them. We stepped aside, huddled for a conference and, within seconds, curiosity won out over caution. We walked back giggling and nodded "Yes." Each of us was hoisted up onto a saddle, and off we went.

The view of the mountain Popocatepetl was breathtaking, and I was thrilled by the strong arms around me and the stranger's moustache tickling my cheek. But, as we galloped on, my bottom began to get sore, and my bouncing stomach told me that I was about to get sick all over my cowboy's horse. Smiling in desperation, I motioned my caballero to put me down. He did and I staggered feebly away to sit on solid ground and recover. I doubt if I've had an equestrian fantasy since.

Having seen no ballet since Pavlova's last tour there in 1925, the Mexicans bombarded the box office with demands for tickets. Still in very shaky condition, we were grateful for the enthusiastic applause we received opening night, but our success did not quite satisfy the colonel, who was aware that only a small number of Mexicans could afford the price of a ticket. Since he was driven as much by the urge to broaden the ballet audience as by the need to make a profit, de Basil decided that we should do something to make performances available to working people. So on the following Sunday (our day off) we made what was probably the first appearance of a ballet company in a bullring since Pavlova had danced in one for a crowd of 32,000 people.

Our stage for the matinee at the Plaza de Toros was a specially built wooden platform covered with canvas. It was made in such a hurry that there were no curtains to hide us or the stairways leading down to the earth of the bullring. The sky was ominously gray, and the makeup on our faces looked ghastly. We were only a few steps into *Les Sylphides* when it began to rain. The steady drizzle dampened our billowy, starched tarletans until they drooped and clung to our thighs. Our pointe shoes were so soggy they could barely support us.

The rain, the strong odor of the bulls, the aura of the bullring associated with killing, the running makeup, sagging skirts, and collapsing shoes finally got the better of us. *Sylphides* had become one of my favorite ballets and I always danced it with reverence, but that afternoon I joined the rest of the girls in allowing Fokine's vision of perfect serenity to dissolve into suppressed fits of laughter.

The audience seemed oblivious to the absurdity of the situation and sat through it enthralled. Many children stared open-mouthed. *Petrouchka* pleased them even more than *Sylphides*. But during the third scene, it was the audience that found something to laugh at. Toumanova's pantaloons ripped straight down her backside as she rose from the Blackamoor's lap, and the crowd began to roar. In full view Tamara exited down the wooden steps, still in doll-like character. But the minute she reached her dressing room, lately a matador's, she collapsed sobbing in her mother's arms. No one could convince her that the audience had found it adorable and amusing rather than indecent.

We left Mexico City soon after, relieved to be able to breathe and eat normally again. Ahead of us lay the 1934–35 American tour. On its second transcontinental tour, the Ballet Russe de Monte Carlo would visit ninety cities and towns, traveling twenty thousand miles between September and April, and I would be with them!

n 1934 America was virtually virgin territory for ballet. Neither Pavlova nor the Diaghilev Ballets Russes had been seen in the United States for almost seventeen years, leaving the pioneering work to one Russian and two Americans. Adolph Bolm, my first teacher, had spent years laying the foundation for ballet in Chicago and was now staging works for a small company connected with the San Francisco Opera. Bolm's work in Chicago had been taken over by Ruth Page, who had become ballerina and ballet director of Chicago's Grand Opera Company, for which she not only staged the opera ballets but choreographed her own original works as well. In Philadelphia, Catherine Littlefield was the leading dancer with the Philadelphia Grand Opera Company and was involved in the planning stages of her Littlefield Ballet, probably the first wholly American ballet company, which made its debut in 1935. George Balanchine had recently arrived in the United States and had just opened the School of American Ballet, with the aid of his champion Lincoln Kirstein. Their work was just beginning. So there was only the 1933–34 tour of the Ballet Russe de Monte Carlo, headed by de Basil, to bring ballet to an extensive American audience.

When we started that tour, it was estimated that just over one million people had attended performances of de Basil's various companies both here and in Europe. Boarding the train that would be our "home" for the next six months, none of us dreamed that forty years later the ballet audience in America alone would number more than seventeen million!

The train itself consisted of six Pullmans, one dining car, and four baggage cars, loaded to the roof with eighty-four backdrops and curtains, six thousand costumes, and sheet music for the entire repertory. The stagehands, administrative staff, and twenty-one musicians, although officially part of Sol Hurok's organization, which managed the tour, traveled on the train with the company, which numbered fifty-two dancers, seven mothers, three fathers, four turtles, one monkey, one rabbit, and a dog. Out of all this came a schedule of programs drawn from the following repertoire:

LE BAL
Choreography: Balanchine; music: Rieti;
décor & costumes: di Chirico

BEACH
Ch: Massine; m: Françaix; d & c: Dufy

LE BEAU DANUBE
Ch: Massine; m: Strauss; d & c: Polunin, after Guys

LA BOUTIQUE FANTASQUE
Ch: Massine; m: Rossini; d & c: Derain

LA CONCURRENCE
Ch: Balanchine; m: Auric; d & c: Derain

CONTES RUSSES
Ch: Massine; m: Liadov; d & c: Larionov

COTILLON
Ch: Balanchine; m: Chabrier; d & c: Bérard

JEUX D'ENFANTS
Ch: Massine; m: Bizet; d & c: Miró

LE MARIAGE D'AURORE (AURORA'S WEDDING)
Ch: after Petipa, additional dances by Nijinska; m: Tchaikovsky;
d: Bakst; c: Bakst & Benois

LES MATELOTS
Ch: Massine; m: Auric; d & c: Pruna

PETROUCHKA
Ch: Fokine; m: Stravinsky; d & c: Benois

LES PRÉSAGES
Ch: Massine; m: Tchaikovsky (Fifth Symphony); d & c: Masson

POLOVETSIAN DANCES FROM PRINCE IGOR
Ch: Fokine; m: Borodin; d & c: Roerich

SCHÉHÉRAZADE
Ch: Fokine; m: Rimsky-Korsakov; d & c: Bakst

DANCES

SCUOLA DI BALLO
Ch: Massine; m: Boccherini; d & c: de Beaumont

LE SPECTRE DE LA ROSE
Ch: Fokine; m: Weber; d & c: Bakst

SWAN LAKE, ACT TWO
Ch: after Ivanov; m: Tchaikovsky; d: Prince Schervachidze,
after Korovin and Golovin; c: Golovin

LES SYLPHIDES
Ch: Fokine; m: Chopin; d & c: Benois

LE TRICORNE
Ch: Massine; m: de Falla; d & c: Picasso

UNION PACIFIC
Ch: Massine; m: Nabokov; d: Johnson; c: Sharaff

The train was the great equalizer, subjecting everyone but Massine and his vivacious wife, Eugenia Delarova, to drafts, noise, and cramped quarters. The Massines traveled in a chauffeur-driven Lincoln with a well-outfitted trailer attached, which, in those impoverished years, looked to me like the epitome of luxury.

Nothing about *our* life was luxurious. As months passed we became increasingly inventive about ways to save both energy and money. Sitting upright on the train for hours was one of our worst problems, draining us and making our legs ache. One day Lichine had had enough. He yanked out the musty green velour back of his Pullman seat and laid it across his upturned suitcase, making a comfortable bed from the two facing seats and the cushioned suitcase in between. Dancers don't talk, they imitate. We took one look at Lichine sprawled out, there was a brief pause, and then the Pullman was filled with a "bustle-fuss" of yanking, pulling, pushing, and shoving. Within minutes it was over. The car, from one toilet to the other, was transformed into one long bed. Thereafter, this became common practice. To keep out noise and light while we slept, we wound scarves around our heads, then stretched out, wrapped in our overcoats.

When we weren't getting some much-needed sleep, we read, sewed, gossiped, and watched the country roll by outside our windows. Meanwhile, another car was the scene of more serious activity. Heated poker games ran nearly round the clock, and most of the time

Mamitchka Riabouchinska sat right in the thick of it, betting and swearing with as much fervor as the men. When she wasn't in that smoke-filled car, Mamitchka sat with Tania, breaking off tiny bits of chocolate and feeding them, one by one, into her daughter's mouth, like a protective bird feeding her young. We were never offered any of that chocolate, but it didn't offend us. Having seen her standing in the wings during performances, doing relevés in Tania's stiff new pointe shoes to break them in, we easily understood how her devotion to her daughter overshadowed any other consideration.

Sleeping arrangements at our whistle stops were just as innovative as those on the train. The company was offered special rates of a dollar per night, and even when we didn't stay over, we often rented the rooms anyway to have a place to bathe and rest between matinee and evening performances. To save money, we worked out a "room routine." Two dancers would register for a room, and then, under their breaths, pass the room number along to their friends sitting in the lobby. Half an hour later, ten people were sharing a room for two.

Once settled in the room, we moved the night tables into a corner, pushed the twin beds together and turned the mattresses sideways, making one bed large enough for everyone. Every two minutes one of us would poke a head out the door and say, "May I have another towel, please?" After delivering seven or eight, the chambermaids would get suspicious. Delivering the ninth towel, she banged on the door rather than knocked, and eight dancers jumped into the closet.

It seemed our train always left at six in the morning, and getting up in time to catch it was one of the hardest things about being a dancer. It was especially hard in late autumn and winter, waking up when it was still dark and cold. One of those mornings Prudence, Brigitta, and I just couldn't get up. Not even the constant ringing of the hotel operator on the phone stirred us. It was our instinct that finally woke us. We dashed to the station in a panic and ran onto the platform just in time to see the last car disappear in the distance.

Frantic, we begged the stationmaster to phone ahead and have the train stopped at the next junction. Without waiting for confirmation that it could be done, we jumped into a cab, shouting "Follow that train!" It was neck and neck for quite a while before the train finally stopped. Twenty dollars poorer, we boarded the train hanging our heads as we saw the icy stares of Grigoriev and Tchernicheva. "Trou-

blemakers," he said with disgust as we passed. Standing beside him, his
wife gave us a disdainful sniff.

Between catnaps, gossip, jokes, and sewing, there was lots of time on
the train to learn more about my new "family." I found Colonel de
Basil perhaps the most fascinating of all. Being tall and extremely
pallid, he stood out among us physically. From the stories I heard, his
past was as curious as his appearance.

"De Basil was policeman in Russia," someone told me.

"Not true," contradicted another. "Is Cossack from Kuban in
Caucasus."

"*Da*, is true," added another. "And real name really Vassily
Grigorievitch Voskresensky."

Rumor also had it that he had sold cars in Italy after the Revolution. But in the long run the mysterious gaps in his history made no
difference to me at all. For me this impassive Cossack was the one who
in a few moments had changed my life, and I would always be grateful
to him.

As time went on, I heard that in 1925, de Basil had been assistant
to a Prince Zeretelli, one-time manager of the People's Theatre in St.
Petersburg, who after the Revolution managed several seasons of Russian opera in Paris. After Diaghilev died in 1929, de Basil had seen the
once invincible Ballets Russes fall to pieces. Starting with nothing but
absolute determination and a great passion for the ballet, he decided to
bring back together what Diaghilev's death had shattered. He organized a small troupe singlehandedly which, in 1932, toured Western
Europe in buses. The dancers were paid from the box-office receipts, so
when business was bad, the dancers didn't eat. But Baronova told me
that she and Lichine, who danced in that company, were so happy to
be performing that they really didn't care too much about food or
money.

After the bus company, de Basil joined forces with René Blum
who, under the aegis of the Société des Bains de Mer de Monaco, was
the director of the Ballets de l'Opéra de Monte Carlo. Together they
engaged many of Diaghilev's dancers and the twenty-eight-year-old
George Balanchine, who was both ballet master and choreographer for
the company. Before he left de Basil to form his own Ballets 1933,

Balanchine had observed the students at Preobrajenska's studio in Paris. There he had discovered two extraordinary young girls, Tamara Toumanova and Irina Baronova. For them, he had created leading roles in his ballets *Cotillon* and *La Concurrence*.

Without question, the credit for reviving the Russian ballet belongs to the colonel. It was his fierce dedication that reforged the links of the chain of ballet history that Diaghilev's death had broken. He pushed twentieth-century ballet across the American continent.

Our long American tours gave the Russians their first chances to pick up English, and I gladly translated for them whenever I was asked. Grammar didn't exist. All that mattered was instant communication.

"Vere go autoboos to Broadvay?" they'd call out when we reached New York. At each train station, they'd tell bewildered redcaps, "You. Fellow. Valiss poot here."

They were shocked to see Americans eating meat and sweet things together. "Ham and pineapple? Vat is dat?" But curiosity soon won out over initial disgust, and they were soon ordering their "hamand-pineapple" with "cocacolavidowdice."

They loved drugstores, especially Walgreen's, our favorite hang-out. The service was even faster than in Paris bistros, they pointed out, and in the same place that we ate, we could buy corn plasters for our blistered feet, hot water bottles for sore muscles, and assorted toiletries. We ate many a 6:00 A.M. breakfast at Walgreen's counter, twirling on our revolving stools as our eggs fried, keeping one sleepy eye on the door for the arrival of Tatiana Chamié. Once a member of the Diaghilev company, Tania was one of our best character dancers. She was unusually placid by nature, plumper than the rest of us, and was known as the company's unofficial food taster. Invariably late for breakfast, she would slowly settle herself on a stool and survey everyone's food. "Look de-*lish*-us," she'd coo, just as we lifted our forks. Then, leaning across her neighbor in any direction, she'd pick away at my pancakes, or Prudence's eggs, or anyone's anything. "Hide food, here comes Tania," became the password whenever we saw her heading for the counter. Oblivious to our teasing, she'd smile and continue pecking off our plates.

Another "Amerikanski" store the dancers loved was Woolworth's.

For them "Voolvort's" *was* a fun place to shop. The men were fascinated by the American gadgets in the hardware department—André alone could have spent hours there. The women ran straight to the counters to stock up on jewelry and makeup. From the audience no one could tell that the diamond tiaras of *Aurora's Wedding* or the gold bracelets of *Schéhérazade* came from the dime store. We carried the same kind of stage illusion into our own lives. Stylish as we tried to be at all times, our dresses were $12.95 at Lerner's and our shoes $2.99 at A. S. Beck.

After paying for clothes, makeup and false hair, taxis, meals, and hotels, I was usually flat broke by Wednesday. My first six months in the company, I wouldn't have dreamed of borrowing money and was ashamed that I had to wire home from Paris for fifty dollars. Gradually, I grew wise to the ways of the troupe and began to borrow against my next week's pay. Hurok's transportation man, Joe Fingerman, who also sold our souvenir programs at the theatre each night, was a good friend to me and a regular touch for five dollars. I hated being in debt to Joe or the company but soon resigned myself to the inevitable.

It was rumored that Baronova received a top salary of $150 per week, but I never heard of or saw a checkbook. Grigoriev paid us at the end of the week after performance. Still in our dressing gowns, we would file past his table, sign a ledger, and pick up our brown envelopes. We dressed, left the theatre, and spent what we could on dinner.

Since Grigoriev was responsible to the colonel for every penny of the production budget, he spent the company's money even more sparingly than we laid out our own. The Diaghilev company, beneath all its glamour, had been just as financially insecure as ours, so years before joining the colonel, Grigoriev had become a master of professional thrift.

Tania Chamié remembered an instance of Grigoriev's tight economy during the Diaghilev days. She had gone to him one day with her nymph costume for *L'Après-midi d'un Faune* nearly in shreds. "Sergei Leonidovitch," she wailed. "Look at my costume! Soon I'll be dancing naked!"

"It will be different, Tania," was his cool reply.

I was even more concerned about my pointe shoes than about the scarcity of money. Fortunately, shoes came from the company budget rather than our own. But shoes were a major expense for the colonel, and dancers felt it was their duty to preserve them as long as possible. We had no set shoe allotment, so Grischa, who was rumored to have been a monk, would dole them out on demand. Unlocking the huge wicker trunk which held the entire supply of pointe shoes, he would warn me, "Remember, you vear one pair twelve performance." I'd nod silent agreement, take the precious shoes, and go off, knowing they rarely lasted for four.

Our shoes, made by the famous London cobbler Niccolini, weighed only three ounces. After just a few ballets they began to soften noticeably. My feet were not very strong, and I felt insecure when my shoes lost their stiffness. It hurt to dance in soft shoes, but they were all we had. So someone—Prudence, I think—came up with a great idea. We poured colorless straw-hat lacquer into the shoes and left them standing upright to dry overnight. Once it hardened, the lacquer would keep the shoe strong for a few more days. If any liquid seeped through the satin-covered shoe, we camouflaged the stain with pink body makeup.

Early in the tour I noticed the girls on the train sewing diligently on the hard blocks of their pointe shoes.

"What are they doing?" I finally asked Eglevsky.

"Dat's *shtopatz*," André told me. "Girls sewing pointe shoes."

With that, he went down the aisle to the other end of the car and asked Mama Eglevsky how to *shtopatz*. With Mama's instructions clear in his mind, he came back to where he had left me sitting and showed me how to stitch heavy, pale-pink mercerized cotton tightly across the tip of the pointe shoe as reinforcement. André was more successful in teaching me *shtopatz* than he had been with pirouettes.

Tights were a precious commodity as well. Onstage, we wore only silk tights, which we had to pay for ourselves. They could be bought only in Paris, and a year's supply cost an outrageous forty-five dollars for three pair, which left me with almost nothing to live on for several weeks each spring. Aside from runs, which could be mended invisibly, there was the constant problem of their bagging at the knee. There was an ingenious solution for that as well. When the silk at the knee started to buckle, we sewed loops of elastic on patches of extra fabric at the hip, ran a network of strings through the loops, pulled the tights taut, and then tied the strings around our waists. If there was no time to sew on loops, we placed English copper pennies on our hipbones, where they would be held in place by snugly fitted costumes, and simply wound the strings around those.

Making up for the stage took almost as much time as taking care of our shoes and tights. Because we perspired so heavily, we used the thickest greasepaint available. We used a different shade of greasepaint for nearly every ballet, and once it was chosen, we smoothed the makeup all over our faces and necks, right down to the collarbone, then shadowed on top of it. For a gaunt look we painted a thin triangle of darker shadow between the cheekbone and jawline. We made our noses look perfectly straight by applying tan shadows on either side and, imitating Tchernicheva, dabbed large dots of moist rouge in the corners of our eyes for added brightness. We powdered heavily, removed the excess powder with a rabbit's foot, and then patted cold water all over our faces to hold the greasepaint.

After the basic preparations came the painstaking job of making up eyelashes. First we brushed on mascara, wet with spit. Then we melted special black wax in a spoon over a lighted candle and, using a matchstick, slowly built up bead upon bead of wax on our lashes until they looked like spider's legs.

False noses altered the face most effectively. Baronova often used them to create a forceful or dramatic face to match her character. With a quarter inch of putty on the bridge of her upturned nose when she danced Lady Gay in *Union Pacific*, she was unrecognizable as the girlish and pretty fifteen-year-old we knew offstage.

Like so many other aspects of our life in the ballet, makeup methods were often experimental. If someone had a good idea, we all shared it. No one taught us how to make up, so we were on our own. I observed the more experienced dancers in the dressing room as closely as I watched them in the classroom. From them I learned to treat the face like a blank canvas and to paint it to complement the costumes and décor of each ballet.

In time I found a way to disguise my Oriental features which were, I felt, particularly noticeable in classical ballets. The trick was to change the convex contours of my face to concave, more Occidental ones, which I did with heavy shadowing. This was only one step of my backstage education, since the different "looks" required for the ballets on any one evening varied from performance to performance.

In a single night, for instance, we were sylphs or swans from eight-forty-five to nine-fifteen, whipped off our pale tights and shoes during the fifteen-minute intermission, darkened our faces, necks, and hands with body makeup, and reappeared on stage at nine-thirty as swarthy Spanish peasants wearing black high-heeled shoes and Picasso's heavy linen dresses in *Le Tricorne*. By ten-thirty we were flirting in petunia-colored petticoats in *Le Beau Danube*, with pink-cheeked faces, beaming smiles, and corkscrew curls and ringlets of false hair bobbing as we waltzed.

While the audiences strolled at leisure in the foyer during intermissions, we rushed through the fifteen minutes in near frenzy. No detail of preparation could be abbreviated or eliminated. We squirted large dabs of LePage's glue in the backs of our shoes to adhere them to our tights. As added protection, ballerinas who performed lengthy pas de deux would have Madame Larose, our wardrobe mistress, sew them into their tutus after the bodices had been hooked up.

Still there were accidents. Posed serenely in our straight lines as swans in *Swan Lake* one night, we were watching Baronova and Eglevsky dance the pas de deux, as usual, out of the corners of our lowered eyes. As Baronova lunged into a deep arabesque, her shoulder strap broke and one breast fell out! We must have been a group of wide-eyed swans as André, never losing his cool, pivoted his Swan Queen and deftly flipped her downy breast back into her bodice before she completed one revolution to face the audience.

We went through the same elaborate rituals over and over, whether we danced a night, a few days, or a week in Boston, Springfield, Buffalo, or Scranton. For many of our audiences, ballet was a brand-new experience, and they cheered us across the country.

Massine's extraordinary ballets made up three-quarters of our repertory, and the audiences adored them. *Les Présages* was one of the most popular, along with *Le Beau Danube*, which usually closed the performance.

Présages, a massive work set to Tchaikovsky's Fifth Symphony, was considered revolutionary when it premiered in 1933. Massine's audacity in using a symphony for a ballet score had caused enormous controversy. Some music critics called it sacrilege, but the audiences were enthralled.

The steps of the ballet were quite orthodox, but the stage patterns and arm movements were not. In many traditional ballets the corps is immobilized or offstage during a solo or pas de deux, so attention can be focused exclusively on the soloists. Massine's approach was to reverse this procedure during the melancholy Second Movement. Baronova and Lichine entered on an empty stage, advancing slowly with his arms entwined around her torso and hers around his face and neck. During their passionate pas de deux, large groups swept on and off across the back of the stage. At the peak of their love duet, a discordant blare in the music announced the entrance of Woizikovsky, as the figure of Fate. His rigid, staggered movements seemed even more threatening in contrast to our languid flowing and swooping. The ominous gray-and-black figure, looking like an enormous bat, approached the lovers, weakened them, and drew them apart by an invisible force that radiated from his outstretched arms. At one point, Baronova succumbed, collapsing into the arms of Fate. Yet, inexorable as he might be, Fate was not stronger than the power of love. Fate's grip was loosened and, defeated, he staggered backward stiffly on his heels until he was out of sight. Reunited, the lovers exited in the same cherishing embrace in which they had entered.

Massine broke with tradition by casting his soloists as an abstract but real flesh-and-blood couple, rather than as a romantic duo of swan and prince or sylph and poet. Crowned with a headdress of red velvet hearts, Irina was the essence of warm feminine desire.

In contrast to the symphonic ballets with their monumental themes, Massine could also create moods of gaiety in ballets such as *Beach*, which also premiered in 1933. The slight libretto depicted the boredom of Nereus, a sea god who gets weary of the charms of his splashing Nereids. Cupid's arrow transforms him into a swimmer, and the aquatic lovelies become human bathers who dance with an American sailor, an Arab rug vendor, and two Oriental potentates. Disguised as a harassed bellhop at a Monte Carlo hotel, Cupid encourages Nereus to pursue his love for the Rose-White Maid, danced by Irina in a daring flesh-colored bathing suit and bare legs. The tables are turned when she is changed into a sea nymph, abandons Nereus at the hotel, and disappears into the sea as the curtain falls.

The ballet was more of a divertissement than most of Massine's creations, but European audiences loved the tongue-in-cheek blend of mythology and modernity. American audiences were just as pleased with the touch of history and boisterous fun in *Union Pacific*.

In 1932 Massine combined fantasy with hints of sexuality in *Jeux d'Enfants*, to Bizet's music. The libretto was by Boris Kochno, who had been closely allied with Diaghilev and his Ballets Russes. Riabouchinska danced the central role of the Child dressed in a short blue dress, bare legs above her toe shoes, and a large patent-leather bow in her hair. She was seduced by the worldly older man, the Traveler, danced by Lichine, who flew with abandon in grand jetés between signs reading NEW YORK and PARIS.

Visually the entire repertory was overwhelming. It looked all the more lavish and glamorous against the colorless poverty and disillusionment of the Depression.

Leon Bakst's set for *Schéhérazade*, created in 1910, was still startlingly opulent in its Eastern harmony of ocher, henna, magenta, cerulean blue, and a green Bakst described as "lugubrious." In front of the backdrop were three arched doors from which "black slaves" emerged in peculiar, crouched positions. A pale henna canvas groundcloth covered the stage, and soft cushions, scattered strategically, added a voluptuousness to the exotic setting. Looming stage right was a tall platform with stairs leading to it. In the bloody finale of the ballet, the leading dancer—Eglevsky, Lichine, Woizikovsky, or Massine—dashed desperately up the stairs, and then fell the full length of the flight to the stage as he was slashed to death with a scimitar.

The effect of all these details could be instantly ruined if the set didn't function properly. The staircase had to be bolted tightly to the floor or the audience would hear it rattle as the slave fell, destroying the illusion of an impenetrable stone palace. Props had to be placed securely as well. Cushions only appeared to be casually strewn; each was placed on specific chalk marks. The corps de ballet rushed in and out of the wings throughout the ballet, carrying platters of fruits and garlands of flowers on their heads. The corner of one cushion out of place could send us sprawling.

Some of the greatest artists of the day used our stage as their canvas, designing unforgettable curtains, décor, and costumes. Raoul Dufy designed *Beach* and handed his sketches to the scenic artist Prince Schervachidze, who rendered them to their theatrical dimensions. The set pictured a red-and-white-striped awning, beneath which small boats sailed in different directions on a royal blue sea. Among the waves, a single tugboat billowing black smoke, some crabs, a seahorse, and a large white conch shell could be seen.

The enchanting set for *Jeux d'Enfants* was by Joan Miró, who designed it with some wonderful examples of stage magic in mind. The backdrop was pale blue with several thin black lines running vertically through it. In front of the abstract design stood nothing but two geometric forms: a tall black conical shape topped by a red circle at stage right, and a large white spherical shape with a minute red flag emerging from its roundness at stage left.

As the ballet began, a panel at the lower half of the white sphere slid up like a window to reveal a pair of pure white feet. Behind that set, Eglevsky, who along with Verchinina danced the Spirits Who Govern the Toys, held himself aloft with his hands. All the audience could see were his finely-arched feet, softly rising and falling in tight fifth position. The whimsical touch of Eglevsky's disembodied feet set the magical tone of the ballet before any dancing actually began.

What followed captured the naïve delight of a child's pleasure in playing with rocking horses, soap bubbles, battledore and shuttlecock, and a spinning top (Baronova or Toumanova turning innumerable fouettés). With his almost limitless imagination, Massine was able to create the wonder and innocence seen only through a child's eyes.

Miró, like Massine, insisted that the illusion remain intact and that no production detail should fall short of his standards. Unable to attend the closing performance of this ballet during the Barcelona season, Miró wrote to Grigoriev, asking that certain parts of the décor and costumes be repaired so that the production would keep its original vitality.

Grigoriev had the enormous task of keeping every production as fresh as opening night, with every prop in place and every light in focus. Though his English was rather rudimentary, he managed to make himself understood wherever we traveled. "Now, poot curtain," meant "raise the curtain." To an electrician on the light board, he would say, "Ven orchestra go ta-ta-zoom, go blue, not so fast," and the stage would slowly fill with blue light on the proper musical cue.

Meanwhile the train sped back and forth across the country. The train, the hotels, the rehearsal studios, and the stages were the boundaries of my world. In the nine months since I had left home, my experience had broadened despite its physical limitations. I knew excitement, loneliness, and sharing with new friends. I learned something the night I lost a shoe onstage as well as the day I finally turned three pirouettes in class. I was beginning to feel that I knew what it meant to be a dancer.

We reached Indianapolis in December, and I was impatient to celebrate Christmas with my family during our engagement at the Auditorium Theatre. Our family reunion was happy but not long, since I spent all my time rehearsing in my real home, the theatre. Although Father's business was sparse, my parents were coping with the Depression without complaint. As always, Mother hid her apprehension about money by making a joke of it. "Finish your dinner, children," she'd say each night, "tomorrow we may be in the breadline." Tim was almost ten now, and Teru was becoming a beautiful adolescent. I was thrilled to know they were in the audience for some of the performances, especially when they were there to see me step out alone and do my stint as the Barboy in *Union Pacific*. Later I led them proudly backstage to meet my new friends.

The morning after the colonel's big New Year's Eve party, we learned of a shocking outburst of emotion—our first *"bolshoi* scandale."* In the early hours of the morning following the party, Paul Petroff, one of our darkly handsome, subtly romantic young dancers, was found stabbed near an elevator in a corridor of the Hotel Auditorium. Rumors flew. Although Petroff had a lover already, he had been showing a great deal of interest in the portly, blonde Madame de Basil, who was not a dancer but traveled with her husband. Another dancer had recently developed an interest in Madame as well and let it be known he didn't want competition from Petroff. The tangle of passions and personalities made quite a scenario. While the company buzzed with theories, Hurok kept our little *épreuve d'amour* from reaching the press and police.

Petroff was forced to stay behind in Chicago until his wounds healed, and he stayed for a while with my family. To my knowledge, he never told anyone who had tried to kill him that night. I think his promotion to soloist when he rejoined the company was partly a reward for his silence.

It was not until we left Chicago that I realized how little I had seen my family. Seeing them again brought back to me how much I loved them and had missed them while I'd been away. But however much they meant to me, traveling and performing with the Russian ballet meant even more for my happiness. Despite constant tension and the exhausting routine, I was stronger and more content with the ballet than I had ever been at home as a child. I would never turn back.

A month or so after we left Chicago, we reached Lincoln, Nebraska. The next stop was Omaha. The fact that I was about to appear in my birthplace must have hit Hurok, de Basil, or someone in management as a publicity angle, because shortly after our arrival in Omaha, a newspaperman poked his head into the train compartment, said "Smile, Miss Osato!" and the next day, a front-page story on the Ballet Russe's arrival after "winning the heart" of Lincoln was accompanied by my picture. The caption read, "Former Omaha Miss with Troupe," and a short sketch of my background appeared beneath. This was one of those added bonuses in the frantic life of a dancer. Not only was I dancing, at the age of fifteen, with the world's most famous ballet company—my dream come true—but I was already seen as a viable commodity to help publicize the troupe!

I must have been thrilled with the attention, but it takes time to appreciate things, and there was simply no time. Right after the photograph was taken, I was worrying about bags, hotel rooms, and the next rehearsal. When the picture appeared, I was already preparing for rehearsals and performance. If I had dwelt an extra moment on the new experience of personal publicity, I might have been late for rehearsal and fined a dollar. That would reduce my week's twenty-five dollars to twenty-four, and I'd be in to Joe Fingerman for another few dollars. By the time the extra bit of attention in Omaha had set in, we must have been on the train to Emporia, Kansas.

Over the next three months, the pace became increasingly frantic. There was no union to regulate our working hours, which meant that as New York and the end of the tour came closer, every minute we weren't actually onstage was used for rehearsal. We rehearsed in the aisles of the train. After performance each night, we'd return to the hotel, put on our practice clothes, and still in stage makeup, rehearse in the lobby until one or two in the morning. Hurok always liked the company to arrive in New York with a new piece that would brighten up the season and impress the audience and critics. So Massine was hard at work on a new ballet.

He based the libretto for *Jardin Publique* on a fragment of André Gide's novel *The Counterfeiters*, and asked Vladimir Dukelsky to compose an original score. Along with Auric, Poulenc, and Rieti, Dukelsky had played one of the four pianos at the 1926 London opening of Nijinska's *Les Noces*. But he was better known for his popular songs, like *April in Paris*, which he wrote under the name Vernon Duke.

During rehearsals of *Jardin Publique*, I began to observe Massine more closely than ever. He was a total enigma, a sphinx. Offstage there were no signs of the passionate nature that shone through his stage roles. In daily life he was reserved almost to the point of inhibition. Shaking hands with him, you only held the tips of his fingers. He didn't *wear* his stylish felt hat, he posed it lightly on his head, yet it never budged, not even when he bowed formally when introduced to a stranger. I never saw him laugh out loud or lose his temper in rehearsal or anywhere else. He seemed to channel all his feelings and energy into his performances and his choreography.

Every day Massine would arrive at rehearsal, punctual to the minute, dressed in an immaculate white shirt, a black sweater tossed loosely over his shoulders, and a fine hairnet. Shunning tights, he always wore fitted black trousers, modeled after those Picasso had designed for him in *Le Tricorne*. By his chair Massine kept a large book that he guarded with his life and referred to frequently during rehearsals. When I asked some of the older dancers what was in the book that made it so interesting, they said it was an old Italian text on choreography that Diaghilev had given to him.

Massine came into the room, sat down in front of us, and rehearsal began. He would concentrate in silence for several moments, then get up and lead a single dancer or a group to a certain spot on the floor. Humming a short phrase of the music, he would demonstrate the steps he wanted while the dancer facing him would imitate each movement. Watching the dancer do it alone, he might then say, "Not so much. Too exaggerated," and then repeat the movement himself, experimenting with it until both he and the dancer were satisfied. The process was repeated over and over to each phrase of music, until the dance slowly emerged.

There was a mysterious feeling of suspense during those long hours. Massine spoke very little, with long pauses in between, but no one became impatient. We simply waited in silence, fixed by his concentration. Watching him closely while we marked time, I wondered what he was visualizing. Had he seen the patterns in his dreams, in his dressing-room mirror, or were they just forming themselves behind his still, black eyes? No one asked and no one found out. All that I could see was that he somehow linked one movement to another until the music could almost be seen in our bodies.

Our complete attention was necessary, no matter what time the clock showed. Each movement had to be remembered the next day at rehearsal, regardless of what performances intervened. Music had to be memorized as well, even though we often heard the score for the first time as Massine choreographed to it. Unlike a painter, composer, or writer, who agonizes alone over his work, the choreographer

works in front of others. His ideas can be realized only through dancers' bodies, his tools. As his tools, we were completely in the dark
about our particular function while he created. The movements must
have been conceived and shaped in his mind with crystal clarity, but
because he told us little about his vision, we had to work on his ballets
without a feeling for its motivation. Massine's reticence magnified the
usual silence of rehearsal. We sweated in a vacuum, willingly repeating the movements, but without real understanding.

We arrived in New York, nearly limp with exhaustion, for five
performances at the Majestic, a theatre we learned to loathe. The stage
was covered with treacherously slippery linoleum instead of wood, and
the backstage conditions were crowded and uncomfortable. Our tem-
pers were getting shorter and shorter. When Madame Larose handed
us our costumes for *Jardin Publique*, we nearly gave up. The long
skirts, aprons, and starched headbands that Branitska, Chabelska, and
I were to wear as nursemaids were nice enough, but the padded
bodices were grotesque. Under our chiffon blouses were mammoth-
sized breasts painted with bright pink nipples!

"I'm not going onstage in this!" I muttered.

Grigoriev overheard me. "You vill vear," he snapped.

So onstage we went, with radiant smiles and cursing the designer
in our hearts.

In *Jardin*, Danilova and Petroff, in the roles of a Wealthy Couple,
danced a lively rhumba. Toumanova and Massine came on later,
dressed in rags as Poor Lovers. John Martin in *The New York Times*
was not overly enthusiastic, but he did concede that in the ballet
Massine revealed his awareness of the economic hardships that gripped
America. After months of all that hard work, it was disappointing to
have our new ballet only a mild success. But, if nothing else, the reviews marked the end of a grueling tour.

Free of the constricted atmosphere of the train and all the attendant inconveniences, we gratefully boarded the *Ile de France* for Europe. The crossing was almost an exact repetition of my first trip with the company a year earlier. The moment I smelled the stuffy air and rubber-coated floors of the ship, I took to my bunk, nauseated and miserable, while my roommate flitted in and out all day.

"Oh, what good lunch you miss!" she'd chirp gaily. "I have celery remoulade, zen a divine filet mignon avec sauce béarnaise, et petits pois, et pommes frites, et for dessert, pêche . . ."

"Lulu! Stop!" I'd groan, knowing full well the result of "melba"!

Although she roomed with me, she was officially Mrs. David Lichine. Born Lucienne Kilberg, she was now Lubov Rostova, and everyone called her Lulu. The only French member of the company, she was a slim blonde of tender beauty. Sometimes her eyes were blue and at other times they looked gray. Her pale complexion positively glowed from the sea air. Balanchine, it was said, had loved her, but Lichine had won her.

No longer a stranger to Paris, I looked forward to the prospect of several weeks of relaxation and rehearsals without the pressures of performance. By now I knew that Paris represented the only permanent residence the Russians could call their own. Through my new friend Anna Volkova, one of the corps dancers, I had a moving insight into the life these émigrés made for themselves in their substitute home.

Anna invited me to tea at the apartment she shared with her mother and two brothers in a poor neighborhood in Paris. Climbing the steep steps in a house that smelled like an old church, I noticed that the toilets were on the stair landings. The apartment doors were shabby, obviously unpainted for years. But when Anna opened the door to her home, a tiny glimpse of Russia was revealed. Between windows covered by worn, starched curtains, an icon hung on the wall from a faded blue ribbon. Several family portraits in old silver frames dotted the room. I thought it odd that a bathtub stood near a wall of the small, spotless kitchen.

With quiet grace Anna's mother served tea, Russian style, in tall glasses with strawberry jam, along with dry sweet biscuits and chocolate cake. She chatted easily with me in French, occasionally lapsing into Russian, wanting to know about how the tours had gone and what our next plans were. As the afternoon wore on, I urged her to reminisce about her comfortable life in Russia in earlier days. I marveled that the shocks of revolution, widowhood, and poverty had dented neither her dignity nor her charm and fortitude. "To live life is not to cross a field," she said with a smile.

These same qualities were evident in most of the Russian émigrés I had met. Homeless, but rooted in their art, the dancers radiated a resilience and often a joie de vivre that left no room for self-pity. "Heaven gives us habits instead of happiness," was one of their favorite proverbs. Their Nansen passports marked them as displaced persons, and at times they were treated like second-class citizens, though some were born aristocrats. But the dancers lived and behaved with the same self-discipline that they applied to their dancing. Even at 6:00 A.M., Madame Tchernicheva was always immaculately groomed and perfumed. They were gallant and philosophical in accepting hardship.

When we arrived in Paris, Tania Riabouchinska prodded me to take class with her own teacher, Mathilde Kchessinska, who, in our world, was a living legend.

In 1890, when Kchessinska was eighteen, the Imperial family came to a school performance in which she danced. She and Tsarevitch Nicholas were seated together at a supper following the ballet. They were attracted to each other and, in time, what had been a sympathetic friendship grew into love. They became lovers, but despite her romantic and extravagant life, now having servants and fine clothes,

D A N C E S

Kchessinska did not permit her royal love affair to interfere with her dancing. After late evenings spent with Nicholas, several grand dukes, and famous artists, she returned every morning to the barre for diligent practice, gaining the rank of prima ballerina assoluta at the age of twenty-three. She knew that eventually Nicholas would have to marry a woman of royal rank. But when the dreaded announcement of his engagement to Princess Alice of Hesse came, Kchessinska fell into a deep depression, and withdrew from dancing. Through her strong self-will, she later returned to the stage—and to liaisons with two grand dukes.

Kchessinska danced in a variety of ballets, ranging from *Le Spectre de la Rose* and *Carnaval* to *Swan Lake* and *La Esmeralda*. She dazzled the public not only with her artistry but with her Fabergé jewels and the attention showered upon her by men such as Emperor Franz Joseph of Austria. The world of Russian ballet hung on her every word, and she was a social lioness. In 1902 her son Vladimir, the result of her affair with the Tsar's cousin, Grand Duke André, was born out of wedlock. The ensuing years brought more fame, pleasure in her son's growth—and then, the Revolution. Her St. Petersburg home was confiscated by the Bolsheviks and became their general headquarters. In her salon, Trotsky rested after his impassioned speeches to the city's workers.

Kchessinska and Grand Duke André fled to the Côte d'Azur, where they were wed in 1921. By virtue of her marriage, Kchessinska was now a princess. She was also forty-eight years old, and almost penniless. So out of necessity and with some doubts about her ability, she went to work as a teacher. She found space in Paris, and on the opening day of her studio, the highest official of the Russian Orthodox Church came to bless the room.

By the time I reached this studio, I was literally speechless with awe at the thought of meeting a legend. Tania presented me, explaining that I was an American but spoke French and could follow class. I only curtsied. Following Tania to the barre, I suddenly realized that we were alone, the only pupils in class.

Kchessinska was slim and tiny, hardly more than five feet tall. She came to us with pert, light steps, the hem of her soft gown gently wafting well below her knees. She wore a band around her sleek little head and tiny pink ballet slippers. Her lively brown eyes scrutinized us throughout the hour-and-a-half class. When she approved of our work, she'd give us a radiant smile.

I was so awed by Kchessinska's presence that I frankly don't remember how or what she taught in those few classes. And even if I did remember, I was, at fifteen, hardly prepared to judge *any* teacher, let alone the great ballerina who had taught dancers like Tania Riabouchinska, Lulu Rostova, and David Lichine. What I *do* remember was the exciting moment at the end of the barre work when she placed one perfectly straight leg on the barre, with the other standing well turned out on the floor. From this taut position she did a port de bras, lowering her torso and arms so smoothly that she might have kissed her small, raised foot. I almost applauded for this sixty-three-year-old woman, who was as supple as I at fifteen.

We left Paris to tour again, and my greatest regret was having to leave Kchessinska. To have been her pupil for those ten days was one of the great honors of my life.

We arrived in Barcelona, and the routine was the same as during our previous stay—more *langostas* at Los Caracoles and many more glasses of Manzanilla at late-night suppers. The same little girl at the pension again brought me a pitcher of water and a basin, and there were siestas in the hot afternoons.

One day, Massine and Grigoriev canceled rehearsals. We were given permission to attend the bullfights. I had been in a bullring only that one time in Mexico to dance, and that day I almost fainted when I saw the first bull killed. Everyone screamed and cheered and, as the minutes went by, I thought it would be wiser to concentrate on the daring of the men in the ring rather than focus on the fate of the bulls. By the end of the fierce competition between Spanish and Mexican matadors, I was on my feet along with the Catalans, shouting "Olé!"

One young Mexican, dressed in a pale-blue suit of lights, swirled his cape magnificently. He stopped suddenly, lunged with an outstretched arm, and "hissed" at the bull. The bull stopped in its tracks, mesmerized, as the matador slowly turned his back and knelt on one knee. The crowd fell silent. Very slowly he made the sign of the cross, then rose and strode away from the massive bull. The crowd went wild. I left the arena exhausted by the noise and excitement of seeing the bravery of those graceful young men face death that afternoon.

We left Barcelona, driven by a cross-eyed driver who somehow maneuvered our bus safely to Valencia for a one-night stand, and then we went on to Madrid. I remember little of that city except a visit to the Prado Museum with its remarkable treasures. Zorina and I roomed together in an old pension, and between periods of work, we pored over the passions of D. H. Lawrence's *Lady Chatterley's Lover*. Too young to appreciate Lawrence's analysis of British upper-class morality, we skimmed through the audacious novel, searching for "sexy parts," which we found hilarious. We never got beyond the passage where the heroine winds flowers in her lover's pubic hair, since we were laughing so hard we dropped the book, and burst into hysterical guffaws every time we tried to reopen it again.

We returned to London for a two-month summer season at the Royal Opera House. With a feeling of great relief, I unpacked my trunk in the room that would be the closest thing to "home" that could be had on tour. It was in a boarding house on Montague Street, within walking distance of Covent Garden. It was a grimy place, neat but not clean, filled with the smell of stale bacon. There was a common bathroom for all the lodgers, and by the time I usually got to the tub and inserted my pennies into the meter attached to the hot water tank, there wasn't enough water to reach even my navel. But since I was in the house only to bathe and to sleep, the little inconveniences weren't important. Whatever shabbiness surrounded me in that little house was forgotten the moment I closed the front door behind me. Flowers and fresh vegetables scented the cool early-morning air as I hurried to the theatre past the vendors, carts, and a tall bobby or two.

During the previous month word had filtered through the company that part of our rehearsal time in London would be devoted to a new ballet by the famous sister of the great Nijinsky, Bronislava Nijinska. We heard that the ballet would be called *Les Cent Baisers*, based on Hans Christian Andersen's *The Swineherd*, with a revised libretto by Boris Kochno. Nijinska chose Irina to dance the Princess, Lichine for her Prince, and Edouard Borovansky, a fine character dancer, as the

King. Secondary roles were given to Roman Jasinsky, Yurek (George) Lazowsky (another Pole who had recently joined us), and the Czech Vania Psota.

The first time I saw Nijinska was at Covent Garden, that day in June when she selected dancers for the corps de ballet of *Cent Baisers*. We sat in straight-backed chairs placed around the edges of the rehearsal hall with our eyes fixed on the small, plump woman. From the start it was obvious that she was all severity. Her pale green, faintly Tartar eyes peered at us from an impassive face, totally free of makeup. Her nondescript blondish hair was pulled back tightly into a small bun, and she wore a long, shapeless navy-blue garment resembling a sailor's uniform, and spotless white gloves.

"Why the gloves?" I whispered to Branitska.

"She don't like feel sweat," she whispered back.

The girls Nijinska called onto the floor would be the final choices for the ballet. Those left sitting would be understudies. So I was thrilled to see her point to me, but the thrill quickly passed. When she began to choreograph, I saw that although my technique had improved, I wasn't prepared for the kind of movement Nijinska demanded.

Her torso and arms writhed like sinuous snakes, their movement phrases often ending in a sudden snap of the wrists. Simultaneously her iron-strong legs whizzed through glissades, brisés volés, and innumerable entrechats six. Though plump, Nijinska was incredibly light and fast on her feet. Her unorthodox combinations were assertive, syncopated, and wriggly in the torso, while sharply classical in the legs. Nijinska's movement was imbued with a brisk humor that was distinctly different from Massine's broader comedy.

We had five weeks before the premiere in which to master her unique and unfamiliar style, and every afternoon we struggled with its weird juxtapositions. Taking our wrists daintily in her gloved hand, Nijinska led us to our places and said, "Now, do." She spoke Russian and always whispered in an attempt to hide the fact that she was quite deaf.

We never waited with Nijinska. Every step was clearly organized in her mind. As soon as one detailed phrase had been danced to her satisfaction, she would move on to the next sequence. Irina could be very mischievous during rehearsals and often burlesqued her dramatic roles. But during those days she rehearsed on pointe, full out and completely serious. She quickly captured the Nijinska style, with all its strange subtleties, without losing her own fluidity of motion.

Nijinska smoked constantly, using a long silver cigarette holder. Becoming more and more engrossed in her work, she would absent-mindedly let her cigarette fall, still lit, to the floor. One man or another would run and pick it up, returning it to her with a slight bow, murmuring respectfully, "Here you are, Bronislava Fominichna." She would nod without a word and grip the holder, only to let it drop again moments later, when the whole process would be repeated.

Looking at me one day, Nijinska pointed and muttered something in Russian to Grigoriev.

"What did she say, Anna? What did she say?" I asked Volkova.

"'What can I do with the foreigner? She's neither fish nor fowl,'" was her quick if rather embarrassed translation.

At first I felt humiliated, then angered by her words. I didn't mind so much being called a foreigner, but I never thought of my dancing as so vague. I resolved on the spot not only to improve my technique and work on my own character in dancing, but also to learn Russian immediately. If people were going to talk about me, I was going to know what they were saying!

After that comment I expected Nijinska to replace me in the ballet, but she never did. "Neither fish nor fowl" was dancing with the other Maids-in-Waiting when Les Cent Baisers opened at Covent Garden on July 18, 1935. Rehearsals had gone along smoothly right up until the day of our first orchestra rehearsal. At the eleventh hour we found that many of the nuances we had rehearsed so carefully disappeared under voluminous tutus with bulky leg-of-mutton sleeves that hid the droll twitches of our shoulders. We also wore wigs, feathered hats, and white gloves, just like Nijinska's. It was disheartening to see that our hours of working on fine details were now lost in fussy excess.

Les Cent Baisers was designed by Jean Hugo and had a score by the banker-composer Baron Frederic d'Erlanger. It had a mild success and was kept in the repertory for several years. When we reached New York, John Martin summed up Nijinska's work with us by saying, "She has been merciless in her demands on the dancers, but in a number of places it has been worth the pains, for she has achieved a somewhat frantic staccato that makes for an extremely amusing style." I thought that having the chance to work with Nijinska was the most worthwhile thing about *Cents Baisers*, although her interest in us seemed strictly academic. It was impossible to gauge her reaction to our performances from her perpetually inscrutable face. Did we or didn't we please her? No one could ever tell.

Several of our performances that season at Covent Garden were attended by British royalty. At one *Swan Lake* matinee, we were all leaning on the shoulders of our huntsmen, commiserating with the pleading of our Swan Queen that day, Baronova. As she sank to the floor, gracefully bending her head and draping her torso and arms over her extended leg, a young voice hissed loudly from the darkness of the theatre, "Get up!"

It was Princess Margaret Rose, the younger daughter of the Duke of York, leaning out of the Royal Box, carried away by her excitement with the performance. The child's imperious command made the audience burst out laughing. I'll never know what kept the "swans" in character!

All London was gossiping that season about the romance of Margaret's uncle, the Prince of Wales, and Mrs. Wallis Simpson. From my position on the floor during the Prelude of *Les Sylphides* one night, I had a perfect view of the Royal Box, where I spotted the prince himself, Lady Cunard, and both Mr. and Mrs. Ernest Simpson. At one point I saw the Prince, at the rear of the box, bend towards the dark-haired woman. After the ballet, I rushed into the dressing room yelling, "He kissed her on the neck!" There were a few blasé remarks, but no real surprise. "But she's *married!*" I insisted.

"*Nu, dushka,* so vat?" an older dancer shrugged.

"Vy you all late?" Grischa barked, appearing in the doorway. "Onstage, all of you!" Conversation and speculation on the prince and the commoner ceased as we raced back onstage to the lights, sets, and costumes of our more familiar fairy tales.

Between hectic rehearsals for the new ballets and performances, I was spending all my free time with Roman Jasinsky. Courteous and modest, he was more attractive to me than the more aggressive *moujiks* who teased the girls unmercifully with suggestive remarks like, "Vy you save it? Come vid me, I teach you!"

Roman was naturally polite to everyone. I used to feel tremulous sighs of a kind of pride inside as I saw him pick up more of Nijinska's cigarettes than any of the other men. I was as drawn to him by his courtesy as by his fair complexion and beautiful body. He treated me so protectively that I felt totally serene and secure in his care. His attention to me was quiet and unaggressive.

We were soon having late suppers together every night. Although we were drawn to each other, Roman tried to explain to me that an almost ten-year difference in our ages inhibited him sexually. He told me that at his age he didn't feel comfortable pursuing a fifteen-year-old girl. Rather than convince me it was wrong, I loved him all the more for being so considerate of my youth and my welfare. In August, just as the season ended, Roman and I gracefully and untraumatically became lovers.

Yasha, as we called Roman, adored the sun and always knew where to find it. Leaving London together for our month's holiday, we went to Nice and then by ship overnight to Calvi, a tiny town at the northern end of Corsica. There we found a cheap but very clean pension. By day our sparsely furnished room seemed very romantic. But at night our bliss became a battlefield as swarms of mosquitoes divebombed through the netting that enclosed our bed. By morning I was covered with large red welts and was itching all over. Roman sweetly ignored the blotches and made me feel even prettier than I tried to be for what was, in essence, my honeymoon.

Outside the mosquito-infested room, our romantic holiday was perfect. We discovered a tiny, deserted beach and baked the year's exhaustion out of our bones in the blazing sun. Hand in hand each morning, we bought fresh bread, salami, and cheese to take to a cool pine grove near the water for a picnic lunch in the deep shade. Sitting there in our little haven, Roman told me all about himself. At Christmastime in 1932, only three years earlier, he had been too poor to buy food. Half-fainting with hunger, he went to ballet classes at Egorova's studio in Paris just to be able to have the sweet tea and cakes she would give him after class. I listened to my lover's dramatic story in awed silence, thinking how brave he had been.

For a month we slept late every day, swimming, eating, talking, and laughing whenever we chose. Talking over company life, we swapped gossip about all the romances, a few of which were homosexual. Dancers were in such close physical contact all the time—touching, holding, and lifting one another—that sexual involvement developed quite naturally out of their familiarity and trust of each other's bodies. Roman told me that many couples had been together for years, with or without a marriage license, some since the Diaghilev years and the lean uncertain days that followed his death.

Our holiday drifted by and I began to understand the feelings those couples must have shared over the years. I felt completely at ease with Yasha, and luxuriated in the comfort of his tenderness. Sharing my life with him became as natural as dancing, and I felt a happiness I had never known.

September came and we returned to Paris to buy our coming year's supply of silk tights and to take some classes to loosen up our brown, long-idle bodies. For once we didn't mind having to give up our holiday to begin work again, because at the end of our voyage back to the United States on the S.S. *Lafayette* was to be the first appearance of de Basil's Ballet Russe de Monte Carlo at the Metropolitan Opera House in New York.

ol Hurok had taken special care with the plans for the New York engagement because the Metropolitan meant something very special to him. And Hurok meant something very special to me. I was only fifteen years old when I first met him, but I was instantly charmed by this dashing, rather chubby figure of authority and fame. "Solchik" had flair. And when he'd flatter me with the special diminutive "Asatichka," I'd think how wonderful it was that this great man, with such a remarkable story, had noticed me.

Hurok came to America in 1906, an immigrant from the village of Pogar in the Ukraine, and, like other Russian immigrants of that time, arrived clutching his cherished goose-feather pillow and one dollar. When he discovered the Met a year later, he became a permanent patron of the gallery, sitting night after night in his eight-dollar suit to hear Chaliapin's every performance. His first jobs in America—as a bottle washer and hardware salesman, among others—were only temporary. His passion for the musical arts and dancing, combined with tireless initiative and keen intuition, produced astounding results. By 1935 Hurok had become the world's greatest impresario of musical and dancing talent. He had managed Isadora Duncan and Anna Pavlova, and his ceaseless pursuit of the greatest performers available carried the one-time immigrant many times around the world.

Hurok needed all the patience and fortitude he could muster to cope with the illnesses, injuries, and temperamental outbursts that plagued us no less than any other ballet company. In addition to the unavoidable pressures of touring, unforeseen clashes of personality now jarred the company management and began to unnerve us. What we began to sense was the mounting friction between the colonel and Massine. De Basil was determined to maintain sole charge of the company's artistic policy and refused to give Massine the title of Artistic

Director. Massine was not satisfied to remain with only "collaborator" status in artistic decision-making. Casting of ballets brought further clashes. Massine wanted his vivacious wife, Delarova, to dance the Tarantella in *La Boutique Fantasque*. De Basil insisted that *his* vivacious *new* wife, Olga Morosova, dance the role. (His first wife hadn't been seen for a long time.) The men reached a stalemate and the two vivacious ladies alternated in the part. For the present at least, Massine would turn away while de Basil sat enthralled watching Morosova, whose legs, he said, reminded him of bubbling champagnski.

I doubt if Massine had more to contend with than the colonel did. For quite some time, de Basil's long association with René Blum had been coming to an end. Ever since the company's first transatlantic tour, the colonel had spent more and more interest and energy on America, while Blum—the gentle and cultured brother of the French Socialist premier Léon Blum—chose to remain on the Continent. Unwilling to hold back his effort to give us worldwide exposure, de Basil broke away from Blum and with that had to relinquish the words "de Monte Carlo" from the company's title. We were renamed Col. W. de Basil's Ballets Russes.

But despite whispers of intrigue in the company management, our main concern remained the opening night at the Metropolitan Opera House. It was certainly no surprise to us that the Met was a vast improvement over the Majestic Theatre. The slightly raked stage was enormous and deep enough to allow the simultaneous hanging of several backdrops that sprang to life as Grigoriev's directions regulated the colored lights which brought perspective to the painted canvases. During those technical rehearsals we examined the badly pitted stage carefully, making note of the dangerous ruts.

The only undistinguished feature of the Met was the stage-door entrance, an inconspicuous slot in the drab, exterior brick. Just inside it, doors led to the stage and the dressing rooms from a narrow passageway covered in metal as a fire protection. Beyond that passage, the dressing rooms for the leading dancers were small and stuffy, but quite near the stage. Massine had one to himself. Danilova and Riabouchinska shared one; in another were Irina and Tamara, who, in the midst of tutus, feathers, and wigs, had to make room for the mamitchkas. Soloists and coryphées were assigned much larger quarters one flight above the stage. In a single room, makeup tables bordered in lights ran around all four walls, leaving the center of the floor free for a costume rack bristling with hooks holding our freshly ironed costumes.

Each of us had her own place before the makeup mirror and arranged her dressing table for personal convenience. On the table we laid a towel or piece of oilcloth, then covered it with tubes and pots of greasepaint, cakes of rouge, and cans of glue beside boxes of newly invented false eyelashes. Large bottles of cheap eau de cologne stood beside tiny ones of precious French perfume. The Russian girls reserved special places for their little icons, which they kissed before rushing onstage. My place was as crowded as the others, but in my place of honor was a talisman of superstition rather than a Russian Orthodox icon. In "Voolvort's" I had found a Russian doll of a little boy, made in Kazakhstan, that stood just six inches high. I treasured it as my good-luck piece.

Unlike crowded theatres elsewhere, the Met had ample wing space that allowed us to rush through our entrances and exits easily. There was even room for a large screen, which enclosed a makeshift dressing room where we made lightning-fast changes. Very often we appeared in more than one scene of a ballet, especially in Massine's symphonic works, but the music left us only a few minutes to change costumes. True to form, the mothers helped out as dressers during the frantic rush. Many times we'd stand half-naked, moaning, "Hurry, Mamitchka, hurry! We're late! We're late!" Hooking us up calmly, they'd say to soothe our nerves, "Don't worry, *dushka*, you make, you make." And somehow we always made it onstage, fully and properly costumed, with only the vaguest idea of how we had got there on time.

Before the curtain each night, the stage filled with nervous dancers, each warming up and calming himself in his own way. Massine wiggled his slim hips from side to side and jiggled his fingers. Baronova bounced, jumping from a well-turned-out second position into the air, landing in the same position, and up again. Danilova rose on pointe in relevés and nervously ruffled the edge of her tutu. Riabouchinska circled the crowded stage in flashing leaps, while Lichine and Roman pranced in place like racehorses in the starting gate.

Mamitchka Toumanova, wearing her perpetual black dress with a collar spiked with safety pins and threaded needles, stood next to her daughter and repeatedly made the sign of the Russian Orthodox cross

DISTANT

over Tamara's heart. The girls bent to retie the ribbons of their pointe shoes more securely. The men spiraled straight up, lips compressed, practicing their double air turns. The overture ended and we scattered into the wings for still another step in the rosin box.

The Met opening-night audience gave us a reception far beyond our expectations, and every night thereafter the theatre was packed to capacity—from the Diamond Horseshoe to standing room. We received enormous publicity in the press, which dubbed Tania, Irina, and Tamara the "Baby Ballerinas." Tamara was also called the "Black Pearl of the Russian Ballet," and every bit of human-interest value was wrenched from the hair-raising story of her birth in a boxcar in which, along with seventeen White Russian officers, her parents fled the Revolution via Siberia. Group interviews invariably ended with the brash reporters yelling, "Lift up your skirts, girls. Give us more leg."

Our twelve days at the Met grossed $75,000, and launched us into our 1935–36 tour of 212 scheduled performances in 110 different places. Added to the repertory that season were revivals of:

CARNAVAL
Choreography: Fokine; music: Schumann;
décor & costumes: Bakst

CHOREARTIUM
Ch: Massine; m: Brahms (Fourth Symphony);
d & c: Terechkovitch and Lourie

LES FEMMES DE BONNE HUMEUR
Ch: Massine; m: Scarlatti; d & c: Bakst

FIREBIRD
Ch: Fokine; m: Stravinsky; d & c: Gontcharova

SOLEIL DE NUIT
Ch: Massine; m: Rimsky-Korsakov; d & c: Larionov

THAMAR
Ch: Fokine; m: Balakirev; d & c: Bakst

To top our Met success, Hurok engaged the great Leopold Stokowski to conduct some of our performances at the Philadelphia Academy of Music. We heard that Stokowski conducted without a baton, so, curious to watch the maestro's unique method, the company went to the first orchestra rehearsal with more than usual interest.

Stokowski was even more devilishly attractive than his pictures. With his aureole of fair hair and graceful hands, he looked like an archangel leading the musicians through Chopin's preludes, nocturnes, mazurkas, and waltzes in *Les Sylphides*. Stokowski was an arresting sight, but our ears told us that something was wrong with the music. He was conducting at a funereal pace. As Irina executed a series of arabesques en relevé ending in a deep plié, he drew the music out like a dirge.

Posed in our *Sylphides* formations, we whispered in amazement: "How can she balance that long?"

"Is not possible!"

"Vat he doing?"

"Is crazy. Hold music forever."

When she finished her variation, Irina was stopped by Stokowski. "Does my tempo suit you?"

"Mr. Stokowski," she replied coquettishly, without batting an eyelash, "vat you do, *I* do."

That night she danced the performance at the same speed without losing a trace of her marvelous control and fluidity. The next day the headline of a Philadelphia newspaper read, "Baronova Says Stokowski Nice Man But Lousy Conductor." But Stokowski didn't mind. A few nights later he invited Irina to dine with his family.

Our Philadelphia engagement over, we headed west on the train. Living with Yasha in Corsica had been simple and romantic, but I wanted to avoid the lies and embarrassment of registering in hotels across the country as Mrs. Roman Jasinsky. So I decided to register instead with Anna Volkova and an American girl, Patty Thall, now called Kyra Strakhova. Patty was born in St. Louis but was brought to Paris by her mother to study with Kchessinska. She was an attractive blonde who spoke and probably wrote fluent Russian. What I particularly liked about Patty was her wry sense of humor, but as much as I enjoyed her company, and Anna's, I'd no sooner sign the hotel register and go upstairs before I was knocking on Yasha's door to spend the night with him.

It was on those long train rides that I became good friends with Patty and Anna. Between mending tights and "*shtopat*zing" pointe shoes, we pored over movie magazines and first heard two examples of Patty's hobby of inventing words.

"She's *so* 'John Canoe,'" Patty would say, studying a picture of Jeanette MacDonald.

"What do you mean by that?"

"Well, Katharine Hepburn is 'Redurr' and *she's* 'John Canoe.'"

I soon caught on. 'Redurrism' was best exemplified by President Roosevelt, Mary Astor, Ronald Colman, and Hepburn. Beside such style and dash, Nelson Eddy and his singing companion could never hope to be more than "John Canoe" in our opinion.

But even more than movie stars, legendary stars of the ballet were our true idols. I had by this time built up enough courage to approach Mme. Tchernicheva once in a while. When I spoke to her on a few of those train rides, I asked her to describe the immortal dancer most of us had only seen in photographs.

"Lubov Pavelovna," I inquired, "how exactly did Nijinsky jump through the window in *Spectre de la Rose*?"

"Vell, I tell you. In middle of last jump, ven legs open," she said, "he raise torso from hip—he stay in air—I never see no dancer do dat vay." She told me further that after Nijinsky had regained his breath, he still had strength enough to unwind by doing innumerable small changements backstage. I thought this was all the more fantastic when I later saw dancers who performed *Spectre* barely able to stand up after their exit. Lichine used to slump to the floor in a heap, gasping for air.

Tchernicheva herself was as impressive as her stories. Naturally she was not as limber as the younger ballerinas, but she didn't need to be with her stunning beauty and dramatic stage presence. I'll never forget her as Zobéide in *Schéhérazade*, reclining langorously in the arms of the Shah as the curtain rises, or sitting straight-backed on the cushions, the turban on her head spouting white ostrich feathers, watching with imperious hauteur as her lover departs. Once onstage she was always in command, but Tchernicheva performed so rarely that the opening notes of the overture always made her nervous, and she would pace back and forth like a caged lioness. Knowing how difficult she was to please, we became even more nervous than she was whenever she performed with us.

When she danced the sadistic Queen of Georgia in *Thamar*, several English girls and I as her handmaidens dressed her onstage quite close to the footlights, with only a few bars of music to finish the job. We had to slide an elaborate lamé jacket over the many rings and bracelets that covered her hands and wrists, but the silk always caught on the ornaments. Under her breath she would mutter in Russian, "*Bozhe moy!* My God! These foreigners!" and we would tremble. If looks could kill, we would have been as dead as her stage lover, who, at the ballet's end, was thrown out of a window as Thamar, settling herself on a divan, beckoned still another victim by slowly waving a crimson scarf.

It was said that Tchernicheva had had as many lovers offstage as she had on. The older dancers told me that during one of the Diaghilev seasons in Barcelona, she had been discovered on the floor of a box in the Teatro Liceo, frolicking in the arms of one of the theatre's firemen. Another time, in Monte Carlo, the whole company was witness to a *bolshoi* scandale. One morning Tchernicheva and her current lover failed to show up for rehearsal. Diaghilev walked in rather grandly and noticed who was missing.

"Sergei Leonidovitch," said Diaghilev, summoning Grigoriev, Tchernicheva's husband. "Go get them."

Grigoriev did, and, when all three returned, there was a scene that culminated with the lover jumping up (in an entrechat six, someone said) and slapping the already humiliated Grigoriev in the face, in front of the entire company!

I was learning more and more Russian, and one of my teachers on tour was Hurok's road manager, David Libidins. Libidins was a friendly, unflappable man who waited by the train every time we were ready to move on. As I rushed to the train lugging my bags, he would call out, "*Nu*, Sonitchka, what's the verb, 'to sleep'?"

"*Ya splu*," I'd say with my eyes half-open. The third-person plural past tense took weeks to learn, but I came up to Libidins on the platform with a little more energy than usual the morning I knew it.

The poker games resumed, and several new American male dancers and a Cuban, Alberto Alonso, joined Mama Riabouchinska and the boys. Soon they were yelling out, *"Chort vazmy! Devil take it!"* when they lost. Roman played occasionally, but most of the time he was with me, the two of us lying under our overcoats, sleeping on the long, long bed.

The closer we came to Chicago, the more apprehensive I became about revealing my love affair with Yasha to my parents. Would Father try to kill him? Would Mother embarrass him with a sarcastic remark? I didn't know what to expect, which did little to lessen Yasha's anxiety. When we finally arrived at the apartment on Michigan Avenue, we were taken completely by surprise. There was no mention of my loss of virginity, no talk of marriage, no imposing of guilt. My parents welcomed Roman warmly and invited him to dinner at home with us whenever our schedule permitted. I sat beside him at the table relieved and elated that our relationship had been accepted.

While we were eating supper at home, the company's attention had turned to a stranger who entered our midst in Chicago. His arrival caused quite a stir, not only because it was unexpected, but because he was tall, dark, and extremely handsome. "Look like movie star," more than one person commented. His name was German Sevastianov, and like any newcomer to the troupe, he was given a thorough going-over.

Gerry, as he was called, was Moscow-born and spoke fluent French and English. He had first seen a ballet performance at the Bolshoi Theatre when he was five years old, and fell in love with it. As an émigré, much later, in 1933, he saw the first London season of de Basil's company and was so impressed that he decided to do anything to get involved with it. After several jobs he came to New York and told Hurok he would take any job available, and wound up with a subconcession selling our souvenir programs. Colonel de Basil offered him a job as his own secretary awhile later, but the wages were so low that Sevastianov declined the offer. Disregarding the refusal of his offer, de Basil had all of his clothes removed from his hotel room and sent to Chicago, knowing full well that Gerry would have to come after them and that, once there, he would get caught up in the life of the company.

We soon became accustomed to seeing Sevastianov at the colonel's side backstage before performances, both men freshly shaved and in full evening dress. The colonel looked us over carefully, then warned us, "Gardez la ligne! Watch the line!" meaning to make our crossovers in *Swan Lake* with the precision of a Cossack regiment. Following the colonel from performances to meetings to press conferences, Gerry quickly absorbed what he needed to know. With his knowledge of English (the colonel's vocabulary was still pitifully small), added to what he was learning on the job, Sevastianov was soon de Basil's indispensable right-hand man. It wasn't long before he was shouldering managerial problems on his own, dealing with lawyers, accountants, and conductors with charm and intelligence.

The two conductors who traveled as regular members of the company were the tall Russian Efrem Kurtz and Antal Dorati, a former pupil of Zoltán Kodály. Despite his youth, Dorati allowed nothing to shake his composure. If an agitated dancer demanded a specific tempo, Dorati smiled agreeably, then conducted precisely as the music was meant to be played. Only if he saw that the performance was running late would he accelerate the tempo of the finale. At those times it was amusing to see one of the complaining dancers come up to him and say, "Oh, Tony! Dot much, *much* better!"

The tour went on its routine course until we reached Columbus, Ohio, when another *bolshoi* scandale disrupted our common life.

Irina Baronova was by now a beautiful young woman whose dancing had supported herself and her parents for four years. She was almost seventeen and aching to have her own life, but Mamitchka had her lorgnette aimed at Irina's every move on and off stage. Irina had had enough of tending her little pet monkey in its cage and decided she would break out of hers. When she boldly announced that she had fallen in love with Gerry Sevastianov, Mamitchka gave her a black eye. De Basil was outraged when he heard of this and decided to take the Baronova family business into his own hands. On a prearranged day Gerry sat waiting in a taxi outside the theatre after a matinee. The colonel himself diverted Mama Baronova's attention while Irina bolted out the stage door and into the waiting cab.

For some reason the cabdriver suggested Cincinnati for the wedding, but when they got there, the courthouse clerk told them that the bride had to be twenty-one to "get hitched in Ohio." So the lovers drove on, crossing the bridge over the Ohio River into Kentucky, where they were married in Newport, with two obliging strangers as witnesses.

The next morning, headlines read "Baby Ballerina Elopes with Manager." Mama Baronova rushed to the police in a rage, demanding just retribution—exactly what, no one knew. The older dancers in the company were, for once, shocked at Baronova's daring, but I thought it was wonderfully romantic. The episode titillated us for weeks after.

Our train continued westward through the snow, carrying ballet, Borodin, and Bakst to Joplin, Sioux Falls, and Des Moines. In Butte, Montana, we performed in a movie theatre where our sets, costumes, and props had to be squeezed onto a stage barely big enough to fit a movie screen and a few vaudevillians. Assigned to a coal bin in the theatre's basement, Patty and I made up under a single, unshaded light bulb hanging from the ceiling. Hitching up our court gowns for *Aurora's Wedding*, the opening ballet, we carried our toe shoes in hand and tiptoed through the filthy cellar and up to the stage. We knew that where we dressed was never any excuse. Grigoriev expected us to be immaculate at every performance.

Keeping clean was nothing compared to trying to keep warm. Dancing in the bitter cold of the Northwest in January and February meant coping with legs and the soles of our feet feeling almost numb. We had to warm up for at least an hour dressed in layers of sweaters, leg warmers, and bathrobes, and even then many a swan in the first ballet entered with inappropriate goose pimples. Just off the uninsulated baggage cars, our grease paint felt like ice cream on our faces. One of our consolations was the colonel's superstition that if we were working on January 1, we would work the coming year. I often wished he had chosen a warmer date!

But the audience saw only the glamour of our lives, which lasted exactly as long as the orchestra was playing. Our own idea of glamour, as it was for millions of others, was the glamour of Hollywood, and we spent as much of our free time at the movies as possible. Escaping the penetrating cold one afternoon, Lulu and I went to the movies to see Charles Boyer and Loretta Young in the torrid film *Caravan*. For a few hours we were lost in the warmth of the theatre, Boyer's "bedroom eyes," and the passion of gypsy life, complete with violins. The film ended and we wandered up the aisle, only coming back to reality when the cold outside the theatre hit us. A clock read 8:12. We ran with hearts pounding to the theatre only to hear the opening Prelude of *Les Sylphides* half over as we fell in the stage door.

"*IM*-possible," said Grigoriev, waving us off without even listening to our feeble excuse, "I fine you dollar, boat of you."

It was only in extreme cases of "unprofessional" behavior, such as our being late for performance, that a dancer was ever singled out for personal attention. Otherwise, our learning and development were absorbed subliminally. We worked and watched and listened. No one even ran after the ballerinas to commend them on their performances, so I never received or expected praise for dancing well as one of the three Odalisques in *Schéhérazade*, let alone for staying in line in *Swan Lake*. Among us dancers there was seldom time for artistic conversation, especially on the road, where our primary concerns were maintaining our strength, keeping warm, and getting enough rest.

After dancing in Boise and Portland, we saw the bright sun and orange groves of California as an Eden, and greeted the state with shouts of joy from the train. Everyone was excited about our opening at the Auditorium Theatre in Los Angeles.

The first ballet that night was *Aurora's Wedding*. The opening Polonaise over, the corps stood at the side of the stage during the variations scanning the audience for movie stars. I spotted one in the second row with a scarlet mouth, and one eye hidden beneath a black velvet beret. It was Marlene Dietrich, with Josef von Sternberg next to her. I passed the news along under my breath, and soon the whole corps de ballet was squinting against the stage lights to look at the Blonde Venus in the second row.

Later, during the Bluebird pas de deux, I caught sight of a shimmering figure in white satin seated in a box to the left of the stage. As she adjusted her ermine coat, I realized it was Jean Harlow and lost my breath. I wanted to gape openly but knew it was too unprofessional. Besides, I might have been seen by the colonel and Gerry, who were there in the box, hovering over her like birds.

Mother had always forbidden me to see any of Harlow's films, claiming they were too suggestive for a child. Until now I had contented myself with a photograph of her in a barrel, bathing under Clark Gable's admiring eyes. She was even better in the flesh!

Le Beau Danube ended the performance, and we all raced back to the hotel to dress for a party in our honor at the Ambassador Hotel. Hoping to get an even closer look at more stars, I tore into my room, where my pale-blue crepe dress and orange kimono with matching blue lining lay waiting for me on my bed. I had a fresh gardenia all ready to wear in my hair, and I was finally going to have the chance to use the silver nail polish I'd been carrying, unopened, wherever we went. I had just about finished drying my hair and doing my nails when all the lights in the room blew out. Cursing, I stumbled around in the dark, gathered my things, and stormed out of the room.

The party was in full swing when I arrived, and the rushing had been worth it. Cary Grant was there, tall, dark, and sunburned, waltzing with dapper grace and charm. Our hostess, Tatiana Tuttle, a beautiful, dark-haired woman in a white satin gown cut down the back to the base of her spine, danced with Randolph Scott, tall, tanned, blue-eyed, and rugged. Most of us wandered through the crowd, dancing occasionally, giggling behind our hands at the sight of each new star. A week later Marlene Dietrich followed us to Santa Barbara. Rumor had it that she, too, wanted to be carried onstage as a rail in *Union Pacific*. But she never got beyond sitting under the amber lights in the first wing, dressed in gold lamé, to watch *Prince Igor* with Warriors dancing with more fury, and Maidens wafting their red veils more absently, than they ever had before.

We left stargazing in California and started weaving our way back East, traveling south through Denver, San Antonio, New Orleans, Birmingham, and Savannah. In April we arrived in New York for our closing season at the Met physically drained from six months on the road. Trains, hotels, rushed meals, and overworked muscles left us fit only for collapse, but we couldn't afford that luxury. New York meant new ballets.

Entering the vast and very cold rehearsal hall atop the Met, the colonel announced to us matter-of-factly, "In next ten days, we do Nijinska *Les Noces*." We forgot our shivering for a moment and looked at each other in disbelief. There were groans, moans, and eye-

balls raised heavenward. Older dancers who had danced *Les Noces*
with Diaghilev knew the enormity of the work that lay ahead. Years
later I found out that our struggles were modest compared to the years
of labor it took Stravinsky to have his ballet produced.

Stravinsky was six years old when he was taken to the Maryinsky
Theatre to see *The Sleeping Beauty*, and by the time he was sixteen, he
was spending six nights a week there watching ballets and operas. In
1914, after directing most of his energies to the score of *Le Sacre du
Printemps*, he began to work on the scenario of a cantata, based on the
subject of a Russian peasant wedding, that he had been thinking about
for several years. He called it *Les Noces*. The score was completed in
1917, but Stravinsky continued to polish the orchestration. In 1922 he
added a xylophone, tympani, two crotals, a bell, cymbals, a bass drum,
and a triangle to the choral work, and completed the rest of his revisions in Monaco in April 1923.

Diaghilev had shown interest in this music since 1915, when he
was moved to tears as Stravinsky played it for him. When Diaghilev
was given the completed score, he chose Nijinska to choreograph it.
Nathalie Gontcharova had known of the work for seven years, and
Diaghilev commissioned her to do the décor and costumes. To capture
the essential qualities of the music, Gontcharova, famous for her vibrant colors, pared them and all other ornamentation down to a stark
setting which consisted of a door, three benches, and a backdrop that
was bare except for one small painted window. She dressed the
women in theatrical versions of their rehearsal clothes, shapeless cotton tunics that fell below the knees, kerchiefs pulled low across the
brows, and cotton tights, giving the dancers the unadorned look necessary to the spirit of the work. The men wore high-necked Russian
blouses, tight-fitting trousers fastened at the knees, and cropped wigs.
The costumes, including those of the soloists, were identical; they were
in two colors, white and a blackish-brown.

Stravinsky came to all the early rehearsals, at first indicating in
terse phrases what the music was meant to convey. It soon became
clear that his meaning was beyond the dancers' immediate understanding. His frustration reached such a pitch that he began to wave his
arms. He threw off his coat, sat down at the piano, and banged out the
music, singing in an almost terrifying voice. The dancers watched his
frenzy in amazement. Inspired, the company would rehearse again

with as much fervor as they could muster. Stravinsky, exhausted by his own demonstration, would watch until he was satisfied with the day's work. At the end of rehearsal, he would put his coat back on, turn up his collar, and walk off to a bar.

Still, the dancers were so confused by the strange, complicated rhythms of the work that they rehearsed for three months with the counts of the music written on strips of paper they held in their hands as they danced. But on the opening night—June 13, 1923, in Paris, at the Théâtre de la Gaieté Lyrique, with Ernest Ansermet conducting— all the elements somehow came together. The success of *Les Noces* earned its choreographer the title "La Nijinska."

Three years later, in 1926, *Les Noces* was given its London debut by the Diaghilev company at His Majesty's Theatre. Not one critic showed enthusiasm for the "modern" ballet. The reaction of the general public was probably best represented by the two people in the stalls who walked out in the middle of the performance. Ten years passed before the ballet was seen again.

We started work on *Les Noces* on a day so cold that Grigoriev sat huddled in his overcoat as he watched us warm up in the Met's rehearsal hall. As we stood hugging our chilled bones when we weren't dancing, it was clear that we would have to forget all our classical training for *Les Noces*. The movement Nijinska demanded from us was spare, primitive, and earthbound.

In the first dance Grigorieva (formerly Sidorenko), as the Bride, stood starkly immobile on pointe, six girls on either side of her, holding eight-foot braids in their hands. As they moved in unison, she held her head rigid, staring directly front. This dance, "The Consecration of the Bride," was for the most part built on the pas de bourrée, but with the feet and legs kept facing straight ahead, not turned out. At top speed we had to come off pointe to a flat foot, but never at the same count. Some steps were accented on the count of one, some on three, some on five. We counted out loud, but we were still terribly confused.

With only ten days to complete the mounting of the ballet, Nijinska worked with extra determination. She never changed a movement. Again and again, she took our damp arms in her gloved hands, pressing them down with the command, "Down, more down!" Impatient with our failure to grasp things immediately, she'd yell, "Poot feet in ground, *more!*" Then, grunting, she would crouch her small plump body, rounding it over her knees, and inch forward like some animal in search of food. At night in my dreams, I heard the counts and Nijinska's voice shouting repeatedly, *"Zemla! Zemla!* Earth! Earth!"

Without any time to have the ancient Russian peasant rituals explained to us, we had to let the pulsating music and bizarre choreography teach us what we had to know. Dancing in a haze of exhaustion, we were mesmerized by the peculiar sounds and throbbing energy of the score. We drove ourselves relentlessly, almost fanatically. The ten days passed in one huge effort, sustained by a curious sense of exaltation.

The first orchestra rehearsal took place just a few hours before the opening. A sixty-voice choir, organized under the auspices of the Art of Musical Russia, had been practicing the score for nearly a year. They were crowded into the pit with four grand pianos and the usual orchestra. The conductor, Eugene Fuerst, took his place in front of them. We took our positions onstage and Fuerst gave the downbeat. We were appalled at what we heard. A woman's voice sang plaintively, sometimes the whole chorus sang or chanted, or a voice let out a long wail. The human sounds were mixed with drum beats, ringing bells, crashing cymbals, or periods of silence.

"Where's the music?" we cried. "What happened to the music?" The precious counts that we had learned so laboriously from the rehearsal piano had disappeared in the jumble of voices and percussion.

"Where is music? Can't find music," one dancer after another would moan, as we moved from one scene to the next in growing despair. All afternoon we counted and swore in confusion, while the well-rehearsed chorus sang and yelled with total clarity and precision. De Basil kept rushing onstage to placate Nijinska in her mounting distress. At one point towards the end of rehearsal, the colonel found Tania Chamié so exhausted that she had fallen asleep onstage during one of the breaks. Amused, he bent way down and, gently prodding her, said, "Tanitchka, Tanitchka. *Icho rass*, one more time." Waking, she looked into his pale gray eyes and rose groggily to her feet and found her place with the rest of us.

A few hours later we were putting on our costumes. Despite the fear of what was to come, I was thrilled to find that my costume still

had in it the name of Kouchetouska, the Diaghilev dancer who had
worn it at the ballet's premiere in Paris.

Waiting backstage, I found my throat bone dry. The Russians kept
crossing themselves, and everyone was rechecking the thongs that
crisscrossed around the calves. Nijinska, impassive as usual, was wearing an evening dress. She stationed herself in the first wing and there
she remained. The curtain went up, the ballet began, and as we struggled through it, she became more and more agitated, hissing the counts
so loudly that the audience might have heard her. She had worked
herself up to such a pitch that by the last movement, it wouldn't have
been surprising if she had plunged onto the stage and led us through it
herself. In the final scene she yelled out, "Zoritch! Platoff!" and the
two tallest men instantly snapped their heads in line with the shorter
dancers.

When the great golden curtain fell, we were thoroughly spent.
Through its thick folds we heard nothing. Then the applause began,
slowly at first, but then growing and swelling into a low roar, punctuated by shouts of "Bravo!" Our fear and fatigue turned into pure
joy.

The next morning, John Martin in the *Times* wrote that Nijinska
"has couched her composition in terms of the starkest design, and her
movement is characterized by a general inhibition which only serves to
mark the bits of violence which break through from time to time. Here
is in essence a peasant ceremony, though there is only the merest hint
of actual peasant material in it. It is overcast with profound mysticism,
almost with a kind of terror for the solemnity of the occasion."

"The stillness of the whole company at the end after all their
frenzy," said poet-critic Edwin Denby, "is a climax of genius."

Les Noces remains one of the most powerful ballets I have ever
been part of, and to this day, I get chills when I hear the score.

e sailed for France on the S.S. *Paris* late in April. Once there, Roman and I took a room in Pigalle, where it was nice to have some privacy after months of crowded Pullmans. Six months of touring made even a few days without performances feel like a holiday, but it was still a long time until August, and we had no time to become absolutely idle. Tchernicheva taught class every morning, and rehearsals went on until late afternoon. Since Roman was loyal to Mme. Egorova, who had fed him during his days of poverty, I went along with him to take class.

Another famed alumna of the Maryinsky, Lubov Egorova was eight years younger than Kchessinska, and plumper, darker, and much less dynamic. She taught quietly, in Russian, while sitting on a low stool. Keeping her soft dark eyes alert for errors, she coached us patiently through the class, giving gentle instructions.

After an hour, changing from ballet slippers to pointe shoes, I tackled the difficult final half hour of work. Egorova wanted pirouettes, then déboulés and piqué turns, all executed in the widest circle around the room. I barely managed to keep up with the others, and finished the rapid sequence gripping the barre tightly to steady my dizzy head and queasy stomach. But since I didn't make mistakes that were noticeably atrocious, Egorova, like so many Russian teachers who had been teaching class after class, day after day, since the Revolution, did not single me out for individual criticism.

After the turns we paired off with partners to practice lifts and adagio work. I carefully followed Yasha's whispered directions. Dancing only as a part of the corps de ballet had given me no practice for standing in arabesque, supported only by a partner's hand, which many of the girls seemed to do with ease. Partnered adagio work was not a standard part of the class, but we were expected to master it just the same. Sooner or later we would be called upon to dance with a partner, so we prepared for that moment expectantly. If you couldn't learn adagio fast enough, you'd be quickly replaced by someone who could.

Partnering was especially important to a man. Apart from requiring brute force, he needed split-second timing if he was to lift the woman in one seamless motion to his shoulder or into the air. His hands had to be sensitive enough to feel for a woman's proper balance and placement to support her multiple pirouettes in place. He had to learn when to assist his partner and when to leave her alone. He had to discover that the secret of supporting his partner on pointe in a pose or in a promenade lay not in the extended hand but in the precise position of his elbow. If he held her hand too long once she had balanced with his help, the breathtaking moment in which the audience saw her, perfectly poised in space and unsupported, would be lost.

The classical repertory always calls for more women than men in the corps. Because there were fewer of them, the men were in constant demand as cavaliers, and Yasha had already gained a good deal of experience. Fortunately for me, he was a patient and skilled partner, so my first tentative efforts were not too embarrassing.

There were no showers in ballet studios, so we rubbed ourselves down with eau de cologne before leaving Mme. Egorova's studio each day. Between classes, rehearsals, and our time alone together in Pigalle, our days in Paris whisked by, and soon we boarded the train for Spain.

We arrived in Barcelona late in May and were surprised to see the train station practically deserted. We were told that the porters had gone on strike. With no knowledge of what the real situation was, we peevishly picked up our bags and carried them ourselves to our pensions. Once settled, we heard that in recent months Spain had had over one hundred general strikes.

Another surprise came during performances at the Teatro Liceo. While we danced, some of the boxholders turned their backs to the stage and held lengthy conversations with one another. Outraged, we thought longingly of our American audiences who, though inexperienced, had never been rude, even when they were confused.

Even more annoying was the problem of the stage itself, which was raked, or sloped, so that the back of the stage was several feet higher than the front. Dancing at such a perilous angle made us throw our weight constantly backwards to avoid pitching down the incline into the orchestra pit. Between class and rehearsal, we spent every moment of our break onstage, turning and jumping repeatedly in an effort to find a balanced position.

During a performance of Massine's *Choreartium* one night, our fears became reality. For some time the dancers, picking up the comment of some wag in the audience one night, had referred laughingly to the ballet as *"Crematorium."* But no one felt like laughing in Barcelona when Yurek Shabelevsky lost his balance while dancing on the raked stage, fell, and broke his elbow. With his arm contorted and an agonized look on his pale, sweaty face, Yurek sat backstage smoking a cigarette as he waited for a doctor. As we passed him in the wings, we not only felt terrible for him but realized that, at any moment, it might happen to us.

Woizikovsky and Eglevsky had left the company several months earlier, vacating several roles. In those roles, Yurek had emerged unexpectedly as an outstanding character dancer. He was small, extremely handsome, and pale as parchment. Offstage he was as silent as he was attractive, but when he assumed the character of a stage role, his transformation was as startling as Massine's. Painting his face and body a silvery-gray to dance the Slave in *Schéhérazade*, Shabelevsky lunged and darted about the stage with the desperation of a hunted animal. His caresses of Tchernicheva as Zobéide were absolutely lascivious. And, in my opinion, he suffered the most amazing death of all the men who performed the role. Fleeing down the stairs at the ballet's close, he was cut down by a scimitar as he raced past the Shah's brother. In one motion, he fell, then rose on his head, spun perfectly upright, and collapsed, quivering. In those terrifying moments the audience witnessed the death of a crazed animal rather than a man.

Shabelevsky was also brilliant in *La Concurrence*, created by Balanchine with Georges Auric and André Derain in 1932. *La Concurrence* comically depicted the competition between two tailors who vied with each other by furiously reducing the prices of their lavish clothes on sale. Their rivalry over the gathering of curious customers (including the Chaplinesque outcast, the Tatterdemalion, who bobbed among them, gleefully jangling newfound coins in a pouch) grew bitter; the crowd broke into a free-for-all and mounted into such a commotion that the well-ordered citizens of the town had to take matters into their hands and disperse the throng. The competition over, the tailors found themselves alone. Counting up their profits, they were delighted and, reconciled, congratulated each other on a good day's work. As the Tatterdemalion, Yurek showed he would have been right at home in vaudeville. Shambling onstage in a suit of rags and a hat full of holes, he danced his jerky, syncopated solo with a cocky wit that made the audience laugh out loud.

Cotillon, our other Balanchine work, was less comic than *La Concurrence*. Boris Kochno conceived the simple scenario, which began in a ballroom where introductions were being made. Woizikovsky, as the Master of Ceremonies, turned up late in a desperate hurry. He and Tania Riabouchinska, the Mistress of Ceremonies, demonstrated the first dance, which the guests repeated. Next came a series of short dances in which dancers assumed the characters of harlequins, jockeys, and Spaniards, simply by putting on hats. The central pas de deux, the Hand of Fate, followed. Next, a young girl read the fortunes of the guests, and then there was the apparition of the Bat and the *"coup de champagne."* Then came the Grand Rondo, which concluded the Cotillon.

Christian Bérard, the famous French artist, created a stylish yet simple set consisting of three shallow boxes that bordered the three sides of the stage. Delicate gold chairs were the only props. Into the subtle mood of gaiety that permeated the ballet, Balanchine injected a note of mystery far more ambiguous than the well-planned drama of the Fokine works so familiar to us. It was a ballet of youth and perfume and whispers, with moments that had the same effect as the sudden skipping of a small stone across a still pool of water—passages where the women dancers held hands and wove their way through the upheld arms of the men to pause briefly in deep, bending stretches. They were interrupted by Lichine, who at one point leaped through a box, his legs tucked sideways below his rounded back, and, after landing center stage, vigorously galloped in this crouched pose around in a circle. When the general movement seemed calm and formal, it was broken, as in the Spanish pas de trois, by the jutting of the dancers' hips to one side or by the flick of a wrist. These sudden, quirky gestures gave the ballet its special allure.

For the Hand of Fate pas de deux, the ballroom emptied of all but a single man who stood still while a large, pale-blue cloth wafted center stage as if by magic. He became curious, but cautious, and approached the cloth in long, slow arabesques, holding the sides of his thighs with both hands, first right, then left. He touched the cloth tentatively. Suddenly a black hand from behind the cloth clutched his wrist, the curtains parted, and a woman stood alone. She was dressed all in black and wore a shining half moon on her head. The two began dancing together. She lifted her leg in a slow, high développé and then lowered it. He did the same. She repeated the motion; he did too. The languid overlapping of their legs was then changed into flat-footed steps as they faced each other, first shuffling away, their torsos arched backwards and arms touching each other's wrists, then coming towards each other as their backs flattened upright, coming together chin to chin. (The same shuffling steps can be seen today in *Apollo*.)

Balanchine created the alluring Black Hand role for Lulu, who danced it with beautiful ease, since it was made for her bones and muscles. Later the part was danced by Zorina, who had a wonderful extension and a sharper attack. I particularly loved this pas de deux and would always stand in the wings to watch it.

After Zorina left the company, Grigorieva and I assumed the role. I was thrilled. Here was not only a part that I loved but one that I knew was right for my kind of dancing. I was more suited to dancing legato than allegro. It was not a technically difficult dance—there were no beats, jumps, or turns. But it needed a flow of motion, for the movements did not look strongly structured, as later Balanchine ballets do with their incredibly fast, precise, difficult positions and patterns. It had to look as light as a glance and have a scent of vague sexuality, for there was no "real" passion ever intended. Paul Petroff partnered me, and since there were no lifts in the choreography, our main contact was through our eyes and hands, and for those few minutes, we were almost in love.

When the pas de deux ended, the ballroom filled again with wheeling dancers, the women in their velvet-bodiced, long, multicolored tarletans, wearing long white gloves; the men elegant in scarlet, yel-

low, and green jackets and black satin breeches. And, at the hub of the
huge circle of rushing dancers, there was Toumanova, spinning in fast
fouettés, her long black hair whipping her face, as the curtain closed.

We had almost adjusted to the Liceo stage when it was time to return
to Paris. We were aching to stretch out in wagon-lits, but the privacy
of an entire compartment was a luxury reserved for first-class passengers. So we had to invent another "routine." I put on my kimono and
then dotted lipstick all over my face and neck. Leaning back on the
seat, I began to moan piteously. Nodding sadly at my spots, Yasha
would tell anyone who slid open the glass door of the compartment
that I had a highly contagious disease. They backed away, muttering
nervously, as Yasha struggled to keep a straight face. For once we
could spend most of a train trip in comfort and privacy.

When we boarded the ferry for England, I no longer feigned illness but crossed the Channel draped miserably over the rail. Back in
London, Roman and I found a one-room apartment near Shaftesbury
Avenue where, he promised me, he would teach me to cook. After
class at the Opera House, we would market in the stalls just outside the
stage door, Yasha squeezing and sniffing and pinching like an experienced cook, showing me which tomato was best and which chicken
was freshest. I followed his example in cooking as carefully as his
advice in dancing, and I could soon prepare plain meals of broiled
meat, vegetables, and huge salads topped with the spoonfuls of glucose
powder we consumed for added energy. After months of bistros and
drugstores, home cooking was a luxury, but it never stopped us from
accepting invitations to the Savoy Grill, where the menu listed among
its famous offerings dishes named after our ballerinas.

There had never been a company doctor, so we were elated with
the news that the company had suddenly engaged a professional masseur. Our thighs were caressed by a Polish masseur who sweated and
breathed heavily as he worked. When he heard about the panting
masseur, Roman swore he would find someone more "qualified." He
found one very soon. For a small fee, a large, white-haired English-
woman, who told us she was a yoga's disciple, came to the apartment
and massaged our muscles with a small ebony iron.

We felt the massages were an extravagance we more than deserved, because once again we were deep in rehearsals for two new works. Massine was preparing another symphonic ballet, *Symphonie Fantastique*, based on a libretto and music by Berlioz. It portrayed an artist's morbid, opium-induced fantasies and his obsessive desire for his Beloved, danced by Toumanova. In the early scenes she appeared to him as an ethereal spirit, and in the fifth scene, "Dream of a Witch's Sabbath," as a fury leading a grotesque orgy. Massine would dance-act the Young Artist. It was an ambitious undertaking, but throughout the rehearsal period, he maintained his usual inscrutable demeanor and took class diligently with the company every morning.

Massine was already well into rehearsals for *Symphonie* when David Lichine started to choreograph his third ballet, *Le Pavillon*. Boris Kochno wrote the libretto, and Cecil Beaton designed the décor and costumes. Before even showing us a single step, Lichine announced that his ballet would be a *chef d'oeuvre*, but after only a few rehearsals, it was clear that the artistry of Lichine's ballet lay in his talk about it, not in the movement. Neither the steps nor the overall choreographic design were as interesting as the great deal he had to say about them.

All this talk was topped, after one particularly hot rehearsal, in a speech by Kochno. *"Mesdames,"* he announced grandly, *"ce ballet doit être dansé comme un bijou!"*—Ladies, this ballet must be danced like a jewel! First the choreographer had been telling us *what* the ballet was about; now the writer was telling us *how* it should be danced. It struck me as a curious reversal of roles, and it didn't make me like working on it any better.

The overall nature of the work shifted from the pretentious to the outright ridiculous when Beaton's set appeared at the first orchestra rehearsal. It looked like the ladies' room of a swanky nightclub rather than the trysting place for a poet and his beloved. Irina put it bluntly, "Look like *pissoir!*"

We wafted about this dubious setting as Spirits of the Garden, striving to look "spiritual" while nearly being choked by the elastic bands under our chins that held large flowers onto our caps. The constricting headdresses made it impossible to hear as well as to swallow (the ballet itself was hard enough to swallow!), and Dorati's orchestrations of Borodin drifted by us scarcely heard.

Not even the prestigious reputations of Lichine, Kochno, and

Beaton could make *Pavillon* a success. The promised *chef d'oeuvre* received only mild approval, confirming my consistent lack of real interest in it.

Whenever a ballet is added to the repertory, a dancer gets an instinctive sense of its worth quite early in rehearsals. A certain movement may be singularly arresting, or a sequence of steps, invented that very instant, may reveal an elusive but exciting quality of the steps to come. The future development of the ballet is unknown, sometimes even to the choreographer, but when a movement rings true, the dancer knows intuitively that the next movement, whatever it may be, will be thrilling. I never put this notion into words or discussed it with my friends, but I found it to be true, time and again. My intuition told me, within the first few rehearsals, that *Pavillon* would be a disappointment and that *Les Noces* would be a revelation.

Compensation for my lack of interest in Lichine's ballet was the news that the colonel had planned a gala to highlight our London season. Originally it was to include Lydia Sokolova, Kchessinska, and Egorova with Volinine, one of Pavlova's partners. But only Sokolova and Kchessinska finally appeared on July 14. Kchessinska was met at Waterloo Station after her trip from Paris by de Basil, Lichine, and Tania Riabouchinska, with enormous bouquets to welcome her.

Appearing in London for the first time in twenty-five years, Kchessinska had chosen a Russian boyar dance that she had last performed before Tsar Nicholas II on the eve of World War I. Before they were abolished by Peter the Great, the boyars were an aristrocratic class of Russian landowners, next in rank to royal princes and roughly equivalent to the barons and knights of Western Europe. It seemed appropriate that a princess should appear in a role so close to her position in society. I couldn't wait for our part of the performance to be over so I could find a place among the dancers jammed in the wings to watch Kchessinska.

The red curtains parted, and Kchessinska, in the traditional boyar costume, stepped from the wings. She was welcomed by thunderous applause. She wore a *sarafan*, a long satin dress embroidered with pearls, and a *kokochnik*, a gilded, arched headdress resembling a full Russian tiara, trailing a satin bow with ribbons falling to her waist.

From both sides of the bejeweled headdress, long strands of pearls looped under her throat. A soft chiffon blouse covered her slim arms.

Exquisitely poised, she glided effortlessly around the big stage. Not one step was exaggerated or tense. Her glowing smile radiated an aura of such joy that we could barely contain our own rapture. Nearly sixty-four years old and making her last public appearance that night, Kchessinska received eighteen curtain calls. As the last curtain fell, she stood proudly with her small feet buried in a sea of flowers.

In her memoirs Kchessinska wrote that her husband was so nervous during her solo that he asked Serge Lifar, his companion in the box, if he dared keep his eyes open to watch. I'm grateful that mine were open to see Kchessinska display such control, such grace, subtlety of gesture, and assurance, such indisputable greatness without the use of a single jump or pirouette.

Several days after the gala, I passed a crowd of demonstrators in Trafalgar Square, waving banners and shouting slogans I didn't understand. None of us was interested in the news, which we had such little time to read anyway, so learning that civil war had broken out in Spain only made us thankful that we had gotten out of Barcelona when we did.

Symphonie Fantastique was a more pressing problem for us than war, since the premiere took place just ten days after the gala. We arrived at the theatre early that night to dress, only to be told that most of the costumes had not been delivered yet from Mme. Karinska, the costumer. Onstage, the dancers in the first movement had been dressed as visions of melancholy and gaiety, while the rest of us paced anxiously in the dressing room, wearing only shoes, tights, and makeup, with our jitters mounting as each bar of music brought us closer to an unclad entrance. At the last minute a caravan of taxis came screeching into Floral Street. Karinska's assistants jumped out, arms bulging with white hoop-skirts and tall, transparent headdresses. As they rushed into the dressing room, we snatched our gowns out of their hands, pulled them over our heads, and ran through the basement in a flurry of pale petticoats, reaching the stage just as the lights came up on the second movement.

Christian Bérard, the designer, had created a magnificent scarlet ballroom for the waltz movement. Live blackamoors, standing at attention beside soaring black archways, held golden candelabra in their uplifted arms. The dancers swept through the archways in a kaleidoscope of shifting patterns, intensified by the contrast of our billowing white skirts against the crimson walls.

Prolonged applause for the waltz gave a little extra time for us to change for the next movement. Stripping off the ballgowns, we saw that our bare waists were spotted with blood. In the last-minute rush to get Bérard's costumes to the theatre in time, Karinska had had them pinned together rather than sewn. Between our opening-night nerves and the costume scare, we had never noticed the pain!

As I stepped into my tattered gray costume for the last movements and saw the men in white hooded monks' habits, the phrases "March to the Scaffold" and "Dream of a Witch's Sabbath" suddenly made sense for the first time. In rehearsal we had learned every convoluted step of the two final movements without ever knowing who we were or why Massine wanted such twisted and tortured shapes. The costumes gave meaning to the grotesque movements we had practiced without understanding.

Symphonie Fantastique was a huge success and a triumph for Massine, both as its choreographer and as its leading dancer, but part of the impact of the ballet was surely due to the contribution of Bérard. He had an exceptional talent for designing costumes and sets that enhanced movement. The pastel leotards and chiffon draperies George Zoritch and Verchinina wore in the Pastorale movement were perfect instances of how carefully he combined fabric and texture to reinforce the choreography rather than hindering or hiding it. While the costumes were light and comfortable on the dancers, accentuating the lines of their bodies, they naturally offered the audience an unobstructed view of the choreography.

Many nights we dressed as hurriedly before leaving the theatre as we did between ballets, because our balletomane friends would open their homes to us after performances. The renowned portrait painter and his wife Sir Oswald and Lady Birley were particularly gracious, inviting us to one party so grand it rivaled Bérard's décor. Sir Oswald had cleared his large studio for dancing. He had green-and-white-striped tents erected in his garden, where we saw the Duchess of York, the present Queen Elizabeth's mother, among the distinguished guests. Pinned to a royal-blue sash at the waist of her white gown she wore a diamond brooch the size of a saucer, without a doubt the largest mass of glitter I had ever seen. Lady Mendl wore emeralds to match her dyed green hair. Everyone seemed to be having fun looking at each other.

We went to a lot of parties like the Birleys'. At every one of them, the colonel wouldn't stop looking at us, then at his watch, and, at about 1:00 A.M., he'd try to gather us together like a father with his large brood of children. *"Allons,"* he'd urge us, *"il faut partir. Répétition demain très tôt."* Russian goodbyes took a good half hour, with vital conversations and sudden phone calls to Barcelona or New York in the hallway. Then we'd leave, walk around the block, wait for a few minutes until we were sure the colonel had gone, and run back for more fun at the party.

We loved these parties, considering them not only as celebrations of the affection of our British friends but as rewards for eleven months of hard work.

Once again, Yasha and I decided to go south for our August holiday. This time we traveled to the Côte d'Azur with a hodgepodge of friends, including Alberto Alonso, two Russian sisters, one Hungarian, two Poles, and an American girl, Shirley Bridges. Now called Anna Adrianova, Shirley got carried away by her new Slavic identity. She wore high red boots and embroidered tunics like a Russian peasant girl. I thought Shirley Bridges, from Rochester, New York, looked a little ludicrous in such a getup, and the native Russians looked at her askance, if somewhat amused, since they dressed without a trace of their homeland.

We headed for St. Aygulf, where Roman assured us we could live cheaply. We arrived early in the evening and trudged down the dusty road from the railway station, hunting for a place to stay. Suddenly someone spotted a long flight of narrow steps leading up from the road between twin banks of cypresses towering like black obelisks against the mauve sky. At the top of the steps, a sign reading À LOUER hung over a rusty bell on an iron gate. Through the pine trees we could see an old villa, its once-hennaed walls faded into a soft pink, and surrounding it a large garden filled with a haphazard design of mimosas and geraniums.

Moments after we rang the bell, an old woman appeared out of the shadows. Squinting at us suspiciously, she grudgingly told us the month's rent. I was earning thirty-five dollars a week by then, and the others didn't make much more, but by pooling our money we could meet her price. We shook her hand, picked up our bags, and moved in.

Accustomed to a life run by organization and routine, we broke up the party into work groups. The men rose every morning to throw stones at the trees to loosen the pine cones. With these for tinder, they built a fire in an old iron stove, the likes of which I had never seen before except in cowboy movies. Two men brewed coffee for breakfast, while the other two cycled to market in the village. The girls planned the menus a week at a time and shared the housecleaning. We all made up our own rooms and did our own washing, which dried quickly in the garden under the hot sun. Too tired to cook, we indulged ourselves by hiring a friendly cross-eyed woman from the village, who entertained us with tales of her popularity during the First World War. She told us that, according to superstition, making love to a cross-eyed woman protected a soldier from death, which is why, she proudly claimed, she had been much in demand!

Time was forgotten as we luxuriated, lying inert, drenched in the hot sun. Sometimes we cycled to the sea to swim or into the hills to explore the wild countryside. Evenings, we played cards, talked, read, or darkened the house for hilarious games of hide and seek. Our only extravagance was an occasional trip to St. Raphael for afternoon teas. We'd ride our bicycles to our favorite patisserie and load up with freshly baked madeleines and mille-feuilles. Taking these delicacies to a nearby café, we'd order tea and hot water. We never failed to annoy the waiters by picking surreptitiously at the pastries from the boxes in our laps. As we cycled off, laughing and calling back and forth to each other, the waiters would look with disgust after us, and then at the few pitiful sous we could afford to leave for tips.

My pale body turned brown, and fresh color came to my cheeks, hidden for a year under shadow, powder, and perspiration. Fatigue melted away during those lazy, sun-filled days. But three weeks later, all too soon, a cool night air began to fill the garden with the smoky scent of approaching autumn.

Returning to Paris before sailing again for America, we faced our most difficult classes of the year. In thirty days of lying in the sun, the muscles of my limbs had relaxed while my torso had stiffened. Back in class, everything needed readjusting and realigning. My breath came in short, shallow gasps the minute I began to jump. My joints ached as I tried to stretch elasticity back into them. My bare toes, after a month of spreading comfortably in the sand, had to be forced back into cramped pink satin boxes. But slowly the flexibility and balance returned. The men found their placement again, practicing dozens of tours en l'air. Once more, my pointe shoes began to feel like natural extensions of my feet, as they would for the rest of the year.

We arrived in New York in the fall of 1936. Hurok was disturbed by our new billing, Colonel W. de Basil's Ballets Russes, because he though part of our glamour had been lost in giving up "de Monte Carlo" when de Basil had broken with Blum, who had rights to that name. But he didn't waste time on what he couldn't change. Instead he planned to get the most out of the scandalous reputation of the revival planned for our opening at the Met. Nijinsky's *L'Après-midi d'un Faune* hadn't been seen in New York since 1916, when the Diaghilev company had danced it at the Century Theatre.

In 1911, a year before the ballet's premiere, Diaghilev and Nijinsky attended a demonstration of eurythmics by Emile Jaques-Dalcroze and his pupils in St. Petersburg. Nijinsky wanted to try to choreograph a ballet, and Diaghilev wanted to introduce his protégé to a style of movement totally removed from ballet. Archaic Greek art and Debussy's shimmering *Prélude à l'Après-midi d'un Faune*, suggested by a poem by the Symbolist poet Mallarmé, inspired Diaghilev, Bakst, and Nijinsky. Debussy gave Diaghilev permission to use the score, and the twenty-one-year-old Nijinsky began to choreograph.

By the time the company reached Paris in the spring of 1912, rumors of the ballet's sexual undertones had already crept into the salons of Paris. Diaghilev was warned that Nijinsky's final erotic pose might cause a scandal, but he refused to have it changed. Word that the ballet had required one hundred and twenty rehearsals also aroused interest, and balletomanes rushed to accept invitations to the final dress rehearsal. Auguste Rodin, then seventy-two years old and quite frail, came into the theatre leaning on Diaghilev's arm. When the rehearsal ended, the audience sat in such total silence that Gabriel Astruc, French music publisher and longtime associate of Diaghilev in arranging the Paris seasons, stepped in front of the curtain and announced that since the ballet could not be understood in a single viewing, it would be repeated!

Opening night at the Théâtre du Châtelet, May 29, 1912, was quite a different matter. All eyes were riveted on Nijinsky's earthbound gestures. The spectators saw placid, controlled movement but not one of the famous dazzling leaps they expected of Nijinsky. When the curtain fell, with Nijinsky stretched suggestively on the nymph's veil, a storm of shouting broke out. Half the audience leapt to its feet, cheering and applauding. The other half hissed and booed in protest.

The next morning *Le Figaro* accused Diaghilev of immorality, stating, "Decent people will never accept such animal realism." In the ensuing uproar, many artists rallied to defend the ballet. Odilon Redon, the painter, wrote that Mallarmé would have been so happy "to recognize, in that living frieze . . . his faun's very dream, and to see the creatures of his imagination wafted by Debussy's music and brought to life by Nijinsky's choreography and the passionate color of Bakst."

Rodin wrote in *Le Matin,* "No more jumps—nothing but half-conscious animal gestures and poses. . . . His eyes flicker, he stretches his arms, he opens his hands out flat. . . . His beauty is that of antique frescoes and sculpture. . . . I wish that such a noble endeavor should be understood as a whole; and that, apart from its gala performance, the Théâtre du Châtelet would arrange others to which all our artists might come for inspiration and to communicate in beauty."

The scandal grew to such a point that the Prefect of Police was asked to close the theatre, but both politicians and artists petitioned to keep the doors open. *Faune* was given three more performances in Paris.

Ten years later, Nijinsky was hopelessly insane, a tragic loss to the dance world. Lifar danced the leading role in the revival, for which Diaghilev commissioned Picasso to design a new backdrop. When the sketches arrived late and consisted of nothing but plain gray cloth, Diaghilev was so infuriated that he deleted Picasso's name from the program.

The stately Tchernicheva had danced the chief Nymph opposite Massine as the Faun in 1916, when Diaghilev's company brought the ballet to America. Massine, now forty, was no longer suited to the role, and was probably not interested in performing it. With Grigoriev's help, Tchernicheva was in charge of our 1936 revival. Because she was tall and beautiful, Grigorieva was given the role of the chief Nymph, and Lichine would dance the Faun. I was made an understudy to Lara Obidenna, one of the six nymphs, so I worked with the other understudies at the back of the same studio where, a few months earlier, we had worked with Nijinsky's sister on *her* masterpiece.

While the famous brother and sister shared a strong attraction for turned-in feet and legs, nothing else about *Faune* resembled *Les Noces*

even in the slightest. Like the music, the movement flowed in un-
broken continuity, each step seeming to evolve organically from the
one before it. Nijinska had forced us to become part of the floor; now
we had to glide across it with our slightly bent knees like levers to raise
or lower our stiff, upright torsos. The plastic vitality of the ballet and
the sensuality that colored it were expressed by restrained energy
rather than by thudding heels or abrupt, emphatic gestures. At first we
thought the familiar music and deceptively simple choreography would
make the ballet easy to learn and to dance. But the exceptional control
needed to maintain our archaic poses was unexpectedly difficult. It
wasn't technically hard, but we weren't familiar with finding ways to
convey emotion eloquently with a minimum of dancing.

Unlike all our other ballets, *Faune* was staged in the narrow space
between the proscenium and the first wing, and all the steps were
linear, executed parallel to the footlights. We moved in two groups of
three girls each, our arms interlocked, our bodies square to the front
and our heads and feet turned in profile to face the wings. Since we
even ran with our arms linked, one jarring move could throw all three
girls off balance. During those first rehearsals, we continually stepped
on each other's heels, looking like anything but our Grecian ideal. Our
necks began to ache from being turned constantly counter to the direction of our bodies. Our fingers became stiff as we kept them held
tightly together with our palms lifted flat beside our torsos.

Tchernicheva remembered not only the choreography but also the
finest points of the overall work. She told us to rouge the heels of our
bare feet for performance and to keep our faces pale, impassive, and
expressionless ("You know, must look like Greek frieze"). Gradually,
we caught on to the sculptural tension the work required. By opening
night, we were transformed into nymphs.

Being an understudy, I watched the trios of linked nymphs glide in
perfect unison. With their immobile golden wigs they looked as two-
dimensional as Bakst's geometric borders painted on their pleated tunics. In her final, fleeing exit, Grigorieva, in her long golden tunic, flew
past me, standing in the first wing. Left alone onstage, Lichine gathered
her fallen veil in his arms and slowly climbed the hidden stairs to the
mound on which he had first been seen as the curtain rose. Keeping his
body upright and holding a fold of the chiffon in his teeth, he sank to
his knees and stretched it out on the ground before him. Arching his

neck downwards, he extended his body full length and lowered it very slowly onto the garment. He gave a small thrust of his pelvis, quivered in a brief spasm, and then slowly relaxed the clenched fist of his right hand.

I heard a woman scream and then footsteps running up the aisle. From where I stood, I had no idea of what could have happened until Tchernicheva came storming into the wings moments after the ballet had ended, her face red with anger. "David," she spat out in Russian, "I've seen many things in my life, but you've outdone yourself tonight!" Lichine grinned and thanked her, very pleased at the disturbance his last gesture had provoked. Later we learned that Hurok, always the showman, had planted the screaming woman himself, paying her fifty dollars for the outburst.

"The de Basil company danced the Faun beautifully," said Edwin Denby. "Lichine in the title role excelled. It is a part that demands exceptional imagination, as well as a great plastic sense. And Lichine had besides these a fine simplicity."

Despite its being our most static work, the audience enjoyed the simplicity of *Faune* without screaming to have the theatre closed down. I admired the ballet so much that I hoped Obidenna would catch cold so I might dance with the other nymphs, but Lara stayed healthy throughout the tour. A year or so later, another dancer left the company, and I finally had the opportunity to rouge my heels and glide into this fragment of the Nijinsky myth.

Faune quickly became a staple of our repertory, not only because the audience liked it so much but because it provided a maximum effect for a minimal expense. Its small cast, simple scenery, and light-weight costumes guaranteed its appearance in many towns across the country whose theatres were too small to stage our large, elaborate productions. Unfortunately the situation was the opposite for *Les Noces*. Because the orchestral and choral requirements for the ballet were so great, and so expensive, after its revival during the Met season, we never danced it again.

Hurok's publicity campaigns preceded our arrival in every town, stirring up previous interest and new curiosity in our many personalities and the rich repertory of Fokine, Massine, Nijinsky, Lichine, and Balanchine. With the month's holiday already far behind us, we began to wonder if we could live up to our own press releases. After mile upon mile of too much travel and too little sleep, it was more and more difficult to give a performance that was fresh, alert, and spontaneous. But the ballets themselves came to the rescue. Works like *Firebird* kept our spirits up at the same time that they thrilled the audience. The brilliance of Fokine's choreography, Stravinsky's splendid score, the magical story, and the artistry of Danilova as the Firebird made performances memorable for us onstage as well as those in the audience.

I stood in the first wing every night, just to admire Danilova's first fast, long jetés across the stage. Wearing a short orange tutu, her head wrapped in a sleek turban adorned with a jeweled feather, she *became* the shimmering creature of Fokine's folktale. The instant Massine, as the Prince, trapped her in his arms, Danilova's entire body recoiled, so repelled by her captivity that even her nostrils quivered. Their pas de deux, during which the Firebird is forced to reveal her magical secrets, described a frantic entrapment rather than a seduction. Bewildered and taut with wonder, Massine seemed to move in two directions at once, remaining emotionally distant even as he crept close to his prey.

Transfixed by the fear in his huge, dark eyes, I barely tore myself away from the shadows of the first wing in time for my own entrance as one of the twelve enchanted princesses. Supposedly stealing from our bedrooms, we were all barefoot and wore dull-gold lamé *kokochniks* and white calf-length nightdresses, still labeled with the names of the Diaghilev dancers who had last worn them in 1926. Hand in hand, we filed onstage through Gontcharova's perforated backdrop depicting the forest. We danced in the moonlit scene, lightly tossing golden apples back and forth. Playing catch on cue was not as simple as it appeared, the apples often colliding in midair. Squinting because of her poor vision, Branitska often sent a few apples sailing into the orchestra pit, which broke our poses of maidenly reverie with girlish giggles, as we stretched our arms out towards the audience and then brought them close to our chests.

Sobriety returned with the crash of cymbals and bass drums that announced the entrance of the evil sorcerer, Kostchei, dressed in trailing black robes, with matted gray hair straggling around his black and greenish-white face. With six-inch claws, he beckoned the Prince malevolently for questioning. Algeranoff usually performed Kostchei with red cellophane patches glued to his eyelids to make his downward glance as frightening as a direct look. When Lichine took the role, he made every effort to outdo Algie with even more disgusting makeup. Into his nose he pasted white strings, which dangled from his nostrils like revolting pale worms.

Kostchei's trainbearers, in papier-mâché heads that lolled peculiarly with every step, were the most hideous members of his grotesquely shriveled entourage. But by the final scene the ghastly Kikimoras were transformed into Princes, who took the Princesses as their brides. Reverently we knelt in pairs for the stately wedding ceremony of the finale. Massine, with his noble bearing and eloquent upraised hand, stood at the center of the tableau, as waves of iconlike figures of the colossal Russian culture entered to Stravinsky's mounting cadences of majestic jubilation, ending in a monumental fanfare, as the curtain fell, like a benediction.

Fokine had written his own libretto for *Firebird* and developed every sequence of steps in the closest collaboration with Stravinsky. For days they worked together in Fokine's living room. Stravinsky played through the entire score as Fokine acted all the roles, climbing over the piano as the Prince in the mysterious garden, then fluttering nervously as the Firebird herself. Originally Fokine proposed a sequence of standard divertissements for the grandiose music of the final scene. But Stravinsky suggested the more static ending, the formal coronation, where his music would dominate. Acknowledging the intrinsic power of the score, Fokine agreed to Stravinsky's suggestion and created this scene of near stillness.

There have been other versions of *Firebird* since that time, but I have never seen any as moving as Fokine's original work. And although other dancers have jumped higher or spun faster, no one, for me, has ever matched the volatile elegance of Danilova as the bird of legend. The intense power and range of feeling she brought to this role made her performance riveting then and unsurpassed now in my mind.

Danilova was the finest example of an artist to which a novice could aspire. Before every performance, she did a half-hour barre, then adagio work followed by jumps, never satisfied with her preparations until she was perspiring heavily. Her self-imposed regimen never altered, even before one-night stands, when she used a part of the set or a packing case as her barre.

Danilova was as impeccable in her dancing and appearance in

Sioux Falls as on opening night at Covent Garden. Incapable of cheating her audience, she gave herself fully in performance every night, regardless of the conditions. Some dancers grumbled about late hours and extreme cold—in Winnipeg it was below zero one night—but Choura let nothing interfere with her dancing. I don't remember her complaining. Many nights, she danced twice on the same program. Her discipline was blind to circumstance, and her dedication never wavered. Choura always found the time, despite the demands of her own work, to encourage the younger dancers who regarded her with such respect. As I came offstage one night after replacing Chabelska in *Le Beau Danube* on a moment's notice, Choura stopped me. "Sonitchka, vy you not dance better? Must try more."

"But Choura, I don't know Chabelska's part. No rehearsal," I defended myself, surprised that she had even been watching me.

"You know, makes no difference," she said. "You try more."

Performing new parts without rehearsal was becoming commonplace for me. I was now dancing in many ballets I had previously only watched from the wings. If another dancer was ill, Grigoriev would walk over to me, poke me on the shoulder, and command, "Asata, *vous pouvez*. Tonight, dance Third Movement."

"But Sergei Leonidovitch," I protested at first, "I don't even know it!"

"Yes, yes. You know, Asata, you know," he'd say with a wave of his hand. And onstage I would go, more guessing than dancing my way through the choreography.

The other girls would help by murmuring under their breath, "When you get to Petroff, kneel, he lift you on three, run to Patty. Stay twelve counts, follow Chamié in second wing, quick change Fourth Movement."

Performances like these quickened my wits but boosted my anxieties. Soloists and principals enjoyed the privilege of company rehearsals when they learned new roles, but there wasn't time for every dancer in the corps to be coached in every ballet in our repertory. After you had been with the company for a while, it was assumed that you knew the older ballets and could dance them as originally rehearsed. So whenever Grigoriev's hand landed on my shoulder, I either had to go on cold or not go on at all. If my visual memory served me well and I got through a performance without incident or noticeable error, the spot was mine thereafter. Everyone but me seemed satisfied just to have the correct number of dancers onstage.

But there was nothing particularly unusual about this unforeseen, abrupt method of learning ballets, and complaining would have been unheard of. My contract said that I was a dancer, receiving thirty-five dollars a week, whether I danced in a movie theatre in Butte or a hockey arena in Montreal. And I was not an exception to learning in crisis. When Toumanova injured her foot, Irina replaced her the same day without a single rehearsal. Thrilled with the drama of one rival helping another, we crowded into the wings to watch. Tamara sat almost onstage, in her dressing gown and holding her bandaged foot, and talked Irina through every moment of the ballet. "Chaîné . . . now arabesque . . . hold . . . wait. Now, penché . . . slow . . . and up. Wait. Come to me—big jeté. *Horosho, daragaya, horosho.*—Good, darling, good," Tamara whispered loudly, echoed by Mamitchka close behind her.

Of course the press played up the rivalry of Toumanova and Baronova, which no doubt sold some tickets. But Tamara's directions were so earnest and specific that it was impossible for us to detect any real competition between the adolescent ballerinas.

Rivalry did exist in the company, as it does anywhere in life, but in dancing, I feel, it is also infused with admiration. How can someone be truly jealous of another when, onstage, the so-called rival moves you to tears or joy in a very special way? At such moments, petty emotions dissolve when a soul is revealed. It is then, I believe, that you truly know another.

Making little allowance for crises, injuries, or last-minute substitutions, Tchernicheva sat in the audience every night, watching with critical objectivity performances for which she herself had trained us. Her comments, whether to individuals or large groups, were always to the point. "You," she'd say with a hint of impatience in her voice, "you sit down too fast. Take time." Pointing to another girl, she'd say, "More épaulement, Fokine style. Not flat like you do."

Suddenly my everyday concerns and pleasures vanished. I discovered I was pregnant. The last thing in the world I wanted was to stop dancing. Marriage, children, and motherhood might have been part of some women's plans, but certainly not mine. In my panic I realized that this terrible mistake had to be erased before it destroyed everything I valued most. More frightened than embarrassed, I asked for help from the other women and desperately tried the abortion remedies they advised.

I swallowed huge ergot pills, which contract the uterus, and drank whole bottles of witch hazel as I sat immersed in near-scalding baths. The ergot altered my vision and hearing but had no effect on my pregnancy. Onstage, with my senses muffled by the drug, I danced as if I were trying to push through curtains of lead. Nausea, delirium, and dizziness twisted through me as I moved.

My panic grew daily, although I tried to console Yasha, who was more considerate than ever, but distressed and probably bearing a great burden of guilt. In despair I finally wrote to Mother. She had left Father again and was living with Teru and Tim in Santa Monica. The minute she read my letter, she caught a train to San Francisco where, through friends, she found a doctor. One morning, with the sun shining brightly, Mother took me, deathly pale and frightened into silence, to the abortionist.

As the anesthesia wore off, I could hear the doctor's low voice urging me to leave the office quickly. When I could stand, I stumbled out to Mother, who put her arm around my waist to support me, and took me to the hotel. Later she took me home with her to Santa Monica, where she nursed me through my recuperation, never speaking a word of reproach, but beneath her solicitude I sensed a disapproval of my carelessness. Physically weak but emotionally relieved, I recovered quickly and spent an enjoyable week with the family, picnicking and roller-skating with Teru. The week went by quickly and I was soon back with Yasha and the company.

My pregnancy was not an isolated case in the company, where nearly every month, someone in the dressing room would say, "I'm two days late." There was only silent empathy, for we all knew her fear could easily be our own the next time. Having danced only hours after her abortion, one dancer suffered a hemorrhage so severe that she bled through pillows as we sped to our engagement on the train.

It seems a sad irony that women who knew so very much about their bodies, and whose lives revolved around successfully controlling them, could also be so ignorant. Birth control was chancy at best. A diaphragm was an exotic object that we heard could be procured only in Switzerland. We left the matter of prevention to the men, and only stamina and luck saved us from fatalities during those frequent, frightening episodes.

hen I rejoined the company, the big excitement was that Michel Fokine had come to polish his ballets. Still one of the greatest choreographers in the world, his ballets unrivaled portraits of dramatic and poetic expression, Fokine joined us early in 1937. Overweight and almost bald at fifty-seven, he stood before us in street clothes to demonstrate every step of each ballet, growing more disheveled as he urged concentration on the natural elements that surrounded us. He told us that the individual dancers and their steps must always be subordinate to the dance itself and to the feelings the dance expressed.

In 1916 he had said, "The artist of the dance should admit the life and art of all humanity and not confine himself to a few poor rules and old-fashioned traditions of the ballet school." He applied those words to the rehearsals he directed. Altered over the years to suit the whims and the techniques of dancers around the world, Fokine's ballets had lost some of the individual style and beauty that had marked them as masterpieces in the early days of Diaghilev's Ballets Russes. Now Fokine was striving to retrieve those lost nuances down to a single turn of the wrist.

For *Petrouchka* he reviewed each character's occupation and rank in St. Petersburg life. He showed every member of the crowd precisely how to stand, and even reproduced a specific bit of stage business he wanted to preserve from the 1911 production. A woman, one of the extras, had stood alone, away from the crowd, mesmerized by the simple hypnotic tune of the Charlatan's flute. Looking at Fokine, with one hand cupping his chin just so, his eyes glowing with enchantment as he listened to the flute, was seeing truly great acting.

Before he left de Basil, Woizikovsky had danced Petrouchka with forceful energy and great musicality. The role was now taken by Massine alternating with Shabelevsky, whose extreme pathos as the puppet made him my favorite. As the Blackamoor, Lichine looked cruder and had greater sharpness of attack than Eglevsky, now also gone from the company. Of the four principals dancing the Ballerina, I favored Toumanova, since her movement came closest to looking like an automaton's.

When I had entered the company in 1934, I'd been given the part of a cadet, originally performed by Baronova. I loved wearing Irina's costume and darting impetuously around the "fair" with Patty, our hair tucked under our military hats. We had more freedom to improvise than the other dancers, but Grigoriev reminded us of our low rank in the Russian Imperial Army and drilled us in the correct salute.

Now, three years later, my part was larger but less fun. Genia Delarova and I played two gypsies who staggered drunkenly onstage with Grigoriev as a rich merchant sandwiched between us. Tossing our petticoats, we danced the fast, bosom-shaking gypsy dance lustily, gold necklaces jangling around our necks as we did swooping renversés. Disguised behind a reddened nose, a false beard and brows, and a battered top hat teetering over one eye, Grigoriev lost his usual reserve and danced with drunken abandon and true Russian spirit. At those times it was impossible to recognize him as the stern disciplinarian who governed our lives.

With paper snow dusting my head and Stravinsky's exhilarating score filling my ears, it was hard for me to believe that I was born in Omaha rather than in a village on the Neva. Even Sol Hurok found it hard to resist the insistent charm of *Petrouchka* when he came to see the company during our engagements in the larger cities. He appeared onstage several times as the Bear Trainer, with gleefully rouged nose and cheeks.

Mme. Fokine, Vera Fokina, came to every one of our rehearsals. Draped in silver fox furs, she sat before us without speaking a word, her face painted dead white à la Theda Bara, her black hair shiny as enamel under her huge hat. Meanwhile Fokine worked away, throwing himself passionately into one role after another. His own performance in *Les Sylphides* was an inspiration, a seamless composition of oblique arcs into which the stiff neck and spine he hated so much were never allowed to intrude. First standing straight as a ramrod, he would slowly curve his neck and tenderly lift his beautiful hands to his chest.

In an instant his paunchy stomach seemed to disappear, and a slender sylph materialized on the spot.

He was equally captivating in other female roles, especially Columbine in *Carnaval.* I felt no woman among us could match his furtive glances or the arch of his rounded shoulders as he ran delicately around the room, his shirttail flapping from his rumpled trousers. Partnered in rehearsal by Shabelevsky as Harlequin, Fokine was the quintessential flirt.

He would shove the dancer performing Papillon in *Carnaval,* urging her, "Flutter. Flutter . . . fast . . . more . . . faster!" as she ran on pointe. It would seldom be fast enough. "Not good, one more time," he'd repeat. Then, jumping to his feet, he'd say, "I show," and skim across the floor, almost in a blur, as if defying her to equal his speed.

In trying to please Fokine, we concentrated on techinque, placing our arms, legs, and hands in almost textbook positions. But this academic approach only annoyed him. For him, perfect fifth positions, straight backs, and turnout only got in the way of choreography. "You exhibit yourself," he'd say with impatience. "Dis not classroom. I don't vant see preparation for pirouette. Onstage you are *artistes!*" He especially despised fouettés. The symmetrical arms called for to keep our balance while doing them offended him. He wanted the whipping turns to express ecstasy. Nothing mattered but the emotion of the motion.

Dancers, Fokine reminded us, were only instruments for expression, their bodies valuable not in themselves but in the contribution they made to the overall atmosphere of a ballet. Our ability to convey feeling interested him far more than the height of our leaps or the number of pirouettes we turned. "Feel de air," he'd say at *Sylphides* rehearsals. "See trees!"

During that spring season he also restaged *Cléopâtre,* the first ballet I had ever seen. In casting me as a Jewish Maiden, Fokine unknowingly made it possible for me to transcend the passage of time by dancing in the very work that had inspired me to dance. I was flattered that he chose me for a small role, and danced the steps exactly as he instructed. But after a few rehearsals I began to feel that the ballet was sadly dated. Its passion seemed histrionic and the choreography florid in comparison to the subtleties of *Carnaval* or *Petrouchka.*

In performances of *Cléopâtre*, my dancing lacked the very inner motivation and honest conviction Fokine demanded of us.

Just before the end of the tour, we gave one performance of *Cléopâtre* at the Brooklyn Academy of Music. As usual, Tchernicheva, as Cleopatra, was wound in many veils and laid in the casket for her imposing entrance. That afternoon, by mistake, her litter was placed backstage right on top of a hot air vent in the floor. Warming up, we heard low, muffled moans coming from somewhere in the semidarkness. We finally traced it to Tchernicheva, trapped in the ornate box, wailing in Russian, *"Bozhe moi, my God, it's hot in here!"* But, by then, there was no time to move her before the curtain rose.

When she was finally unveiled onstage, Tchernicheva stood regally, her eyes glazed under unglued eyelashes drooping towards her nose and her lip rouge running down her chin. Her submissive Egyptian handmaidens broke into titters; the titters later became guffaws when the men appeared in the Bacchanale wearing not only their usual animal skins but, for this performance, false eyelashes as well. By the time the Slave's grieving lover lay over his inert figure, our bodies were heaving with convulsive laughter rather than frozen with horror.

Slightly ashamed by our lack of discipline, we all agreed that only the end of the season and our imminent departure for Paris had rescued us from even more hysteria and unprofessional behavior. We sailed on the pride of the French Line, the S.S. *Normandie*. She had made her maiden voyage two years earlier, in 1935, crossing the Atlantic in a record-breaking four days and three hours, with Colette as her most celebrated passenger.

As always the corps dancers traveled tourist class for a one-way fare of $143.50 apiece. The luxurious ship was the most romantic setting imaginable in which to share our few free days. We were told that the *Normandie* was 175 feet longer than the tallest building in Rockefeller Center, and Yasha and I set out to investigate every inch.

I thought our four ballerinas and Zorina were the most beautiful women on the ship, even though their clothes were more modest than those of the fashionable women in first class. The night of the ship's gala, we were all in the spotlight when we performed *Le Beau Danube* on the stage of the four-hundred-seat theatre.

After six months of dollar-a-night hotel rooms and revolving stools at Walgreen's, a mere five days in this cornucopia of luxury was all too brief. I'm sure I was not alone in wishing that the *Normandie* had not been the fastest ship afloat.

Rested and fortified by our transatlantic voyage, the company arrived in Paris. Yasha and I had barely kicked our shoes off and put our feet up for a few quiet days together in a Parisian pension when news reached him of a death in his family. The colonel let him go immediately to be with his family in Warsaw. Without him, time lay heavily on me, still shaken by the memory of Yasha's distress. I wanted to go right back to work, knowing that performing would leave less time to dwell on my lover's grief.

Because of the revolution in Spain, our annual appearance in Barcelona was cancelled. Instead we were booked for our first engagement in Berlin. At dawn on the day the company left Paris by train, Shabelevsky, his mistress Chabelska, Alonso, and I piled into Yurek's brand new Packard with whitewall tires. The Packard began to break down somewhere between Coblenz and Braunschweig. Since Alonso was clever with machines, he tinkered with the engine when it stalled, while we laughed and swore. The car chugged along for a while through the dark, rainy night. Finally it stopped dead, and our spasmodic laughter stopped too. We had no choice but to get out and push the car to the next town. After banging on several doors in the cold, drizzling rain, we finally found a small hotel, where we spent the night.

The clouds had broken by morning, and from the narrow window of my room, I looked down at the sunlit town square. Under a spreading tree, a fair-haired woman in a long blue dress and white apron sat watching her children play. Two men in brown uniforms and armbands sauntered into the square and jerked their arms up in stiff salutes as they passed the woman. On their armbands were the first swastikas I had ever seen. Not knowing fully what they symbolized, I couldn't understand why I felt there was something oddly wrong about that peaceful scene. The men seemed vaguely disturbing to me, but the woman had greeted them with a bright smile.

As I watched, I suddenly remembered where I was, and why. I

jumped up and hurried to the garage where we had left the Packard. Walking up to a mechanic, I tried to speed up the repairs with my feeble but emphatic German.

"You Germanishes, *gut* mechanishes. *Schnell, bitte*," I said brightly, then tried to pantomime the word "fix," convinced that they would understand. The sound of my words and the imaginative gestures brought nods and smiles of amusement from the mechanics, but no rush of activity. We had to wait most of the day for the car.

To pass time, Alberto and I strolled off to tour the picturesque town. We soon found ourselves surrounded by small crowds of fair blond children who giggled at my Max Factor makeup and stared at my red nails. At first we thought a Cuban and a Eurasian were probably curiosities for them, but the disdainful glances of plain, stern women made me realize that my outfit and cosmetics were the cause of their consternation. I considered my tweed suit, brown felt hat, and high-heeled A. S. Beck shoes rather chic, but the new order in Germany frowned on anything so "stylish." Those women made me feel like Sadie Thompson strutting through a set for Hansel and Gretel.

As soon as we reached Berlin, I took a room in a spic-and-span pension near the Scala Theatre. While both the city and my room were clean and orderly, I missed the dusty charm of Paris, where our lodgings had been papered with moon-sized roses. I sat there, in that antiseptic room, missing Yasha more than ever, since we had rarely been separated in over two years. Fortunately there was no time to mope. We hadn't danced much since we left New York, so intensive rehearsals were under way to prepare us for the Berlin audience.

The Scala was an unusual theatre. It was a long, narrow oblong, with odd-looking boxes right in the middle of the orchestra section. Filled with upholstered armchairs and enclosed on all four sides by waist-high partitions, each box was entered through a little hinged door. Once inside, the occupants looked as if they were waiting to have their shoes shined.

We didn't know what to expect of the Berlin audience, nor did they know what to expect of us, so there was mutual surprise when they responded to us with tremendous enthusiasm. The caressing that went on between the "black" slaves and white concubines in *Schéhéra-*

zade particularly appealed to the Germans, getting loud applause each time we danced it.

As the sweat ran down our alabaster- and brown-painted bodies one night, we could see the ferret-faced Joseph Goebbels, who looked even smaller than Kchessinska, applauding energetically from his "shoeshine" box. Surrounding him was an entourage of tall, blond young Aryans, all dressed in black with swastika emblems. They cheered as loudly as their little leader, obviously delighted with the very elements of our ballet—which they decried in public as degenerate.

Because few of us spoke German, we spent most of our free time at a Russian restaurant called the Troika. A black-uniformed Nazi chilled the restaurant's warm, Slavic atmosphere when he entered our noisy hangout one evening carrying a metal cup. He passed from table to table, shaking the cup in our faces vehemently, demanding money for the "Winter Relief." Not knowing which winter and to what relief he referred, we nevertheless hastily dropped a few coins into his cup rather than challenge his cold, ugly manner.

Leaving the Troika late at night, I would be walked home to my pension in Lutherstrasse by my Russian friends. On the way we passed Horcher's, a famous restaurant, and peered through its lace curtains at the Nazi officers, whose lavish suppers covered the large tables. Their joviality was a startling contrast to the fearful suspicion in the eyes of my landlord a few doors away, who would let me in the chained door only after opening it a crack and identifying me by a slow look from head to toe. Eating my cold meal alone in my room, I would pause to wonder what made that man so apprehensive, and sigh at the thought of being separated from Roman for so long.

Behavior like my landlord's prompted many questions. Most of us regularly ate in our rooms to save money while on tour. In Berlin the butter we bought, imprinted with quaint figures of cows, turned out to be tinted whale blubber. We were sure that the Nazis at Horcher's were *not* eating whale blubber. Why couldn't we buy butter? The "wool" jacket I bought that April was also imitation, actually made of wood pulp, which I discovered when I began to shiver with cold. Where was the real wool?

While we were ignorant of politics, we couldn't mistake the eerie tension that permeated Berlin when it came right into our lives in the theatre. Before we opened, Gerry Sevastianov and the Scala management met several times to discuss whether *Schéhérazade* would be included in the scheduled repertory, since its décor was by a Jewish designer, Léon Bakst.

Lichine was half-Jewish, and he became more nervous every day. During his entrance in *Pavillon* one night, the stage went inexplicably dark. David's terrified voice whispered, "My God, what's happening?" as we inched into the wings. The audience stayed seated, and the lights came on again in a few minutes. We finished the performance without further confusion, but we never found out the cause of the blackout. David was convinced it had been a personal threat to him.

The pervasive power of the political situation touched the entire company on April 20. During Fokine's rehearsal for his new ballet, *Cinderella*, the theatre manager burst into the studio and told us rather nervously to stop the rehearsal because it was Hitler's birthday, which the entire city was honoring. Rushing to the window, we looked out and saw blood-red banners emblazoned with swastikas hanging in every window, as far as the eye could see. Above, a mass of droning bomber planes, flying in tight formation, filled the sky. We were amazed and bewildered at the sight of a birthday celebrated with instruments of war instead of music and fireworks.

Fokine was furious with the interruption of his rehearsal and ordered us to resume our places. With puzzled glances over our shoulders, we picked up where we had left off. We directed our attention to Fokine, dropping back into the habit of silent concentration so quickly that we had no time to ponder the disquieting significance of what we had just seen. Surprisingly there were no repercussions because of our disobedience. Goebbels continued to attend our performances faithfully, showing his appreciation by sending large bouquets, always of lilacs, and effusive notes of thanks to the ballerinas.

One of the evenings he failed to appear, Crown Prince Wilhelm, a member of a German order much older than the Nazis, attended the performance. When the prince came backstage, wearing a gray flannel suit with a red carnation in its lapel, his informal appearance astonished me almost as much as his truly remarkable resemblance to King Edward VIII. We lined up in rows to greet the prince, curtseying as he passed. Danilova bent in a deep révérence. Tania Riabouchinska must have been much less impressed—she shook his hand instead of bowing. Later we agreed that our ballerinas, though still wet with perspiration, far outshone his dowdy wife, Princess Cecelie, who didn't have a fraction of their grace and composure.

The Berlin season came to an end soon after the prince's visit. We packed as quickly as possible and left Berlin without a backwards glance. Without Yasha, I felt the train trip back to Paris would be unbearably lonely, so I gladly drove back with Tania and Lichine. David's understandable anxiety to get out of Germany affected us all. Though he drove through the traffic on the pristine Autobahn at maniacal speed, Tania and I kept still, our eyes, like his, peeled for the French border.

Compared to the tension that gripped Berlin, the freedom of Paris could almost be touched. The grumbling shopkeepers and my sullen concierge seemed positively cheery in contrast to the apprehensive citizens and menacing soldiers dressed in black whom we had left behind. We relaxed in our favorite bistros and willingly donated our few extra sous to passing gypsies instead of to Nazis.

There was just time for a class or two with Egorova, Preobrajenska, or Kchessinska before we were on the move again. This time we traveled by train to our first and only season in Florence, where we were to appear from May 10 to 20 at the International Festival of Music. The annual festival was under the patronage of the Princess of Piedmont, who requested an opening program that, she said, Mussolini had personally selected: *Aurora's Wedding*, *Le Tricorne*, and *La Boutique Fantasque*.

The golden beauty of Florence was so exhilarating after Berlin that we snatched every spare moment between rehearsals to explore. Bursting with curiosity, Lulu and I carefully choreographed our first visit to Michelangelo's *David*. Gripping each other's hands, we squeezed our eyes tightly closed and shuffled through the doors of the Galleria dell' Accademia. Pausing just long enough to whisper "Now," we opened our eyes and saw before us the most exquisite man imaginable, bathed in soft light. The beautiful male bodies I was accustomed to seeing paled to insignificance beside his sublime marble form. We marveled at the lifelike details, examining the veins and tendons from every angle, and tried to stroke the smooth, cool ankles when the guards had their backs turned. As we left the museum, I couldn't help feeling our experience had been somewhat more erotic than cultural. As much as we appreciated Michelangelo's other work, it was to *David* that we always returned. At the Pitti Palace several days later, Massine's interest in the corpulent female nudes of the paintings seemed prurient as well.

Lulu and I found a café in the Piazza della Signoria which we adopted as our own because it had a Polish name, Pazkowski. Today it is a parking lot, but in May 1937, neat boxes of privet divided tiny tables from a small string orchestra that played gay waltzes all afternoon. The café was filled with military officers, wearing flowing green capes over their uniforms and spotless white kid gloves. They so dominated the café, as well as much of the city, that, being curious, I finally asked a waiter where all the women of Florence were. "At home, naturally, *signorina*, making babies," he answered with a wink.

Lulu and I scanned the faces at the other tables. Mussolini's uniformed supporters, dressed all in black, looked dull and pot-bellied, so we eyed the more elegant officers instead, and they eyed us right back. I thought one bronzed officer was especially attractive, and for several afternoons flirted with him over my teacup. One Sunday he arrived at the café with a fat woman in black and a child in a voluminous dress of garish pink. The three of them sat over their tea in rather bored silence, while the officer looked everywhere but at me. From his evasiveness I decided he was *en famille*. And remembering that Italy had invaded Ethiopia the previous year, I assumed my romantic officer had probably gotten his tropical tan while killing Abyssinians. After that, whenever I went to Pazkowski, I purposely ignored him.

It was harder to ignore the more persistent advances of the men in the streets. Unescorted women in Florence often received the *mano morto*, the casual touch of a man's inert hand on some part of her body. Propriety demanded that she ignore the hand, which would stay on its chosen spot while the man attached to it looked heavenward, innocent as an angel of Raphael. Someone stroked my rear end one day with a hand more lively than "dead," but that was only my introduction to the quaint Italian custom. As Lulu and I strolled along the Arno River one night, a young army recruit, hardly older than a schoolboy, detached himself from his buddies. He sauntered up to me, cried out *"Mamma mia!"* and grabbed my breasts. Blind with rage, I charged, thrashing and punching wildly, taking the whole group on at once. At the sight of me flailing my fists, Lulu rolled back and forth on her heels, holding her stomach and laughing hysterically, leaving me to slug it out alone.

The news of the "assault on my person" traveled through the company like wildfire. When I entered the rehearsal hall at the Teatro Communale the next day, shouts of *"Mamma mia!"* greeted me. Half-laughing and half-embarrassed, I ducked without punching and was more than ever grateful for Yasha's tenderness and courtesy.

These brief encounters were only interruptions in our daily round of practice and performance. Sightseeing was incidental. Work was our real purpose. I knew my parents had been concerned when I cut short my formal education so abruptly, but after three years with the ballet, I felt that my schooling had been more extensive than it ever could have been in Chicago. We danced ten hours a day, six days a week, eleven months a year. Music, design, and human nature were the subjects I studied with some of the greatest choreographers, dancers, musicians, and artists in the world as my instructors. Outside the theatre, our peripatetic existence constantly exposed me to whole continents with nations of different languages and customs.

I was dancing considerably better as the months passed. I was training my body, through constant use, to move more precisely at my will. I became more outgoing, able to speak with Yasha, with my friends, and even with strangers. In our working lives silence took the place of casual conversation. Instinct guides dancers far more than words, and their eyes are their speech. Talking about dancing and actually doing it are as different as day and night, and only *doing it* yields results. The more I danced, the better I danced. As I watched more and concentrated my efforts more, my awareness of myself and my ability increased. Whether assaulted by a *mano morto* or by six different ballets to perform in one day, I was learning to absorb the difficulties, to trust my instincts, and to act with more confidence.

Our adaptability was indispensable to the colonel, who could keep performances going only by asking us to substitute for each other constantly. Zorina had left the company to star in the London production of Richard Rodgers's musical *On Your Toes*, choreographed by

Balanchine, whom she married a year later. Danilova, who had a demanding repertoire of her own to dance, also had to replace Baronova in many roles while Irina recovered from an emergency operation she had undergone in Berlin. The rest of us went on in whatever parts needed filling, praying that our muscles and our memories would be equal to the often unexpected demands.

The unexpected was rapidly becoming the rule. As we left Florence, we heard that our London season now included participation in the coronation festivities for the new King George VI, brother of Edward VIII, who had abdicated to marry Mrs. Simpson. We would dance first with the opera in Gluck's *Orfeo ed Eurydice* and Borodin's *Prince Igor*, and afterwards in two ballets that were being choreographed or restaged especially for the royal celebration. Our stay in London would be unusually long, July 1 to 31 and September 6 to October 13, with our month's holiday in August the only interruption. One of the new ballets was not even scheduled to open until September.

My childhood exposure to opera had been a single perfor- mance of *Madama Butterfly* at Ravinia, outside Chicago. Even with such a limited knowledge of the art, I somehow expected opera to be as thrilling in its own way as ballet. But when we got to London, I was soon sadly disappointed. Our short stint as dancers in opera ballet was like partici- pating in a comedy of errors.

The choreographer for *Orfeo* was a stranger to us. She posed us around the singers in drooping, mournful clumps. We wore long, bulky gowns and moplike wigs, so that when we did do the little movement she gave us, we looked like phantasmagoric advertisements for Bon Ami rather than grieving Grecian maidens. The lead singer in *Orfeo* had a powerful voice but no physical coordination. Groping around the stage, as if searching desperately for the men's room rather than Eurydice, he got so carried away with the music that he ended up with his hands splayed across the breasts of one of our dancers, a shy girl from Cleve- land. The basso in *Prince Igor* sang with such force that he knocked off his own false nose during an impassioned aria.

In contrast to the effusive overacting of the singers, Fritz Reiner's conducting was superbly controlled. He stood absolutely still, holding his baton close to his chest, yet drew sounds of immense power from the orchestra with a minimum of movement. His performance was more musical and exciting to me than all the emoting singers put together.

We spent our nights barely moving on the opera stage, but our days were filled with whirlwind rehearsals. Fokine was reviving *Le Coq d'Or*, which he had originally choreographed for Diaghilev in 1914.

The Russian authorities had seen Rimsky-Korsakov's opera as a dangerous satire of their conduct during the Russo-Japanese War of 1904, so the opera itself had not premiered until after the composer's death in 1908. De Basil insisted that the ballet last no longer than forty-five minutes, so Fokine and his former collaborator, Nicholas Tcherepnine —himself a pupil of Rimsky-Korsakov—pared down the score with the help of Antal Dorati. Tcherepnine eliminated the vocal soloists and chorus in the opera by distributing the vocal roles to various instruments in the orchestra. Before we even began dance rehearsals, they had arranged the music so the ballet would proceed without a hitch.

For the role of Tsar Dodon, Fokine chose a lanky, red-headed American, Mark Platt (Marc Platoff), who, after watching Fokine mime and dance the first scene, threw himself into the part with such Russian verve that Fokine shook his head in amazement.

According to Benois, the Queen of Shemakhan, who seduces the Tsar, "must be of enchanting beauty and must walk and dance like a fairy." Irina easily filled both these requirements, and injected humor into the difficult role as well. She had to dance unclassical steps on pointe, with knees bent and overly turned out, and manipulate a tambourine at the same time. In rehearsal, with pigtails bobbing over her black tunic, she was the picture of an impish schoolgirl. Yet, watching her, I knew that with her extraordinary artistry, she would transform herself, in performance, into an Oriental enchantress.

Though not a classical dancer in the truest sense, Tania Riabouchinska was the perfect choice for the title role, the Golden Cockerel who warns the Tsar of his enemy's approach. Tania's line was not as long as Danilova's or Baronova's, and she wasn't fully turned out. But her great strengths were speed, lightness, stamina, and, most of all, spontaneity. Blending these with her ethereal beauty, she was able to convey the deepest emotions exclusively through movement. Whatever technical flaws she might have possessed became irrelevant when she began to dance. Fokine said, "She born to do part."

I was one of the four women and two men in Irina's undulating retinue. Being part of Coq d'Or gave me yet another opportunity to observe, work with, and learn from Fokine at first hand. He was a passionate man, unselfconscious, and unlike Massine, he showed his feelings immediately. He hadn't danced onstage for many, many years, but when he showed a movement, it was *performed*, not merely demonstrated. So, when he choreographed the role of Tsar Dodon, he *became* a very big, slow man. When he rehearsed Baronova, his movements lightened, he smiled as seductively as she did, and his eyes sparkled as he arched his neck and raised his arm. His use of the torso, neck, and arms molded his choreography in a unique way. They were the parts of the body that conveyed emotions, and photographs of Nijinsky in *Petrouchka* and *Le Spectre de la Rose* show the Fokine style perfectly. Nijinsky's legs are not extraordinarily taut, but pain is visible in the *Petrouchka* picture, and the relaxed wrists and curved neck of *Le Spectre de la Rose* reveal a stance of reverie, all ease and delight.

Rehearsals with Fokine were inspiring because he threw himself into his creations totally. He seemed to love every one of his characters, male or female, big or small, and at the end of the work day, though tired, I also felt exhilarated by his great ardor and the magnitude of his artistry.

Every day we hurried from *Coq d'Or* rehearsals onstage to the studio where Lichine was at work on his new ballet, *Francesca da Rimini*, set to Tchaikovsky's famous symphonic poem. Lichine collaborated on the libretto with a wealthy American balletomane, Henry Clifford, who was a member of the curatorial staff of the Philadelphia Academy of Art. Based on Dante's story of the warring factions of Rimini and Ravenna, it focused on the love affair of Paolo and Francesca. It was the most ambitious ballet Lichine had ever undertaken, yet the reviews of *Pavillon* had taught him an important lesson. This time he did not declare his ballet a masterpiece before even showing us the first plié, revealing that perhaps a new maturity was replacing his original cockiness.

Adjusting every day between Pushkin's mythical golden bird and Dante's Renaissance romance kept us more than usually busy. But we truly liked both ballets, and were also encouraged to work especially hard by the fact that we would perform them for the Londoners, whose devotion and behavior towards the dancers was unique in our experience. The theatre's firemen and stagehands, for instance, always made a point of complimenting their favorite dancers. Working women saved their wages all winter to have enough money for gallery seats at our summer performances. A few had spent months embroidering scarves that they presented to their favorite ballerinas to place on their makeup tables.

One gallery dweller surprised me one night as I entered the stage door. "Miss Osato," he called out, "you've improved since last year!" This was good news. I always assumed the audience was interested only in the leading dancers, but this stranger's encouragement made me realize that although I was in the corps de ballet, I was being noticed.

I could enjoy London more fully now, because Yasha had returned from Warsaw. On Sundays we spent time with friends in Surrey. Our hosts were very informal and didn't mind our puttering around the kitchen. Irina liked to cook and prepared real Russian dishes with ease, and Lichine always made *gogel-mogel*, a zabaglione-type dessert of eggs, brandy, and sugar, which he insisted on stirring for half an hour. After lunch we played tennis, serving barefoot, with one foot fully turned out on the white line. Our whooshing lobs ended with us in arabesque, or a more grotesque position, and the ball in some distant rosebush.

Back in London our most steadfast admirers occasionally took us out or had us to their homes for dinner. A most special friend was Lady St. Just, a devoted ballet lover since the days of World War I, when she had entertained Diaghilev and Nijinsky. Diaghilev called her "ma fidèle." We called her Florrie. Surrounded by lovely antique furniture, fresh flowers, and fine paintings and attended by her butler, Charles, Florrie lived in a fine house in Cavendish Square. Charles was also a balletomane. When he left the dining room, Florrie would lean towards Choura and whisper, "My dear, Charles thought you were *marvelous* in *Boutique* last Wednesday!" Choura was always pleased to hear it, but we never saw Charles display any of his own enthusiasm. He stood silent and erect, without uttering a word, behind Florrie's chair until it was time to serve the next course.

On the day of the premiere of *Francesca da Rimini*, the gallery audience stood patiently waiting outside the theatre, while the company was still rehearsing inside. The costumes had just arrived, and one angry complaint followed another.

"Sleeve too big," sniffed Tchernicheva, who had the title role.

"Jeté im*poss*ible, dress too heavy," said another.

"Look dis! Dis *horr*ible!" wailed yet another, trailing around in one of the beautiful costumes we felt were too cumbersome to dance in gracefully.

Danilova, who would dance Guinevere in a vision scene, was given a dark wig of real hair that fell almost to her calves. Without a fuss she took the wig and was working on a way to manipulate it so that the hair wouldn't fall into her face.

Out front sat de Basil, Grigoriev, Sevastianov, and Lichine, with the English artist Oliver Messel, who had designed the sets and costumes. While we tugged, complaining, at our costumes and headdresses, they remained unfazed, calmly discussing light cues. This dress rehearsal was the first time the separate elements of *Francesca* had ever been assembled. Cockney expletives and the pounding of hammers meshed with the music and Dorati's Hungarian accent, continually starting and stopping the orchestra as he searched for the right tempo. Lichine's shrill voice, screaming directions to the dancers and stagehands from out front, soared over the rest of the hubbub. But out of the din, a kind of order appeared as the finished ballet emerged slowly from the chaos.

Lichine's dramatic romance was warmly received that night. The Cliffords, Messel, Gerry Sevastianov, and the colonel rushed backstage to congratulate us, followed closely by the fans. We all got a laugh when one of the dancers, still caught up in the romantic piece, was asked who the composer was and answered, "Da Rimini!"

One day, I heard a rumor that Raya Kouznetsova, a new dancer from the Blum company who had recently joined us, was cast to dance the Tarantella in Massine's 1920 ballet *Cimarosiana*, which had just been added to the repertory. When I found out the rumor was true, I was furious. In such a large company of dancers, solo roles were hard to come by, and since there were never enough to go around we waited anxiously to be given one. We were all in the same position, but in order to advance their daughters, some mothers pleaded with the colonel to get larger roles for their girls and were often successful. One member of the corps de ballet, who had cried miserably to the colonel, was now dancing one of the leads in *Les Sylphides*. As much as I wanted to get ahead, I just couldn't get myself to stoop to crying for recognition. But seeing Kouznetsova, who I thought danced like a flea, get that role so quickly pushed me beyond restraint. Finally determined to let out my anger, I went to the colonel backstage.

"Why is Kouznetsova already dancing the Tarantella, Wassily Grigorievitch?" I yelped. "She's only been here two weeks and *I've* been here three *years!* It's my turn to have a chance!"

Amused at this aggressive outburst, de Basil smiled down at me paternally and said, "You also learn."

Determined to out-dance the "dancing flea," I decided to go directly for coaching to the originator of the role. Despite the Russian name under which she became a star, Lydia Sokolova was British through and through. Born Hilda Munnings, she was a direct descendant of a man who had fought at the Battle of Agincourt. The only time I had ever seen her dance was the night of our gala the previous July, when she performed a Danse Russe. Pale, slim, and strong, Sokolova was in her early forties when I first met her in London. I can't remember how I got in contact with her, or what she said to me at our first meeting, but she welcomed me to her studio and willingly agreed to teach me the role, refusing to accept payment.

Cimarosiana itself was a series of danced divertissements that Massine had choreographed for the last act of a comic opera-ballet, *Le Astuzie Femminili*, by the Neapolitan composer Cimarosa. Derived from the rapid folk dance of the same name, the Tarantella was a pas de deux that sparkled with hops, small traveling steps, and lively shifts of direction. As Sokolova marked out the dance, I watched her intently, carefully noting every twist and turn she made. She was gentle and encouraging. "Don't stretch your elbows," she reminded me constantly. "The arms are always rounded in the Tarantella." I listened and she seemed genuinely pleased with how closely I tried to capture her posture and shading of the character steps, which she infused with colorful nuances, especially a certain "Italian look" in some of the brief poses I had to assume.

During our breaks I asked Sokolova about the days when she had danced for Diaghilev. She was in the corps of the historic 1913 premiere of Nijinsky's *Le Sacre du Printemps*. The audience started hooting, shouting, and whistling as soon as they heard the first notes of the score. Racing around to the crashing pulsations of Stravinsky's demonic music, the frightened dancers looked into the wings and saw Nijinsky stamping out time for them and Diaghilev holding his head.

ABOVE *Posing on the S.S. Lafayette when we arrived in New York in October 1935. Left to right: Baronova, Adrianova, Toumanova, Grigorieva, Zorina, Riabouchinska, Danilova, Morosova, Verchinina, and me*

BELOW *On board the S.S. Lafayette: Col. de Basil and his company of "Les Ballets Russes de Monte Carlo" in mid-Atlantic on their way to New York (autumn 1933).* 1 *Grigoriev* 2 *Eglevsky* 3 *Danilova* 4 *Toumanova* 5 *Baronova* 6 *Col. de Basil* 7 *Riabouchinska* 8 *Massine* 9 *Lichine* 10 *Woizikovsky*

A FAMOUS DANCING TROUPE RETURN
Ballerinas of the Monte Carlo Ballet Russ
togs

Stars of the de Basil Company: Toumanova,
Baronova, Riabouchinska, and Danilova
"snapped" in Philadelphia in practice dress

One of the Japanese dinner
my father always gave when we played
in Chicago. At the front table: me, Jasinsky
and Shabelevsky. At the table behind us
the painter A. Jacovlev, Danilova, Petroff
and Delarova. Along the wall from
left: Mama Toumanova, Volkova
Nelidova, hostess, Chabelska, hostess
Massine (with sake bottle!), unidentified
and Lulu (Rostova

Olga Preobrajenska and Col. de Basil

Tamara Toumanova   *Irina Baronova*   *Tatiana Riabouchinska*   *Alexandra Danilova*

With Brigitta (Zorina) at a rehearsal in Barcelona, 1935

Roman Jasinsky

With Leonide Massine in Chicago on New Year's Eve 1934–35

Colonel W de Basil
and some members
of his company
taking fresh air
in California

A page from our 1936–37 souvenir book

On the roof of the Teatro Liceo, Barcelona, 1935

On board the H.M.S. Orcades, Suez, November 1939

Union Pacific. Front row: *Borovansky, Branitska, Chabelska, Morosova (in Baronova's role), Hoyer, Toumanova, Massine, and me (kneeling at right)*

ABOVE *At a rehearsal hall, Monte Carlo. I'm in the back, far left, with my right arm raised, Baronova is far right, and Danilova is second from right (kneeling down)*
BELOW *Trying to perform in the bullring in Mexico City, 1935, before the rain*

*In 1939 I was so poor
that you can see where I had to
patch my tights at the heel*

Le Coq d'Or, 1938. Grigorieva,
Rostova, me, and Nelidova

Rear, from left, facing front:
Volkova, Radova, Nelidova,
Serova, me, and Strakhova.
Front, from left:
Riabouchinska supported
by Ladré, Petroff, Delarova,
Grigorieva, Jasinsky, and
Danilova. In the center:
Baronova supported by
Kosloff and Matouchevsky

Cotillon with Paul Petroff, 1938 (my
costume is by Christian Bérard)

*Me, Zorina,
Danilova, and
Lichine*

*As the Siren and
with Lichine (we're wearing
the original Diaghilev
costumes)*

*Cimarosiana,
1937—in the same
Diaghilev costume
by José-Maria Sert)
that Sokolova wore*

L'Après-midi d'un Faune. *Abricosova,*
me, and Nelidova

Schéhérazade, *1937. I'm playing the*
chief Odalisque

TOP LEFT Pillar of Fire, *with Hugh Laing, 1943*
ABOVE *Nora Kaye in the big rehearsal hall at the old Met*
LEFT *Irina Baronova and Lucia Chase*

OVERLEAF
*As Rosaline
in Antony Tudor's*
Romeo and Juliet

Amidst the general pandemonium, which continued even after the final curtain, Stravinsky shouted, "Go to hell!" at the audience and stormed out of the theatre.

Sokolova's most famous role had been that of the Chosen Maiden in Massine's version of the same ballet, which premiered in 1920. In order to synchronize her steps to the music, she and Massine worked for days with only a metronome as accompaniment. She told me that in *Le Sacre*, she had to stand immobile onstage for twelve minutes with one clenched hand held over her head before launching into seventeen minutes of the most strenuous dancing she had ever done. She was so exhausted by her solo at the ballet's end that Woizikovsky and another dancer had to prop her up between them to keep her from fainting during the curtain calls.

Inspired by listening to and watching Sokolova, I worked even harder at rehearsals with her. It was a precious experience, another of those extraordinary opportunities a young dancer may have to work with and be encouraged by a legendary artist.

Seeing Kouznetsova hopping around in her debut in the Tarantella helped me realize even more what I wanted to do. She bounced through it with a lot of energy, but didn't distinguish one moment from another; it all looked the same. I was going to give it more panache, more colorful shading between the fleeting pauses and the saucy, shifting steps.

Sokolova's encouragement gave me assurance, but I was a little disappointed that my first performance was to be a matinee, since I always felt more alert and coordinated in the evening. My debut was on a Wednesday afternoon. I stood waiting in the first wing, dressed in the same ugly red satin tasseled pajamas that Sokolova had worn and detested. I was numb with fear. No amount of preparation or rehearsal can dispel the terror that stage fright imposes on the mind and body. As I stepped alone onstage to begin the duet, my body felt like lead moving in slow motion. Total fear cut off my body from my mind, deaf to the music. My mouth went dry and a sharp dagger of pain pierced my chest. Only the hissed commands of my partner, Lazowsky, penetrated. "Go. Keep going," he whispered. I can't remember a single moment of that performance. The next thing I knew, I was back in the wings, standing next to the colonel.

"Not bad, Sonitchka, not bad," was his reward for me. I knew at that moment that I would share the role with Raya.

Back in our room, Yasha praised my performance, but gave me more explicit, helpful criticism than de Basil's casual comment. He helped me to rethink the process of solo dancing. He told me that memorizing and rehearsing steps was so much wasted effort if my energy dwindled before my exit. I had to learn to gauge myself by "saving" a bit during pauses so that reserve energy could be spent when I started moving again. The length of the solo made no difference. Once you were dancing, the end always seemed just beyond your endurance. Some dancers, like Tania Riabouchinska, seemed to draw their strength from a bottomless well. I wasn't so lucky. Building my endurance in a dance became as crucial to me as learning the steps.

My debut in *Cimarosiana* was draining, both physically and emotionally, but it was another necessary step in my growth as a dancer. With repeated performances of the Tarantella, I learned to build the momentum as Yasha had suggested. I felt more and more confidence in my ability to convey my own feelings through the choreography. Soon, dancing alone onstage became a pleasure rather than something to be dreaded.

The first part of the 1937 London season ended July 31, and Yasha and I, with some friends, took off for St. Maxime, a village near St. Tropez, in the south of France. We spent the entire month in sheer indolence; Yasha fished and I lay on the beach, inert as a stone. Some nights we swam naked in the moonlit sea and then picnicked around a crackling fire. We disregarded Grigoriev's warning to the women—"Don't get too dark in sun. No good for *Sylphides*"—and basked in the hot sun all day until our aches were baked away and we were the color of the slaves in *Schéhérazade*. The month flew by. By the first week in September, we were back in London again, back in class, back in our pink satin boxes and preparing for the opening of *Coq d'Or*.

At the same time, Lichine was busy on yet another ballet, his staging of *The Gods Go a-Begging*. Balanchine had originally choreographed this slight ballet, to music by Handel arranged by Sir Thomas Beecham, for Diaghilev in 1928. Ninette de Valois, the founder of the Sadlers Wells Ballet in England, choreographed her version for that company in 1936. Lichine didn't cast me in his new ballet, but I stayed for a rehearsal one afternoon to watch Danilova, in the part she had danced in 1928, and Shabelevsky, in Woizikovsky's part, rehearsing with Beecham and the full orchestra. Although the music sounded fine to me, Beecham suddenly threw down his baton and yelled, "Play it the way I want, or I'll take the next boat!" I suppose the presence at rehearsal of Beecham's friend, Lady Cunard, was responsible for his choice of transportation.

Beecham's temperamental display looked very childish to me. His concern in getting the correct reading of the music from his musicians was understandable, but he carried on as if he had written the music himself, rather than arranged it. I'd seen choreographers go through grueling rehearsals with dancers, sometimes in front of dozens of observers, without throwing a tantrum. In fact, while Beecham ranted,

Fokine was calmly putting the finishing touches on the last scenes of *Coq d'Or*.

Opening night, September 23, the packed theatre burst into spontaneous applause when the curtain rose on Gontcharova's set, an explosion of flaming orange, red, and yellow, and on the dancers' vibrant costumes, as the characters sprang vividly to life. The lanky young Platoff, as Tsar Dodon, was disguised by a huge, padded stomach, a gray wig, and a bulbous red nose. As Dodon's temptress, Irina wore a jet-black wig of tightly plaited braids that fell to her waist, around which a girdle of lustrous gold lamé was snugly wrapped. Her torso and bare legs showed provocatively through clinging pink chiffon pajamas. Between the way she looked and the way she moved, her bewitchment of Dodon seemed inevitable. Her fantastic tent, rising majestically from the battlefield, framed the seduction in sensuous folds.

Riabouchinska soared across the stage as the Coq d'Or in a yellow leotard, with large golden wings and a tail, her legs slicing the air in jetés as high as my nose. Each time she jumped, pinpointed in a gold spotlight, the audience gasped at her glittering body and awesome elevation.

Lulu, Morosova, Grigorieva, and I, with Yasha and Petroff as our partners, were the Queen of Shemakhan's retinue. The men wore short bolero-type jackets over their bare chests. The women wore sleeveless vests appliquéd with vines and flowers. The silk overskirts we all wore over our tight-fitting trousers were so heavy that it was hard to stop once we started spinning. In contrast to the traditional Russian gestures and erect posture of the dancers portraying boyars, we moved in sinuous, winding patterns. Fokine had coached us carefully in slanting our pelvises and necks like the figures in Indian stone carvings.

The audience was delighted with the exotic spectacle. Although it was more of a pageant than most of our ballets, *Coq d'Or* was suited in its lavishness to the extravagance of the coronation season. Fokine must have been gratified to see his creation endure the test of time. Twenty-three years old that year, *Coq d'Or* was the great success of our London visit.

Soon afterwards, we said goodbye to Florrie, the Henry Cliffords, and our many British friends and sailed for America on the S.S. *Cham-*

plain. By the time de Basil's Ballet Russe started its fifth American tour in October 1937, ballet had become a small but integral part of American cultural life. Since 1933 the company had toured the United States and Canada for six months of every year, thousands of miles every tour, planting the seeds of interest and awareness that continued to grow long after we had moved on. Our previous American season had grossed one million dollars. The two Diaghilev tours in America had lost half a million, but the loss was covered by the financier Otto H. Kahn, who had also subsidized Pavlova's first American tour. In our 1937–38 souvenir program, Arnold Haskell wrote, "Russian Ballet today is truly an international force."

Hurok and de Basil planned each year's itinerary on the basis of our previous successes and their desire to spread ballet farther and farther. Before us, in the fall of 1937, lay 98 towns, 197 performances, and a network of train tracks that would carry us 24,283 miles. Railroad fares alone cost the company $4,500 a week; salaries added another $9,000 a week. With all the scenery, 1,495 costumes, and 2,000 pairs of shoes, the weekly running cost came to $16,000, a formidable amount in the days of the Depression.

The physical and emotional stresses of touring had always been eased by our spirit of unity. We all endured the same hardships; we all shared the same exhilaration when we danced well and were well received. But during the winter tour, we became more and more aware that the unity of the company was a thing of the past. Over the spring and summer of 1937, the deteriorating relationship between the colonel and Massine had gone from bad to worse. Massine's demands to gain complete artistic control of the company got louder and more frequent. Finally, he decided that his differences with de Basil were irreconcilable and announced that he would leave the company when his contract ran out at the end of the year. While we were in Europe, he contacted René Blum about the possibility of starting a new company together and, with Blum's name and the Monte Carlo title to his credit, Massine sought out the necessary financial backing.

Julius Fleischmann and several other millionaires banded together to finance a proprietorship to sponsor Massine's new company. It was first called World Art and then changed to Universal Art. Serge Denham, a businessman, was placed in the company's executive position, despite his lack of previous knowledge or connection with the ballet. They gave Massine the title he coveted, Artistic Director, with complete control over engaging dancers and selecting repertoire.

With his proposed company almost a reality, Massine sued the colonel in Chancery Court, London, not for money or damages, but for legal rights over his own ballets. In order to plan the repertory for the new company, he claimed copyright protection of his works, which we, of course, were dancing regularly. At the end of July, the Honorable Mr. Justice Luxmoore handed down a decision which stated that the ballets Massine had created while under contract to Diaghilev were Massine's sole property and could be legally removed from our repertory. De Basil, on the other hand, had every right to continue presenting the ballets Massine had choreographed while employed by him. Massine seemed satisfied for the moment. In July, before our month's holiday had begun, he and Delarova temporarily left the company to meet with René Blum and solidify their plans. Ignorant of all this at the time, I now realize that it was Delarova's sudden departure that left the Tarantella in *Cimarosiana* available, leading to my solo debut.

When the Massines rejoined us for the American tour, the Monte Carlo Ballet Russe was waiting to absorb them both once they had fulfilled their contractual obligation to de Basil. As Massine approached one dancer after another to ask how happy each one was with the colonel, rumor became more a part of our lives than it had ever been before.

"Will Choura really leave?"

"Irina vill never go! Tamara? She might."

"You hear about Zoritch?"

We were completely demoralized. Only snatches of conversation and glimpses of intrigue dribbled down to the corps. But even without knowing the full details, the dissension disturbed us as much as it did the principal dancers. We kept dancing, but the energy we tried so desperately to maintain for performances was drained by daily confusion. Dispirited and uncertain, we plodded through the tour in a state of bewilderment, never knowing who would stay or who would leave.

All this time, de Basil was closeted away with two lawyers whom we had never seen before. One was a Bulgarian named Lidji, and the other, an unctuous Russian, Philipoff, stood only four feet seven inches tall. We knew little about these two, but none of us could abide Philipoff. He had no prior experience with the ballet yet repeatedly told us how to dance and what errors we had made in performance.

Between Cincinnati and Seattle we danced nothing but one-night stands. Every evening we left our belongings on the Pullmans and hurried to the theatre to adjust to a new stage. The curtain fell, and we ran back to the waiting train, which would rumble off in the dark to our next destination. The never-ending chore of washing tights now had to be done in the minuscule basin of the train's ladies' toilet. So many dripping pairs swung side by side on lines across the ceiling that the tiny cubicle looked like a back street in Naples. As the train sped by a string of sleeping towns, we belted our dressing gowns around us and joined the men in the dining cars for supper, relieved to find the waiters cheerful despite the late hour.

We lived this vagabond life for two solid weeks, dancing our "ham-and-eggs" programs to the point of boredom: *Les Sylphides, Schéhérazade*, and *Le Beau Danube*, then *Swan Lake, Les Présages*, and *Prince Igor*, then back to *Sylphides* again. In Delta, California, the train was snowbound for two days. The tour ground to a brief halt, but the talk went on, question after question without answers. Massine's leaving the company in San Francisco shattered all hope of keeping us together as we were. Following him in short order to the new Monte Carlo Ballet Russe were Danilova, Delarova, Toumanova, Lulu Rostova, Marc Platoff, George Zoritch, and Roland Guérard.

We heard that Hurok was worried about our future and was tempted to switch his affiliation to the new, financially secure company as soon as his contract as the colonel's American manager expired. He was fully aware that our four American tours had made the words "Monte Carlo" synonymous with ballet, and those words now represented the Massine-Blum-Denham company rather than the colonel's. Bringing his acute business sense to bear on the situation, Hurok persistently tried to arrange a merger between the new company and our own. His experience told him that the United States and Canada were not yet ready to support two separate ballet companies at the same time. However, he argued, the strengths of de Basil's repertory combined with Massine's financial backing and dancers could guarantee financial success. But, after complex negotiations, the colonel refused to sign the merger, and fate took its course.

We returned to Europe at the end of April 1938 and danced in Copenhagen, where enthusiastic audiences cheered and applauded us. The presence of Fokine, who joined us that spring on a permanent basis, was also an encouraging sign for our future. His intermittent visits the previous year had been unofficial, since he had had a contract at the time with Blum.* But Fokine clearly had no desire to share the artistic direction of Blum's company with Massine, so he came to de Basil as our official maître de ballet.

With Fokine in charge, we plunged into a wave of rehearsals, trying to fill the roles departing dancers had left vacant. Grigorieva took over Lulu's roles, Morosova assumed Delarova's, Irina did *Firebird* in place of Danilova, and the rest of us were thrown into one ballet after another. It was at this time that I began to dance more important roles. I shared Lulu's role in *Cotillon* with Grigorieva, and danced Danilova's parts in *Choreartium* and *Francesca da Rimini*.

Our Copenhagen success was only a brief respite in the internal turmoil that plagued the company. When we arrived in London in June 1938, the problems got even worse. Somehow the colonel had lost control of the company! Suddenly we found out that we now belonged to a holding company whose principal stockholder was the Baron Frederic d'Erlanger. Our new, totally unaesthetic name was Educational Ballets, Ltd., with Gerry Sevastianov and the late Pavlova's husband, Victor Dandré, sharing the responsibility of running things.

The only relief we had in all this confusion was that we would at least have the Royal Opera House at Covent Garden for our summer season. But just as we prepared to open, Massine's company took up residence in the Drury Lane Theatre, just two blocks away. Alicia Markova, the famous English ballerina who had been a leading dancer with Diaghilev at fourteen, had joined them. Other principal dancers on their roster were Igor Youskevitch, Frederic Franklin, and the

---

* René Blum was arrested in Paris on December 12, 1941. He was sent first to Drancy, then interned at Compiegne. In the summer of 1942 he was deported to Auschwitz, where he died on September 28, 1944.

Yugoslav ballerina Mia Slavenska. Also in the company, along with our former company members, were Nini Theilade, Jeanette Lauret, Nathalie Krassovska, Michel Panaieff, Milada Mladova (an American), and Simon Semenoff.

The London balletomanes ran back and forth between the two theatres like puppies chasing their own tails. Many of them stayed at the Opera House until intermission and then dashed to the Drury Lane to see the other company on the same night. The artistic competition was naturally a benefit to both box offices. It also gave our dancers extra determination to match, if not surpass, our rivals' freshness and vitality, despite the fact that we were just coming to the end of an eight-month tour. Unfortunately, since we performed every night, we had no time to see our old friends who were dancing at the same hour at the Drury Lane. Our only visits with them were limited to chance meetings in Covent Garden Market as we hurried through the vegetable crates to our respective rehearsals.

Then, as if to add insult to injury, Massine went to court again. This time he meant to obtain an injunction against our performing certain ballets. Almost before we knew it, we were seeing reports in the London newspapers of the court dispute, right alongside the dance reviews of the two companies. De Basil remained in seclusion in a tiny house in Shepherd's Market, while his lawyer, Sir Patrick Hastings, and Gerry went to court for several weeks of wrangling that never seemed to get beyond the question of whether Massine's book of choreography could be admitted as proper evidence. In the end Mr. Justice Morton granted Massine the requested injunction. Massine immediately reclaimed some of our ballets for his own use, including *Le Tricorne* and *La Boutique Fantasque*.

The removal of these popular ballets was a serious loss to us, crippling our repertory almost as severely as the formation of Massine's company had depleted our array of dancers. *Boutique* was especially important to the rep, because it often ended the evening on a gay, cheerful note, and we had few ballets to replace it. Ideally the closing ballet of the evening should be not only one the audience likes but one that will send them out of the theatre in high spirits. Without our standby, *Boutique*, we were in trouble.

Our dragging spirits lifted, however, when we saw posted on the callboard a notice stating that, after a brief season in Berlin, we would sail for Australia rather than returning to America—where Hurok had booked Massine's company in our place. The schedule said the trip would take five weeks, so we immediately began to plan our vacation aboard the ship, imagining endless variations on the simple themes of food, rest, and sun. But our fantasies were dashed by Dandré's announcement that, rather than rest, we would spend the five weeks en route rehearsing—without pay!

The very idea was preposterous. We could stand losing our month's vacation to the voyage, since the boat offered its own kind of relaxation. We even would have agreed to regular classes aboard ship, as long as part of the day belonged to us. But we were furious at the idea of working steadily during our only vacation time, and insulted at being asked to work for no money. I was so angry that I threw caution to the winds for once, and talked openly about how outraged I was. The company's discontent reached the ears of management, as we knew it would, and one night Grigoriev ordered us not to leave the Opera House after the performance. A special meeting had been called.

Still in makeup, we assembled onstage after the final curtain in front of a silent Fokine and the white-haired Dandré. Since the day that Dandré had suggested that his own London tailor make some of our costumes in order to save money, we had thought of him as a rather ludicrous figure, not to be taken too seriously. But that night, with his stern face, severe black suit, and polished, squeaky shoes, he told us coldly, "Word has come to us that some of you are dissatisfied with the plan we have made. You should be ashamed. It is an honor to work with Mikhail Mikhailovitch [Fokine]." Getting more and more irate, he suddenly thundered, "Who are these troublemakers, like Bolsheviks?"

I knew from the Russians' talk of the Revolution that Dandré had just offered us the lowest form of insult. But I was too incensed to keep silent. In a small, quavering voice, I said what must have been in many minds, "I think it's unfair to make us work without pay!"

At that, Dandré's anger flared even higher. I thought he would fire me on the spot, but he directed his rage at the whole company, without singling me out. When the meeting adjourned, the plan remained unchanged. As angry as they all were, a few of the older dancers told me it wasn't my place to criticize. They suggested I learn to follow orders without argument, as they did.

I couldn't agree. With no one pushing me or advising me, no stage mother, no husband, I was habitually quite passive offstage. But in this case, perhaps because I had less to lose than many others, I did not regret having spoken out.

While our tiny battle raged within the theatre, all Europe was in a state of alarm. Prime Minister Chamberlain sent an emissary to act as a mediator in the Sudetenland crisis. Racial laws, which had been in effect for a number of years in Germany, threatened to overrule all other concerns in that country. Because of these repugnant rules and the fact that the company included members of many nationalities, including Czech, Gerry Sevastianov sent word to the German authorities that we did not have enough Aryans in the company to fulfill our Berlin engagement. Therefore, he concluded simply, we would not appear. A prompt response from Joseph Goebbels quickly set Gerry straight. It stated that the "Reichsminister für Volksvertretung und Propaganda . . . will decide who is Aryan—and you all are."

So on September 5, 1938, we opened again at the Scala Theatre in Berlin. We danced to capacity houses every night, with audiences even more enthusiastic than the year before. For the hours they watched us dance, the German audiences could forget the ominous aura that pervaded the city.

By chance I arrived at the theatre early on the evening of September 12, the night Hitler made his closing speech at the Nuremberg Rally. A tiny radio blared into the still, empty theatre. Though I didn't understand German, I couldn't miss the note of hysteria in the shrill, raucous voice that reverberated throughout the deserted house. Backstage I saw only the chief stagehand and asked him to explain what was going on. After looking around to check that we were alone, he gave me a long, knowing look and then, without speaking a word, held his nose in the direction of Hitler's shrieking voice. I still wonder what became of this quiet, sensible man, who made such an appropriate response to the ravings of a madman.

Before we left Berlin, Fokine received several cordial invitations to meet Hermann Göring in his box at the theatre. He refused adamantly, telling the theatre manager that he did not "wish to meet that ——!" When Goebbels offered us the Deutsches Theater free of charge for a future engagement, Sevastianov managed to decline more tactfully, saying we had a prior commitment to appear at Covent Garden.

With war an imminent possibility, the end of the Berlin season could not come fast enough. Soon after we returned to London, Chamberlain announced to the world that he had signed an agreement with Hitler which he believed would secure "peace in our time." But no amount of reassurance could erase from our minds the memory of the Berlin skies filled with bombers. Even London did not seem far enough from the dread we felt in every Berlin street. Simply boarding the old British ship *Maloya* for the long voyage to Australia was a relief. It was the first step in escaping the prevailing tension in Europe.

nce aboard the *Maloya*, our life settled at once into the familiarity of shipboard routine. Again Yasha and I had to room
apart. Patty, Volkova, and I shared a small stateroom, ventilated
by a single fan, in which we barely had space to open our
steamer trunks and still maneuver around them.

English officers returning to India filled the ship, also
crowded with the wives and children of military personnel
stationed in Ceylon. They made an interesting assortment of traveling
companions for us, while they in turn found the size of the company,
our various languages, and our informal way of dressing equally fascinating. We began the trip as properly attired as the British passengers,
but by the time we reached Suez, a week or so later, the heat was so
oppressive that we strolled around in our bathing suits.

To avoid the worst heat of the day, class was held on the top deck
at seven-thirty each morning. Hanging on to the ship's rail, we worked
through our standard exercises, paying no attention to the rolling sea
that gently tilted the deck. After class Fokine and Grigoriev conducted
rehearsals of the regular repertory, demanding the same work from us
that they expected under normal conditions. No one mentioned our
disagreement with management. Rehearsal music was banged out on
an upright piano the crew had hauled on deck for us and lashed to the
railing with their best seaman's knots.

While the early-morning sun threw our long shadows across the
deck, the English officers watched our ritualized bending and turning
with open curiosity. After a few days some of them lost their reserve,
lined up with us soberly at the railing, and joined the class. With sweat
dripping from their brows, they did their pliés and ronds de jambe par
terre with a fierce concentration we had to applaud.

The Red Sea, stretching from Suez to the Gulf of Aden, lay flat and
colorless as a sheet of dull metal under the blazing sun. Warning us

that we risked severe sunstroke if we walked around with our heads uncovered, the crew installed tarpaulins for shade over all the open decks. Scorching nights followed scorching days, so depleting our energy that the slightest movement required effort. Too enervated to dance, we lay listlessly in the shade of the tarpaulins, listening to the steady drone of the engines. The news that one of the engine stokers had gone mad from the heat and jumped overboard roused us momentarily from our torpor. Rushing to the rail, we peered anxiously into the sea, hoping to catch sight of him as the ship slowed down, but the poor man had vanished without a trace.

We stopped briefly in the port town of Aden, a spot so desolate that nothing green could grow. Stray goats, grazing along the banks of the water, ate old newspapers. I was overcome by heat prostration soon after we sailed again. Yasha carried me to a deck chair, where I stayed until the cool winds from the Indian Ocean brought back my strength and appetite.

With the heat slightly abated, Fokine resumed rehearsals. He was choreographing a new ballet, *Tannhäuser*, for performance in Australia, but I never saw a single step of it. Still angry at the injustice of Dandré's working conditions, I refused to attend rehearsals. The more the others complained to each other but followed meekly after Grischa, the more obstinate I became. I knew the company could do nothing but fine me, but they couldn't prevent me from dancing, since every able body was needed to perform. And, no matter how much they snarled, I was still carrying my precious American passport.

While I had a home, a family, and an American passport to fall back on, most of the other dancers lacked all three. Much later I decided that their obedience must have evolved, in many cases, from years of working under more stringent circumstances than I had ever imagined. The contract a corps de ballet dancer signed with Diaghilev in 1918 read, in part:

¶. For this engagement M. de Diaghilev will pay to Miss _____ _____ the sum of £4 per week, London; £5 per week, provinces; and £28 per month Continent respectively.

¶. The Management is not prepared to entertain any objections raised by the performer to the part allotted in the production.

¶. Performers are to accept any change made in the piece performed.

¶. The number and duration of rehearsals are fixed by M. de Diaghilev.

In light of terms such as these, the compliance of the older dancers was understandable.

I was the only rebel in the troupe, but I wasn't punished for it. I even felt a bit smug during the tour, when *Tannhäuser* was eliminated from the repertoire before it ever premiered.

The working vacation was over when we docked in Melbourne in October 1938. Immediately we began our eight-week season at His Majesty's Theatre. Classes aboard ship had kept us in condition, but performing full out in such heat was a much greater strain than rehearsing. It took several days to adjust to the Australian summer.

We appeared under the auspices of Williamson and Tate, Ltd., who had also managed both Pavlova's company in Australia and a smaller company than ours which the colonel had sent there in 1937. They had spent eight weeks in Melbourne, three in Adelaide, and nine in Sydney, a city with only ninety thousand residents at the time. The Australians had greeted their first exposure to ballet so enthusiastically that critic Arnold Haskell wrote, "De Basil's ballet has made theatrical history and is alone in being able to compete with the cinema." Dancing to one full house after another, we continued the work started by the smaller company.

Anton Dolin joined us in Melbourne, having flown in hops of twelve to fifteen hours a day for six days since leaving Amsterdam. Shrugging off the exhaustion of the lengthy trip, he was just as cheerful and energetic in class as the first day I had met him in his London studio four years earlier. His solo, *Bolero*, to the well-known Ravel piece, was welcome in our depleted repertoire and was a personal triumph every time he danced it. In addition to dancing with us, Pat Dolin frequently gave lectures on the radio, sharing broadcasts with Haskell, who had also joined our entourage. Their witty and informative talks were wonderful publicity and helped the Australians to understand and appreciate our work.

After a brief stop in the port of Adelaide, we went on to our eight-week engagement in Sydney, a city with a cosmopolitan atmosphere and lofty beauty that reminded me of San Francisco. The temperature rose to 118 degrees, and we shed pounds as well as practice clothes.

Our sweat-soaked costumes never dried between performances, but the applause was recompense for the discomfort.

Lichine developed a badly inflamed knee that forced him to stop dancing. Rather than remain idle, he decided to use the time to choreograph. He propped the sore leg on a straight chair in front of him in the studio and started his version of yet another ballet first choreographed by George Balanchine, *The Prodigal Son*. Lichine had never seen Balanchine's 1929 work for Diaghilev, so his visualization of the Prokofiev score was original. He chose Baronova and Grigorieva to alternate in the leading role of the Siren, and set the title role on Dolin, with whom he would alternate once he had recovered.

Since the corps for this ballet was only men, I didn't expect to be in the ballet at all. But one day, without warning, Lichine asked me to attend rehearsals to learn the part of the Siren. I was too surprised to speak. I could only nod that I would be there.

For the second scene of the ballet, in which the Siren danced with a hoop, I worked with Roman at the back of the hall, while Dolin rehearsed up front, first with Baronova, then with Grigorieva. At one point in the choreography, the Siren had to step in and out of the hoop on pointe and fall repeatedly to her knees. The constant rising and falling was visually effective, but after a while I found it extremely painful. The longer we rehearsed, the more my knees hurt and the harder it was to continue. But I kept silent and pushed on, never mentioning my pain to anyone but Yasha. The Siren was my first starring role, and complaining would only jeopardize my chance of ever dancing it. Neither Baronova nor Grigorieva said anything about any pain, so I was certainly not going to let it interfere with my chance.

Giving in to the pain would have eliminated me from two ballets, not one, since *Prodigal* was not the only new ballet in progress. A year earlier, while visiting his good friend Rachmaninoff in Lucerne, Fokine had discussed collaborating with the composer. They settled on *Rhapsody on a Theme of Paganini*, and Rachmaninoff agreed to write the libretto. After a year of reading and research, Fokine had started to choreograph. A constant stream of letters arrived from Rachmaninoff, discussing the episodic tale of slander and musical plagiarism that plagued Paganini's life. The drama appealed to Fokine, whose works had often been plagiarized or presented as "after Fokine" without his consent.

Fokine was so involved with the new ballet that he often stayed behind at the studio after we left rehearsals. The dancers grabbed those rare free hours to visit Sydney's Bondi Beach, where our swimming was occasionally disrupted by shark warnings. As the alarm spread down the beach, hundreds of bathers splashed out of the surf, rushing like dancers prancing through a *presto* finale. We were sorry that Fokine and his wife never set foot on the beach, because we thought the sun and salt air might give some color to his unusually pale face.

Early in 1939 we brought ballet to Auckland, New Zealand. The opening-night audience convinced us that we were a first in their experience. At the end of each ballet, the audience sat perfectly still and silent, their hands in their laps. The next day Pat Dolin arranged a radio broadcast to inform the New Zealanders that applause was not only proper, but very desirable to the dancers. Another seed was sown. After Pat's broadcast, thunderous applause followed every performance.

We danced in Dunedin, Invercargill, and Christchurch on South Island and in Wellington on North Island. Between performances in Rotorua, we saw Maoris preparing their food over the small geysers that erupted from crevices in the rocks. We heard that the sulphurous waters in the region were supposed to relax and strengthen sore, aching bodies. But as much as we needed it, we didn't have time to take the natural cure.

Dolin injured his ankle in *Schéhérazade* and had to stop dancing until we returned to Melbourne. The first night he was well enough to perform again, but he reinjured his ankle almost immediately while doing the entrechats six in his *Swan Lake* solo variation. Pausing only long enough to change his costume, he reappeared after the intermission and, without showing any pain, was stunning in the premiere of Lichine's *Prodigal Son*. Watching Pat that night, I marveled at how dramatically he commanded the stage. Unlike some dancers, who are primarily interested in solo work, Pat had mastered the subtle and difficult art of partnering. In pas de deux of exceptional fluidity, he and Irina gave the simplest choreography special value, as if their dancing together were the greatest possible privilege. Every pause, glance, and gesture created a haunting aura of tenderness.

Prodigal Son received glowing reviews. Soon my turn would come to dance the Siren. Younger dancers were regularly assigned matinee performances for their debuts in major roles. Before my matinee in Sydney, panic and excitement raced through my mind. Smoothing chalk-white greasepaint over my face and neck, I blanked out my eyebrows with soap and replaced them with two strong black lines across my brow that almost met above my nose. To create a debauched look, I smeared purple shadows under my eyes and made my mouth more sensuous by painting it half an inch wider than usual.

Mme. Larose handed me the same red-velvet costume and tall white headdress that Rouault had designed for the Diaghilev production. I stared at myself in the dressing-room mirror. I now wore the same costume the sublime Felia Doubrovska had worn a decade earlier. As the second scene came closer, I settled myself cross-legged on a large platter in the wings and draped my narrow train carefully over its rim. Four men lifted the platter high over their heads and carried me slowly onstage, my train sweeping down between them from my perilous perch almost eight feet in the air.

I had rehearsed so long and so hard for this role that my stage fright dissolved moments after my entrance. For once I was fully prepared, and my readiness freed me to concentrate on my interpretation. I blessed Lichine for the many rehearsal hours he had allowed me, because, as often as not, the steps were the least of my worries. At many points in the ballet, Lichine had used immobility for the Siren instead of movement. I had to make those moments as dynamic as my dancing. In one such sequence all the men straddled the narrow banquet table on which I stood at one end. Holding a large goblet before me, I fell towards them, keeping myself rigid as a board. The men closest to me caught my stiff body and lifted it straight over their heads, where they passed me from one pair of upheld hands to the next for the full length of the table.

Except for the solo with the hoop, I was often high in the air, because Lichine wanted to dramatize the distance between the aloof temptress and the aroused Prodigal Son. In the closing tableau of the scene, I sat on top of a pyramid of men, who themselves stood on the table several feet off the floor. The Prodigal was alone at stage level, his arms yearning for my unattainable body, as the curtain fell.

Lichine had recovered sufficiently from his injury to dance the title role, and he partnered me himself for my debut. He was very pleased with my performance, and from that day on I shared the role with Baronova and Grigorieva.

Many years later, during a routine physical examination, my doctor put his hand on my knee and said, "Feel that. It feels like a battlefield in there." Just as I had feared, I had permanently damaged the cartilage in both knees by dancing the Siren. But the risk of injury, either temporary or permanent, is one that dancers face every day of their professional lives. Unlike a musician, a dancer cannot trade in his instrument for another. Our bodies are all we have, and we continue to move them beyond their natural limits, exposing them to perpetual hazards. If you want to dance, you learn to bear the pain.

Months passed and we began to think about going back to England. Again and again Yasha brought up the subject of marriage. In Australia I turned down his proposal, as I had several other times. As tactfully as I could, I told him that our work was our only stability. Remembering the unhappiness of my parents, I explained that to me a real marriage was based only on sexual fidelity and lasting affection, both of which we already had; we didn't need the burden of a legal certification. I was sure my refusals hurt him, but in this case I felt honesty was more important than gentleness. I simply loathed the idea of marriage.

Both Yasha and I saw all around us how meaningless legal marriages were. Infidelities ran rampant. One dancer plied his bride with hot red wine on their wedding night and then, when she passed out in a stupor, spent the night as planned with his mistress. Another dancer, well known for her sexual appetite, often whisked her lover into her dressing room before performances. Later, when she made her transition from amour to arabesques, others would watch with arched eyebrows and chuckle, "Look, balance no good . . . Knees shake . . . Too much love."

The most passionate dancers never allowed strenuous work to interfere with offstage lovemaking. One man was romantically involved and living with two women at the same time and had a mistress on the side! The very idea of that *ménage* strained our imaginations.

"*Quelle force!*" Volkova would say with admiration.

"*C'est un phénomène!*" Kouznetsova said many a time, winking.

But despite perpetual sexual activity, a few girls remained chaste, seemingly against all odds. One had such a ferociously devoted mother that we were positive that if the girl ever married, Mama would be right under the bridal bed, supervising her daughter's performance just as critically and enthusiastically as she did when the girl was dancing. "*Dushka*, smile!" we imagined her whispering. "*Dushka*, go! *Dushka*, stop! *Dushka*, too much!" We'd roar with laughter.

Yasha reluctantly let the subject of marriage drop in Australia. We sailed for London, retracing our outbound route back to England, welcoming the five-week voyage as our first break without rehearsal in two years.

After traveling halfway around the world and back again, returning to Covent Garden for June and July 1939 was like coming home. Soon after we arrived, Sir Oswald Birley asked me to pose for him, and he painted my portrait in a costume for *Coq d'Or*. I especially enjoyed those sittings because Sir Oswald would invite me to have delicious lunches with him and his wife, Rhoda, who was so beautiful that all she would have had to do was to put on the costume and she could have danced Thamar. Lichine wanted to dance the first London performance of *Prodigal*, so its premiere was delayed until his knee was completely healed. But even without a premiere, the season was going very well, with packed houses every night. A few weeks later *Prodigal* was finally scheduled. Scanning the casting sheet on the callboard, I saw "Siren—Osato." It was only a momentary thrill. Lichine soon heard that the London critics expected to see Irina in the role, and changed the casting. I understood the change professionally, but inside I was bitterly disappointed. However, the bitterness was momentary too, because I danced my London debut as the Siren several days later.

After that performance, as I was removing the purple shadows from my eyes, Florrie St. Just came into my dressing room. Though I was drenched with sweat, Florrie kissed me, praised my performance, and sat down to chat for a few moments about my promising future. Before leaving, she pressed a small box with a Cartier label into my hand. Trembling, I opened it and, with my vision blurred by tears, saw a tiny brooch of diamonds surrounding a small emerald. Setting it down, I paused for a brief moment, and wept.

The next day I read in the *Daily Telegraph*, "The great event of the evening was the prodigious impersonation by Sono Osato of the Siren in *Le Fils prodigue*. Cold at first, she became, as the scene went on, more and more possessed by her part, till at the climax, the identification was almost terrifying." Reading this made up for all the pain, the fatigue, and the nerves I had gone through preparing for the role.

Following close on the triumph of *Prodigal Son* was the success of Fokine's allegorical *Paganini*. His reported fears that something, or everything, might go wrong were unfounded. At the premiere the production moved like clockwork, and Tania and Irina overwhelmed the audience.

In the second scene, a pastoral setting, I was one of the girls who surrounded Tania as the Florentine Girl. She danced her solo to one of the piano's intricate scherzo passages, skimming the stage with rapid leaps, flinging her torso backwards in a great curve each time she rose in the air. Seemingly inexhaustible, she was in motion continuously. Her body flew as swiftly as the pianist's hands over the keyboard, every movement flowing into the next without visible preparation.

Wearing a diaphanous white costume that swept the floor, Irina was the image of Divine Genius. In a section of the final movement, during which Death approached the aging violinist, she led a chain of similarly clad dancers, including myself, in a long line of slow, sustained arabesques around him. Rescued from the trials of his career by his Genius, Paganini willingly embraced Death, knowing he had fulfilled his function in life by providing mankind with beauty.

These sentiments may sound trite today, but Fokine made every step of *Paganini* a statement of profound conviction. It was the result of an inspired collaboration between two great artists whose careers spanned a more romantic period than the abstractions of our cool, modern one. Freely, both men had dedicated their entire lives to the full expression of the emotions. Their passionate exploration of man's soul breathed life into their ballet. When it premiered that summer of 1939, Fokine was fifty-nine, and the ailing Rachmaninoff, sixty-six.

Shortly after closing night of the London season, I flew, for the very first time, to Switzerland for a holiday with Yasha. We booked a hotel room to sleep in, but joined the Cliffords during the day at their chalet in Mont-Pélerin, high above the town of Vevey on Lake Geneva. Tania Riabouchinska and Lichine were their houseguests, and the painter Eugene Berman and Choura Danilova also came to stay after Choura's season with Massine's company ended at the Drury Lane Theatre.

Through the bright, sunny days, we ate and talked and dabbled with paints, trying to capture the glorious beauty of the Alps on canvas under Berman's indulgent supervision. Dancing was replaced by lazy strolls through the streets of Vevey. The highlight of our holiday was a concert at the Lucerne Music Festival. Under Ernest Ansermet's direction, Rachmaninoff himself hunched low over the piano to play his *Rhapsody on a Theme of Paganini*. Toscanini sat nearby, peering through his fingers.

During the scherzo passage to which Tania had danced, Rachmaninoff attacked the keyboard with such diabolical speed that Ansermet had difficulty bringing in the violins at the proper measure. We were familiar with the music, but we had never heard it performed with such dazzling speed, clarity, and dynamism. At the last notes we jumped to our feet, cheering. Rising slowly to take his bows, the composer looked pale and unsmiling. Acknowledging the ovation with a slight nod, he was obviously not well. The enormous energy he drew from his weakened body made the performance unforgettable.

On September 1, three days after my twentieth birthday, we were all sprawled on the Cliffords' terrace, sipping aperitifs, enjoying the superb view, when someone switched on the radio for the noonday news. A matter-of-fact voice announced that Germany had just invaded Poland. As these words drifted out over the serenity of Lake Geneva, our silent fears of the last year became cold dread. War had come.

As quickly as they could, the Cliffords closed the elegant chalet and left the country. David and Tania departed immediately. Choura flew to London. Yasha and I stayed in Switzerland, fearing that if we set foot in France, Yasha, being Polish, would be drafted into the French army. Amidst crowds of anxious people trying to contact their relatives, we waited at the post office in Vevey for days, hoping for news of the company's future plans. Mother and Father cabled first, urging me to come home without delay. My American passport left me free to travel at will, but I wouldn't think of abandoning Yasha, not even for a moment.

Dorati wired us from America that he was making every effort to arrange passage for Yasha to travel there with me.

The fact that those two cables reached us at all was something of a fluke. The declaration of war had so convulsed Europe that public services were in a state of chaos. Telegrams took several days just to travel between Paris and Vevey. While we waited for instructions from the company, Yasha and I tried to boost each other's spirits. The days grew colder and we became more and more anxious about our dwindling money and the uncertainty of our future. We waited nearly two months in Vevey before, on October 28, we received this wire:

AUSTRALIAN PERMITS SENT BRITISH CONSULATE LAUSANNE. BALLET LEAV-
ING 18 NOVEMBER. DOING UTMOST OBTAIN YOUR PERMISSION COME
LONDON. GREETINGS DE BASIL.

Reading these words, I realized the colonel had somehow found a way to regain control of the company. Suddenly more confident, I cabled my family and told them I was staying in Europe. Yasha and I made our way to Lausanne and hunted down the consulate the moment we arrived. To one side of the foyer, waiting patiently, stood the colonel, who had flown there to meet us. He had set aside his enormous responsibilities for a moment in order to ensure our safety.

With authority he stated our case to the officials, explaining that we were his employees and on our way to dance in Australia. We were both granted permission to leave the country. De Basil's reputation might have been for being devious and difficult, particularly in business matters, but I will forever be grateful to him for his generosity to us during those first frightening months of the war.

The colonel told us to go to Paris, where he hoped to assemble the scattered members of the company, who had gone as far as Italy and Hungary for their holidays. We reached Paris on November 14 and were issued a two-day permit of stay. Neither the blackout curtains nor the encroaching frost disrupted the Parisians' daily routine. They continued to frequent even outdoor cafés, where they heatedly discussed the latest war bulletins. I heard one anti-Communist declare quite grandly, "Après les Boches, ça sera les Rouges! After the Krauts, it will be the Reds!"

Ashen-faced Jews who had just escaped from Germany crammed

the lobby of our shabby hotel. All day they sat muffled in overcoats, their ears pressed to radios announcing the tragic news of their homeland in strident German. Hearing the guttural tones of German in the middle of Paris seemed both incongruous and menacing to me. How much more dreadful it must have sounded to those uprooted Jews, who understood every word.

In the middle of the night, Yasha and I were startled from our sleep by fists banging on our door and the voice of the concierge shrieking, *"Alerte! Alerte!"* Throwing coats over our nightclothes, we ran down the stairs with everyone else to shelter in the cellar. Together with heavily rouged prostitutes, old men and women, and the new refugees, we sat nervously in silence, listening to the anti-aircraft guns getting louder and louder.

No one spoke. Finally a Russian émigré with a thick accent blurted out frantically, "I must see vat happen," and dashed up the stairs. He returned to the shelter with the good news that the planes above were for *"reconnaissance, pas bombes."* Relieved, we all filed warily to our rooms and slept fitfully for the rest of the night.

Our two-day pass expired on November 16, but fortunately someone again came to our rescue. During his long career at the Paris Opera, Serge Lifar, its premier danseur and maître de ballet, had made many friends among the high officials of the French government. His prestigious contacts enabled him to aid many dancers in many ways during those dangerous months. I don't know to whom he spoke, or what strings he pulled, but thanks to his efforts, our pass was extended for several additional days.

Clutching the pass and praying for some word from the colonel, Yasha and I rushed to the company's only European office, which was a single room at 16 Rue de Gramont. We opened the door and saw what seemed to be every ballet dancer in Paris crammed into that small room.

When war broke out, Massine's company was as widely scattered throughout Europe on holiday as de Basil's. The dancers found their way back to Paris only to learn that Massine and Hurok had left for America without them. Stranded and jobless, the many men who had Nansen passports could not hope to escape the draft unless someone could vouch for them. In desperation Massine's dancers turned to de Basil for help.

For several days, quiet but frantic conversation filled the smoky room with anxiety. People came in, but no one ever seemed to leave. Bodies filled every inch of space on the desks, against the walls, and on the floors. Knowing that they must work or be sent, perhaps, to the Maginot Line, the abandoned male dancers begged the colonel to take them along with us to Australia. De Basil listened for hours on end, never speaking, never betraying any sign of his thoughts. He sat with one leg wound around the other all the way down to his ankle. With one elbow propped on his knee, he smoked constantly, characteristically holding the underside of his cigarette between the thumb and forefinger of his cupped hand. Finally a big smile lit his tired face. With a wave of his hand, including everyone in the room, he announced, *"Nu, pai dom!* Well, let's go!" There was an astonished hush. Then he added, "Not much money. Company already too big." At that moment I adored him.

The colonel didn't appear frightened for an instant. Instead he seemed to relish the adversity of the situation. Formerly a captain in Bicherakoff's Cossacks, who fought against the Red Army in the Crimea in 1920, de Basil now took command naturally. Once his decision was made, he didn't discuss money or contracts, nor did he ask any thanks. The very same man whose ego made him climb a ladder in Dubuque, Iowa, to measure the size of his name on the theatre marquee, now acted without a trace of vanity. His compassion extended to the people who had no other hope but him.

With the three words he had uttered, de Basil added nearly twenty dancers to the company. There were almost a dozen men, the most famous of whom were Anatole Oboukhoff, Igor Schwezoff, Michel Panaieff, and George Skibine. The women included the former Diaghilev ballerina Vera Nemchinova, Tatiana Stepanova, Marina Svetlova, Tania Leskova, and the Moulin sisters. The other men were Nicholas Orlov, Vladimir Irman, Nicholas Ivangine, Serge Unger, Simon Semenoff, and Vassily and Oleg Tupine.

On the way to our ship in Tilbury, England, the expanded company stopped briefly in London. The disciplined Londoners had blacked out the city so thoroughly that at night we had to grope our way down the sidewalks to find an open restaurant. Stumbling back to our hotel one night after dinner, we heard a woman's screams echo through the fogbound night. We stopped in our tracks, but there was no way to find her in the darkness. The next day, reading a newspaper headline "Rape in the West End," we linked the screams we had heard to the rape victim. Our helplessness the night before was yet another element added to our growing sense of fear.

As the train for Tilbury carried us quickly from the West End to the eastern suburbs and then into the open countryside, we saw large balloons, attached to long wires weighted to the ground, floating high above the city and piles of sandbags stacked high around historic monuments. The expedient preparations for London's defense lingered in our thoughts for days, long after we'd sailed and left the city we loved behind.

We sailed on convoy on the passenger ship the H.M.S. *Orcades*, which was jammed with the wives and children of military men stationed in Burma and India. The crew told us that tight blackout restrictions were in effect and must be strictly obeyed. After sundown the open decks were pitch black, but small blue lights illuminated the doorways. The colonel strolled calmly among us, saying, "Don't vorry. Royal Air Force on top. Royal Navy on side." He seemed so confident that I believed him. But after a time, there wasn't a sign of the Royal Air Force. The ship's radio announced one evening that the *Blackhill*, a ship we had passed only that afternoon, had just been sunk by one of the magnetic mines the Germans were sending down the Channel from the North Sea. The next day, the *Torchbearer* was struck. Between Tilbury and Gibraltar many of the ships we passed suffered the same fate. As frightening as it was to contemplate, we couldn't ignore the possibility that the *Orcades* might go down too. Life jackets became permanent attire.

Walking down the narrow staircases to my cabin on a low deck, I realized that if we were struck by a mine, I would never make it. Still, I made elaborate emergency preparations. Alone in my small cabin before going to bed, I thought out the best place to put my life jacket, finally laying it at the foot of my bunk. Over and over I practiced plunging into it on the count of one and fastening the straps until I could do it with my eyes shut. Then I compared the width of my hips to the diameter of the porthole. In the event that my side of the ship were directly hit, I planned to squeeze through the opening to safety. Assuming I might possibly escape, I imagined myself among hundreds of screaming passengers thrashing about in the icy sea. Exhausted by my drill and by my fearful thoughts, I muttered to myself, "To hell with it!" and fell asleep.

With the news that Russia had attacked Finland, God knew why, and the knowledge that order was disintegrating in Europe ringing in our minds, the trip through the Red Sea in oppressive heat was a waking nightmare. It was impossible to sleep in the stifling cabins. Women and children were ordered to bed down on one deck and the men on another. I found room to stretch out next to the gunwale and lay with my nose by a small opening at its base, where the ship's movement produced a little breeze of hot air. Despite the hardness of the deck, I preferred it to the smothering stillness that surrounded us. No one got much sleep, but it was comforting to know that each night took us farther from the war.

When we sailed into the Indian Ocean, we heard from the crew that the German battle cruiser *Gneisenau* was somewhere in the vicinity. With a dry throat I watched the gun drill, and wondered how the single gun mounted on our bow could possibly protect us against the enemy. Fortunately, the rumor was false. But a few days later, when our ship began moving in a peculiar zigzag pattern, a sailor told me that a submarine was stalking us. We zigzagged for several days, but our luck held. Miraculously unscathed, we sailed into Sydney Harbor on Christmas Day 1939, nearly four months after the outbreak of war.

We performed in Australia with a different roster of dancers every year. In 1938 the formation of Massine's company had splintered us one way. Now the war reshuffled us all over again. In September, Irina, Sevastianov, and Pat Dolin, who were vacationing in England, had sailed for America to make plans of their own. But Tamara Toumanova, her Mamitchka, Tania Riabouchinska, Lichine, and the American conductor Max Goberman, who was engaged to replace Dorati, had left America in time to meet up with us shortly after we arrived in Sydney.

Serge Lifar also joined us in Sydney. He emerged from his airplane in a dramatic outfit of jodphurs, a rakish beret, and sun goggles. He was utterly charming, although the ten-day flight from Europe had clearly tired him. Nevertheless, shortly after arriving, Lifar danced the strenuous *Spectre de la Rose*, which he had often performed in Paris to unanimous raves. On this occasion, however, one reviewer bluntly compared him more to the "spirit of a cabbage than that of a rose." Lifar's healthy ego refused to concede that he, the Parisian Dieu de la Danse, was a bit out of shape and a bit overweight. After our two lengthy tours, the Australians were a well-educated ballet audience and *did* know, despite Lifar's refusal to admit it, a dancing rose from a flabby cabbage.

During the short period he spent with us, Lifar mounted his 1935 ballet *Icare*, based on the myth of Daedalus and Icarus, for our company. The new piece absorbed us once again in learning a new choreographic style. Lifar's movement was rather unorthodox, relying heavily on syncopated steps that I thought were fun to learn and very enjoyable to perform. The score for *Icare*, a set of rhythms devised by Lifar and arranged by J. E. Szyfer, was equally unorthodox, unlike anything to which we had ever danced. It used only percussion instruments and depended largely on a wind machine that a stagehand cranked backstage to produce weird, unearthly sounds. Muffled at first, then interspersed with staccato drumbeats and ringing gongs, the strange whirring surged into a deafening roar during the finale, in which Lifar, as Icare, plunged headfirst down a slide onto the stage, his upright, broken wing quivering as he died. Lifar's performance was impressive, but after the French government recalled him to Paris, I thought Yasha's interpretation was even more touching.

Over the next three months the news from Europe got steadily worse. On June 14 the Germans marched into Paris and we wept. We wept most of the day. The Russian dancers had no way of knowing if they would ever see their families again, or if their fathers and brothers had been called into the French army. Letters took months to reach us, slowed by distance and the censors. Daily headlines were too appalling to read. We often wondered if the world would survive.

Dancing was our blessing. Civilization was going down the drain, but we carried our own inviolate world with us. Wherever we traveled, the music and the world filled our days, constant and reassuring. Financial conditions in the company at their best had never been secure. Now with the addition of so many new dancers, the colonel cut all wages to the bone. But no one complained. We knew we were lucky to have our work, and the new dancers gave us lots of pleasure to balance the hardships. Anatole Oboukhoff, who had trained at the Maryinsky, partnered Pavlova, and enjoyed a long career in Europe, took over some of our classes from Tchernicheva. He was slim, energetic, and immaculately groomed in his black trousers and starched white shirt. I soon learned that his deadpan face hid a warm sense of humor.

In class, Oboukhoff used a tiny stick. "Call yourself classical dancer?" he'd say, pointing to my feet, "Vat is *dat?*" And with his stick, he nudged my toes into a more perfect fifth position. His expression never changed, but his eyes twinkled with amusement whenever he corrected me. He demonstrated wonderful floor combinations, dancing with the open, flowing Maryinsky arms that mark the élan and elegance of its successor, the Kirov Ballet, to this day. Inspired by his example, we strove to match his style and, for a few hours, were able to forget the horrors reported in the newspapers.

Having arrived from her year in America with a short haircut and a chic wardrobe, the always more glamorous Toumanova inspired us as well. Gayer than ever offstage, she danced with a new softness, bringing rounder contours to her roles. She focused more on the content of her roles yet sacrificed none of her technical brilliance. Free of romantic involvement, Tamara seemed to live only for dancing, working in an aura of splendid fanaticism. Seeing her blossoming womanliness, I felt that all she needed to complete the transformation was a steady regimen of two or three lovers, and I told her so. This great ballerina, truly one of the most beautiful women in the world, actually blushed at the suggestion. Partly shocked and partly pleased, she drew her hand coyly to her mouth, her dark eyes laughing, and said, "Oh, Sono!"

Mama Toumanova had not changed a bit, still hovering like a mother hen over her chick, hands fluttering over Tamara's heart in the sign of the Russian cross, just before the curtain rose.

We went to Adelaide, Melbourne, and Sydney again. We hoped to find some time to explore the great undeveloped outback that stretches across the huge northern portion of the continent, but our heavy schedule wouldn't allow it. For most of the spring of 1940, we were confined to theatres, rehearsal halls, and furnished rooms. We spent our free Sundays at the zoo, amused by the antics of playful koala bears and bouncing kangaroos.

By summer the war had spread across most of Western Europe. Some of our performances were benefits for the Red Cross. Before one of them, we marched through the streets near the theatre, holding an immense French flag. Crowds of sympathetic citizens threw a shower of coins into the draped flag. Thousands of soldiers from Australia and New Zealand packed troop ships sailing out of Sydney Harbor to join the fighting. Although we never had time to establish lasting friend-ships, we met such warmth and hospitality in Australia that we felt our friends were on those ships.

We hadn't the vaguest idea what would become of us after the tour, so we immersed ourselves more than ever in our work, without thinking of what the future would bring. Finally the colonel told us that we were leaving Sydney for a tour of America. Our old friend Sol Hurok, once again our manager, would meet us in Los Angeles.

Amazed at the colonel's uncanny ability to make bookings appear out of thin air during wartime, we continued the eastward journey that had begun in England, crossing the calm Pacific without even a whis-pered rumor of a submarine. After the nerve-racking trip to Australia the previous fall, this trip was like a holiday. Between lazy dips in the tiled pool, we sat down under the mid-autumn sun to four meals a day. I ate breakfast each morning with Nemchinova and Oboukhoff, who, since he had no classes to teach, decided to teach me a scene from Pushkin's *Boris Godunov* in Russian instead. Too busy stuffing myself with fresh pineapple, pancakes, and sausage, I had memorized only twelve Russian words by the time we stopped in Honolulu.

Hurok greeted us in Los Angeles as if nothing had ever happened. He praised the new ballets and urged us to keep up the "team spirit" and to dance as we had never danced before. During our season in L.A., we heard the story of Hurok's reconciliation with the colonel. After only two years Massine's Monte Carlo Ballet Russe had begun to have its own problems. Massine himself was understandably exhausted: He was artistic director of the company and its principal dancer and had choreographed an array of new ballets, some of them to large symphonic scores with décor by distinguished artists:

BACCHANALE
Music: Wagner; décor & costumes: Dali

SEVENTH SYMPHONY
M: Beethoven; d & c: Bérard

BOGATYRI
M: Borodin; d & c: Gontcharova

GAÎTÉ PARISIENNE
M: Offenbach; d & c: de Beaumont

ROUGE ET NOIR
M: Shostakovitch (First Symphony); d & c: Matisse

ST. FRANCIS (NOBILISSIMA VISIONE)
M: Hindemith; d & c: Tchelitchew

His multiple duties were wearing Massine down, and it was rumored that he was at odds with Serge Denham. His dancers became restless. Dreaming of more money and greater fame, many succumbed to the glamorous temptations of Broadway and Hollywood. For the second time in two years, Hurok watched his prize attraction eroding before his eyes.

Reading our Australian reviews for Lichine's *Prodigal Son* and *Graduation Ball* and Fokine's *Paganini* and *Coq d'Or* whetted Hurok's appetite. By deleting the exclusivity clause from his contract with Massine's company, Hurok was free to manage any company he wanted to in addition to Massine's. Lured by our success and by his deep, lasting admiration for de Basil, Hurok once again took charge of our American tour by rejoining us on the West Coast.

With their handshake Hurok and de Basil agreed to overlook their differences and past conflicts and move forward together. Perhaps their undying love for ballet was the strongest, most valuable bond between them, greater than all their differences. Educational Ballets, Ltd., had ceased to exist when the colonel resumed control of the company. To distinguish us from Massine's troupe, we were now named the Original Ballet Russe.

The difference in atmosphere between Australia and L.A. was remarkable. We were amazed that the main topic away from the theatre seemed to be the approaching presidential election and the candidates, President Roosevelt and Wendell Willkie. "Don't these people know there's a war going on?" we asked each other. Their narrow isolationism made us indignant. We danced our season professionally but left L.A. without any regrets for Chicago, where I was reunited with my family. Over the years I had written to them regularly, but my brief letters simply said that I was well, safe, and working hard. Now I could tell them the details of events I had only mentioned in passing.

Time had slipped by. Teru had grown into a beautiful young woman and a talented painter. Pursuing her interest in theatrical set design and construction, she planned to enter Bennington College in Vermont in the fall. Tim was still enthralled by history. At the age of ten, he had deployed his toy soldiers around the dining-room table to demonstrate to me the strategical errors Napoleon had made at the Battle of Waterloo. Now that he was fourteen years old, his extraordinary intelligence qualified him to appear as one of radio's popular Quiz Kids.

I told the family a little about my gradual promotion from the corps to solo roles and arranged for them to see me in one of my newest parts, Danilova's role as Guinevere in *Francesca da Rimini*. Rather than wear her ankle-length dark wig, I decided to dance the role as a blonde, in the platinum wig that had been supplied with her original brown one. My friends laughed at the idea, but I liked the challenge of completely altering my looks. Each time I danced the role, I covered my face in pearly makeup and painted delicate arched blue eyebrows instead of my own. My transformation was so complete that when Mother saw me in the part, she said she only recognized me by my elbows! Characteristically, Mother's enthusiasm was calm and reserved. Father was more captivated by the whole ambiance of the theatre and my involvement in it, but he, too, said nothing. On the other hand, I didn't ask for opinions. I hadn't seen my family for two years, and my rapport with them, which had never been great, had grown even dimmer. In any case, what with going from class to rehearsals to performance and getting home well past midnight, there was no time for lengthy discussions with my family about my progress, either from my point of view or from theirs.

This time around, Hurok had planned the tour in blocks of performances rather than as a string of one-night stands. So after Chicago we had a short engagement in Canada and then moved directly to New York. Hurok booked us for almost eleven weeks at the Fifty-first Street Theatre (now the Mark Hellinger), since the Met was unavailable that season. Our protracted engagement, following four weeks of performances by Massine's Monte Carlo Ballet Russe, would complete the longest season of ballet on Broadway to that date.

When we arrived in New York, we found a representative of the three-year-old American Guild of Musical Artists (AGMA) waiting for us at the orchestra rehearsal. As if it were the most natural statement in the world, he informed us that the curtain would not go up that night on our opening performance unless we all joined the union that same day. We had never heard of such a thing. No one but the colonel seemed to know what a union was. As angry as we had ever seen him, he warned us, "Don't listen. I am like Fadder to you. *I* vill protect!"

The idea that a business organization could supervise our rights and our time was the furthest thing from our minds. The demands of the choreographic process had always structured our working day. When Massine, Nijinska, or Fokine was creating a new ballet, no clock in the world could dictate time off for lunch. We danced whenever we were told to dance. We knew no other way of working. But when we learned that under the union's rules our hours would be carefully regulated and that we would be paid extra for something called "overtime," we grabbed the pen and signed. As it happened, the union, AGMA, had originally protected only opera performers and concert musicians. Our company members, and Massine's, were the first ballet dancers ever to join the union.

In New York, Yasha and I found a dark one-room apartment near the theatre. It was inexpensive and convenient, but right in the middle of the neighborhood known as Hell's Kitchen, a name that came painfully close to describing the private turmoil of our life together.

During our years as a couple, my feelings for Yasha had slowly changed. I was now twenty and he almost thirty. In the five years we had shared, he had shown me nothing but devotion and tenderness. He taught me how to cook, how to live well cheaply, and, even more, a great deal about how to dance; he had always coached me carefully, as a fair and loving critic. I still had the deepest affection for him, but what I had thought at fifteen was love I now realized was physical attraction and a need to be protected. Feeling more confined than in love, I needed my freedom. Although a terrible feeling of guilt about the pain I would cause him grew with each passing day, I knew I had to tell him we could no longer live together.

Added to the miserable burden of facing Yasha with the end of our affair, I was, simply, in a state of total exhaustion. I was dancing the leading female role in *Prodigal Son* regularly. As a soloist, I danced Lichine's *Protée*, Beauty in Schwezoff's *Eternal Struggle*, the Chief Odalisque in *Schéhérazade*, and solo roles in *Choreartium, Francesca da Rimini, Coq d'Or, Paganini, L'Après-midi d'un Faune*, and *Cotillon*. In addition I still danced in the corps of Nijinska's *Danses Slaves et Tziganes* and in *Swan Lake, Sylphides, Firebird, Graduation Ball*, and *Symphonie Fantastique*. On matinee days I appeared in as many as seven ballets. I became so fatigued, guilty, and confused that I couldn't even concentrate enough to read. Finally I admitted to myself that I had reached a crisis, a blind corner, out of which the only escape seemed to be some kind of forceful, deliberate action. I submitted a written list of requests to the colonel. I asked to be removed from the corps in *Sylphides* and *Swan Lake*. I also asked that my sixty dollars a week be raised to seventy-five.

Meanwhile George Balanchine had come to choreograph a new ballet, *Balustrade*, that would star Tamara Toumanova and Yasha. I was cast as a snake, and I spent rehearsals crawling around on the floor, which couldn't have been more appropriate to my mood. Sadly, I spent much more time in rehearsals worrying about my problems than concentrating on the new experience of working with Balanchine.

Twelve days went by without a response from the colonel. On the thirteenth, I came to the end of my rope. I knew he was swamped with problems; still, I told myself, he somehow could have found time to speak to me for a few moments about my simple requests.

That night I walked to the theatre in a cold fury. In my dressing room, I packed my good-luck piece, some worn pointe shoes, and my makeup in a small bag. Then, saying to an astonished dancer, "I'm leaving," I turned on my heels and walked out the stage door. Alone in the street, I felt strangely relieved. I had no plans for the future, but I felt wonderfully serene for the first time in many months. Later in the season I returned to the theatre as part of the audience to see Balanchine's new ballet. In the lobby I ran onto that unctuous little character Philipoff, who called me a traitor for leaving the company.

Treason had nothing to do with it. It had taken me six years to approach the rank of soloist. Would it take another six to advance even further? The hierarchy of the company was absolutely fixed. Looming over me was a full roster of established soloists and ballerinas. Would any choreographer but Lichine ever see my potential as a leading dancer or create new roles for me? Were there any higher goals in the company to which I could realistically aspire? Where was all my hard work leading me? Would it lead anywhere? I felt that my apprenticeship was over. I had replaced Danilova in two roles and had leading roles in other ballets, and I considered myself a bona fide member of the company, with something definite to offer. But a pattern had been set. Unless something dramatic were to happen, I could see ahead of me more years of last-minute replacements and being "familially" exploited.

Even more difficult was adjusting to my breakup with Yasha. We had been a fixture in the company as a couple so long that I couldn't imagine working with him as if we were strangers. I wondered if I could ever "fit in" on my own.

Everything had come to a head in those thirteen days. Leaving the company was not a thinking act but a reflex. I believe the colonel had never stopped thinking of me as a little girl, and at the time I was too angry to forgive his silence. Once I had walked out the stage door, I never saw him again, but to this day I feel gratitude and love and admiration whenever I think of Vassily Grigorievitch.

Thirty-five years later I stood at his grave in Ste. Geneviève des Bois, the Russian cemetery near Paris. (A few yards away, the double-headed eagle of the Romanovs decorates Kchessinska's grave. Beside a neat bed of pansies and manicured grass, a small wooden bench invites those who loved her to rest a moment.) On de Basil's headstone the Cyrillic lettering was almost worn away. At its base lay a basket of artificial flowers. Someone had dropped an empty plastic bottle by his tomb. Though sad, the contrast seemed unimportant. Whatever physical monument marks de Basil's grave cannot dignify him as much as my memory of him does. The enormous work he did and the fierce tenacity of spirit that drove him will live as long as ballet and its history survive.

Shortly after the new year of 1941, de Basil and the company left for a tour of Mexico, Cuba, and South America. Hurok had lost $70,000 during the New York season, but the colonel continued moving on. With him went all my friends, Yasha, and six years of my life.

Leaving the Ballet Russe was a turning point. Growing up with the Russians, I had learned to love their gallantry, their humor, and their passion. From them I learned the value of community purpose, which is much larger and more worthwhile than any individual effort. I experienced the pleasure one gets by giving pleasure to others. The unspoken love the Russians shared for their art gave them the strength to endure any hardship. The depth of their souls and the breadth of their emotions filled their dancing with magic and their daily lives with philosophical acceptance. Without their dedication, America would never have known the ballet.

felt completely numb that winter. In one swift decision I had abandoned my work, my home in the company, my lover, my friends, and my income. I had cut down my old life without for a moment thinking about what new life would replace it. I had definitely reached the end of something, but not a new beginning.

For the first time in years I was alone. I wrote home to tell the family what I had done, and Mother came to New York to be with me. We moved into a one-room apartment in a converted townhouse on West Fifty-fifth Street, which we named the Gas House because the odors from a nearby Chinese laundry and a beauty parlor drifted through its halls. Teru and a painter friend from Bennington joined us there for the "winter period," an educational innovation of Bennington, during which students were supposed to find employment to gain practical experience in their chosen fields. The four of us lived like gypsies in the single room, taking turns sleeping on a borrowed inflatable mattress. Mother cooked for all of us.

In the years since I had left home, Mother had undergone a change. Now she stood at the stove with her hat still on, taking little sips of sherry all the while she cooked our meals. She was obviously under a great deal of strain, and it worried me more for her than for myself. Sitting down to the dinner table, I would feel my heart constrict as the gay repartee I remembered was replaced by Cassandra-like prophecies of doom. "I can see it now. There'll be a war with Japan. We have no money. We'll lose everything! It will be terrible!" Each time she said it, it frightened me more, because I believed her.

Despite being exhausted, I knew I had to go on dancing each day. I would need a job, and dancing was all I was trained to do. To keep in condition, I went to the School of American Ballet on Madison Avenue and took class with either Pierre Vladimiroff, Muriel Stuart, or Balanchine.

Vladimiroff, formerly an outstanding dancer and a partner of

Pavlova, displayed the lovely manners of a bygone era. Regardless of how badly we danced, he would always acknowledge our efforts with a polite, "Very good, ladies," before going on to the next combination. Regrettably, his exceptional teaching was all but wasted on me. Although I regularly went to class, I gained ten pounds in my state of depression. The additional weight made me lethargic, and I danced like a dangling puppet.

I did no better in Balanchine's class. While his manner was more remote than Vladimiroff's, his ability to spot and analyze our faults was uncanny, no matter how many students crowded the studio. He pointed out to me one day that I did not move sharply enough. "You know, dear. Must use legs like scissors. More sharp," he urged me softly. I understood what he meant, but I couldn't shake my sluggishness and never mastered the dazzling, slicing style his dancers display to this day.

With de Basil's company dancing in South America, I saw almost no one I knew. Except for classes, I kept pretty close to the Gas House, Mother, and Teru. The days were getting warmer, and I was still wandering in a daze. Then I heard that Gerry Sevastianov and Irina were also in New York. Having fled together to America when war broke out in Europe, they had recently joined the new American ballet troupe called Ballet Theatre, which Richard Pleasant had founded in 1939 as an offshoot of the Mordkin Ballet. Pat Dolin had danced in the new company since its first season in January 1940 and had introduced Gerry and Irina to Lucia Chase, the former Mordkin ballerina. In March 1941, when Pleasant resigned his post as director of the company, he was replaced by Lucia, who invited Gerry to join her in the direction of the company, and he signed Irina as ballerina. Just after I left the colonel, I had seen one performance of Ballet Theatre at the Center Theatre, in which three girls stood out clearly in my mind. Their names were Alicia Alonso, Nora Kaye, and Annabelle Lyon.

Excited by the idea of seeing a friendly face from my "family" as well as a possible way out of my slump, I phoned Gerry and hurried up to his office. After listening to my story, Gerry offered me a contract to dance with Ballet Theatre for sixty dollars a week, exactly what the colonel had been paying me. But I was thrilled to get it and relieved at the idea of working again. Merely thanking Gerry wasn't enough, but he told me to stop worrying and report for work in the fall.

With a new feeling of security, I went up to visit Teru, who was back at Bennington. The beautiful, calm, green campus swarmed with girls of every description—tall ones, small ones, cheerful, glum. They stayed awake all night, smoking and talking. They swore like men. They talked about Freud, art, and sex, and dressed in a crazy assortment of clothes. Teru wore a cowboy hat most of the time. The only visible men were professors, drama students, or members of Martha Graham's dance company, which was in residence for the Bennington Dance Festival. Teru took me to a performance of Graham's year-old work, *Letter to the World,* for which she had helped design the lighting. To my surprise, one of the dancers, Jean Erdman, actually spoke from the stage, supplementing the dancers' movements onstage with the words of Emily Dickinson.

"What's all the talking about? That's not dancing!" I said smugly to Teru. "And why do they hold their hands cupped like that? It's ugly!"

"That's Graham's way," Teru answered in defense. "Open your mind! See it again!" She led me to a corner of the wings where I could lie down and peer under the scenery. I was proud and impressed with Teru's expertise with the lights and her familiarity with the dancers. I wanted to please her, so I watched again.

Dressed in black, Jane Dudley swept powerfully across the stage, her skirt swirling about her bare legs. When she paused, her tightly reined energy infused her posture with as much force as her motion. Sophie Maslow, Ethel Butler, and Nina Fonaroff moved just as swiftly, but with a gentler, more rounded attack. Led often by the dynamic Erick Hawkins, the dancers fell noiselessly to the floor from a standing position or snapped their upright bodies into concave arcs. Teru later told me that the abrupt, convulsive movements were called "contractions." After the group made their exit, Merce Cunningham bounded mercurially onstage in a bright green jacket, bending both legs sharply up to his erect torso as he jumped.

Towards the end of the work, Martha Graham, in a long white dress, with feet bare and hands cupped, stood alone. Staring from dark, expressionless eyes, she began to move. Her steps were hidden by her gown, but minute tremors shook her body. The tremors grew stronger but never larger as her hands lightly beat her neck, her arms, her breasts, her abdomen and thighs. Gently rocking, she moved slowly across the stage. I witnessed despair. I began to cry.

My visit to Bennington was not only a rest, it was a revelation. Martha Graham's work opened my mind to a new, powerful means of expression, so different from the vocabulary of movement in my own experience. Inspired by a new awareness of the expressiveness of dance, I returned to New York to join Ballet Theatre.

Once there, I was glad to be working again, but the effects of my physical and emotional exhaustion still lingered on. I entered my new job with an unfortunate lack of ambition and confidence. I was re-signed to dancing with Ballet Theatre, but couldn't imagine it as any-thing more than a serviceable outlet for what I knew how to do. I firmly believed my career was at a standstill. But Ballet Theatre was a brighter, breezier home than the one I had had in the last few years. The atmosphere was less imposing and a great deal less exotic than among the Russians. Now that I'd picked up enough Russian for con-versation or rehearsal, the predominant language in my dancing life was, for the first time, English.

A wholly "American" spirit pervaded the company. The dancers were young, fresh, and completely concentrated on trying to build a new American style of dancing and a new American repertory. Only Gerry's and Hurok's devotion to the classics ensured their foothold among the original ballets of Antony Tudor, Eugene Loring, and Agnes de Mille that Lucia was eager to establish as classics in their own right. Lucia Chase herself seemed the epitome of the group's ambition, whether she was figuring out budgets and timetables as a manager, or doing balancés and temps levés as a dancer. While de Basil had reigned over us like a benevolent Russian Tsar, Lucia worked among us like an American pioneer.

The warmth of my friends, Gerry and Irina, and the relaxed friendliness of those dancers who were perfect stangers eased me out of the doldrums. In addition to Irina, the women were Jeanette Lauret (one of Massine's dancers) and Nina Popova from de Basil's com-pany, and Lucia, Alicia Markova, Karen Conrad, Nora Kaye, Anna-belle Lyon, Maria Karnilova, Rosella Hightower, Muriel Bentley, and Miriam Golden. Among the men were Pat Dolin, Antony Tudor, Hugh Laing, John Kriza, Jerome Robbins, Donald Saddler, Ian Gibson, Richard Reed, and David Nillo. The former male de Basil dancers were Dimitri Rostoff, Yurek Lazowsky, Nicholas Orloff, Borislav Runanine, George Skibine, and Simon Semenoff.

Dolin was made regisseur for the classical repertory, and rehearsed each ballet meticulously. He also restaged *Aurora's Wedding* as *Princess Aurora*, adding the Lilac Fairy from the Prologue and the Rose Adagio from Act I to the last-act divertissements. Irina and Alicia Markova would share Aurora, and Pat chose me to dance the Lilac Fairy.

I was shocked, and thrilled. Up to that point, I had had no view of my career's going any further than the next day's rehearsal. Dolin's casting suddenly renewed my damaged spirit—and with what a role! I had always been cast in rather demi-caractère solos, but this was a legendary classical role. Pat's spirit in rehearsal coaxed mine even higher. He was both diligent and amusing, spicing his corrections with sharp, sometimes biting, humor. His friendly vitality was so like the easy-going Americans' that they all called him Pat. I tried to imagine Massine ever being treated with such familiarity by his dancers! Pat's skill, artistry, and great knowledge commanded respect, and his infectious humor made our work a joy.

Princess Aurora was first performed by Ballet Theatre in New York as part of the November 1941 season at the Forty-fourth Street Theatre. It was a success and remained in the repertoire for many years. My performance as the Lilac Fairy was very well received, which amazed me more than a little.

Beyond the momentary fear that strikes me before going on in any role, there was my deep-rooted fear of being openly exposed by the required technical perfection of a classical role. Had I been diligently trained for eight years as a child, as they were at the Maryinsky, the steps of the Lilac Fairy variation would have been a dream to dance. But I hadn't had those years of solid training with Berenice and had only learned to dance as I performed with the Russian ballet. I felt at ease in the relative freedom of demi-caractère and "modern" roles, but the minute that tight classical tutu with the grapes and the puffed sleeves and the powdered white wig went on, I could very easily have worked myself up into a state of panic.

The first half of the lovely, lilting waltz went well, because I loved *being* the music, with languid extensions of my leg and sustained piqué attitudes. But the part that never ceased to scare me came in the last section of the solo. I had to repeat a combination of two scissorlike jumps (sissonnes), a preparation, and a double pirouette diagonally across the stage three times before ending on one knee. I held my breath and clenched my teeth each time I did the preparation, and exhaled only as I completed the turns. I danced the role of the Lilac Fairy the entire time I was with Ballet Theatre, but no amount of practice or encouragement could dispel my fear of turning. Even Nora Kaye's "C'mon, sweetie, cut it out! It's all in your mind. You've been doing it three times a week for two years" couldn't dissuade me. I assume that long before then I had developed a deep psychological fear of turning that stayed with me as long as I danced on my toes.

Seeing that I was back at work and cheering up, Mother returned to Chicago, and Teru and I found an apartment on West Forty-sixth Street for forty-five dollars a month. During that season at the Forty-fourth Street Theatre, Alex March, a friend Teru had made at Bennington, stopped by our apartment late one night after the performance. With him was a tall, handsome dark-haired stranger named Victor Elmaleh, a recent graduate from the School of Architecture at the University of Virginia. Sitting with one leg slung over the arm of the only comfortable chair we owned, this quiet young man seemed older and infinitely more self-possessed than the men I knew of my age. "He's twenty-eight," I thought to myself, "and he has a mistress."

He told me that Elmaleh was a Moroccan name and that his Sephardic ancestors, after fleeing the Spanish Inquisition, had settled in Morocco. Victor had been born in Mogador. His parents wanted him to be educated in America, so at the age of six Victor was sent to live in Brooklyn with his maternal grandparents and their children. His grandmother, who spoke only Arabic, doted on young Victor. His grandfather, a stern Sephardic rabbi, who spoke Arabic, English, and Yiddish, headed a strict orthodox household of which Victor became the youngest member. Despite the religious solemnity that surrounded him, Victor never became religious himself and fled to pool halls, where he became an expert player.

I was immediately attracted to him. But having worked at disguising my most personal feelings for so long, saving my most personal expression for the stage, I automatically repressed my reaction to this irresistible man. I covered up with an almost frantic amount of nervous chatter. I besieged him with questions and inane suggestions. "Are you hungry? Are you thirsty? Would you like a cold drink? A hot drink? Are you comfortable? Would you like to sit on the sofa? The armchair? Oh, you *are* in the armchair. Do you like my tapa cloth from Pago-Pago? Does it look good over there? Would it look better here?"

Through it all, he maintained a charming, dignified composure, which enthralled me even more. Running out of superficialities and feeling a bit more relaxed, I gave Victor a chance to tell me more about himself. I could have listened to his voice and gazed at his beautiful face all night. Wanting the spell to last as long as possible, I mentioned that Alex had told me he had seen the ballet, and I asked him what he thought of it.

Smiling, he told me that he had seen his first ballet only two years earlier. Having come up to New York from Virginia for school vacation, he noticed a poster outside the Met announcing the appearance of the Monte Carlo Ballet Russe and, on an impulse, bought a seat. Sitting high in the gallery, he was totally taken with the music, the color, the dancing, and the red-headed beauty Mia Slavenska in *Coppélia*. Converted by that performance, he became a regular member of the ballet audience and a connoisseur of the beautiful girls in the company. And after seeing several performances of de Basil's company, he had screwed up enough courage to go around to the stage door and ask Nina Verchinina out on a date.

Listening to all this, I felt a surprising twinge of jealousy, even though I had only just met the man. I must have fallen in love on the spot. Continuing, Victor told me that, even more than ballet, he loved music above all the arts. Bach and Mozart, he said, were his favorites. Although I loved music and always tried to be at one with it in my dancing, I was not able to sustain an articulate conversation on the artistic merits of one composer as compared to another. God knows I wanted to, because I hated the thought of leading him to the door and letting him go. I was afraid I'd never see him again.

Several nights later, after I'd returned from the theatre, the doorbell rang. My heart pounded in my chest; there was Victor again. Our second meeting was more relaxed. This time we talked easily and more comfortably. I found out that he was just nine months older than I, and—as important—that there was no mistress and not even a steady girlfriend. His utter lack of pretense or affectation made him more than just physically attractive to me. I soon felt that, somehow, he was more interested in *me* than in what I did. In little more than a week, I felt as though I'd known Victor for years, and before long, we were spending all our free days and nights together.

Dashing from the theatre to meet Victor after the Sunday matinee on December 7, 1941, I was stopped in my tracks by a news bulletin on the radio by the stage door. Japan had attacked Pearl Harbor. I ran home in a state of panic, the horrifying reality of Mother's predictions of doom reeling in my mind. Victor tried to calm me, but I was overcome by terror. Only three hours later, I stood in the wings before the evening performance, still in a state of shock. How could I face the public? Having been publicized throughout my career as being half-Japanese, I feared the tragedy of Pearl Harbor would provoke an outraged American audience to an angry, possibly ugly response to me.

The *Princess Aurora* overture was playing. "Pat, I can't go on," I murmured to Dolin, "It's too terrible."

"You're exaggerating, Sono," he said, gently. "Of course you can."

I went on, but I danced in a daze. I think the audience numbered approximately four hundred that awful night. Although there was no reaction to my appearance, I was still frightened.

The Hurok management also feared that my presence in the company might affect the audience. They suggested that I change my name rather than risk adverse publicity on our upcoming tour. I agreed grudgingly to take my mother's name and performed for a while as Sono Fitzpatrick.

The war now affected all our lives. In a state of deep depression, I left Victor to tour with Ballet Theatre, knowing that it would be only a matter of time before he was drafted. That tour, December to March, 1941–42, was the sixth American tour Baronova and I had made. But the war so completely disrupted the standard travel routine that, despite all our experience, Irina and I were as unprepared as the others for the additional difficulties we were to face.

Our trains were attached to troop trains. The soldiers and sailors traveling with us were, naturally, seated in the dining cars and fed before anyone else, which left us the choice of not eating at all or grabbing stale sandwiches in the station stops along the way. When trains were unavailable, we traveled in buses, which were even worse than the crowded Pullmans. We felt trapped in our seats with nowhere to walk, no space in which to straighten our aching legs as the hours passed. To escape his confinement, Orloff scrambled up into the over-head luggage rack and stretched out to sleep among the suitcases. Many nights I sat upright on the long seat across the back of the bus, wedged between Nora Kaye and Dorati. By morning, we were always grimy, cranky, and stiff-necked from continuous drafts.

Lucia Chase remained indomitable, actually seeming to enjoy these rugged conditions. Day after day she sat with Irina in the front seat of the bus, smiling and chatting cheerfully. You could never tell from looking at her that she bore the heavy financial burden of the company as well as dancing every night with the rest of us.

Every dancer developed a special way to conserve energy under those grueling conditions of one-night stands. When we'd arrive at our destination, we'd spend most of our time before performances doing long workouts to get back into shape. But I discovered that even on the coldest nights, Markova's body was so supple that she needed only her unique method of preparation. I went to her dressing room for some reason one night, knocked, and opened the door. There she sat, in her hand-knit pink woolies, with her feet up on the radiator, gently slapping her calves and thighs in a delicate kind of massage.

"Alicia, what are you *doing*?" I asked.

"Warming up, dear," she answered offhandedly, looking at me with her reserved smile.

My friendship with Nora Kaye began on the road, where her ir-repressible sense of humor relieved the tensions of hard work and fatigue. Rooming with her and Annabelle Lyon, I learned that Nora's whole life had been dancing. She was Fokine's student at seven and danced in children's ballets at the Metropolitan Opera House. At four-teen she was engaged as a member of the Metropolitan Opera Ballet at a salary of twelve dollars a week. In 1939, along with several dancers

DANCES

from the Broadway show *Stars in Your Eyes*, she joined the corps de ballet of Ballet Theatre at its inception. Three years later she was dancing solo roles. I was fascinated that she had changed her *Russian* name, Koreff, to the *American* Kaye, the exact reverse of the process as I knew it.

Nora was not a conventionally pretty young girl. Her pale complexion, striking green eyes, dark, wavy hair, sultry lips, and dimpled smile made her a dramatic beauty. What made her irresistible was the paradox of physical intensity combined with an infectious personality. Nora could poke fun at herself and everything around her whenever life got us down. She was funny, ironical, and down-to-earth. Looking at a tasteless highway billboard while passing by on the bus, Nora would let out a high, cackling laugh and say, in her inimitable nasal twang, "Well, Sweetie, welcome to Dixie!" She detested any kind of pretentious "arty" behavior, thinking life was too serious to be taken seriously.

Our "Dixieland Tour," as we called it, brought along a repertory of twenty-one ballets, which included *La Fille Mal Gardée, Peter and the Wolf, Gala Performance, Judgment of Paris, Dark Elegies, Pas de Quatre, Three Virgins and a Devil, Lilac Garden, Princess Aurora, Bluebeard, Carnaval, Le Spectre de la Rose, Les Sylphides,* and *Swan Lake.* Touring conditions continued to be erratic, to say the least. Since troop transport had first priority on the railroads, we could never be sure if we and our costumes and scenery would reach a theatre in time for a performance. On evenings when we were lucky enough to have arrived on time by bus, we often wondered if *Princess Aurora* would be performed in Karinska's renderings of Bakst's designs or in practice clothes on a bare stage.

One night we sped into Savannah, Georgia, several hours behind schedule to find the audience passing the time by singing endless choruses of "Roll Out the Barrel." We danced that night on the shiny varnished floor of a basketball court in a large gymnasium. While the audience sat in the bleachers belting out one chorus after another, we frantically slapped on our makeup. Still pulling our straps, tugging at our wigs, and yanking ornery hats and feathers, we hurried to our places as the music for *Princess Aurora* began. Hanging on to a stubborn toe shoe ribbon that wouldn't tie, I hobbled, bent over, into my place for the Polonaise. From behind I heard the crisp lilt of Pat

Dolin's voice say, "Oh, by the way, Sono, you have to replace Maggie Banks in Florestan pas de trois. Poor Maggie's rather ill."

I might have pitched forward on my white-wigged head had the horror of the idea not made me spring straight up.

"But, Pat!" I gasped. "The dance has fouettés in it. You *know* I can't *do* fouettés!"

"Nonsense," he snapped brightly, and was off before I could utter another sound.

The early section of the pas de trois went well enough, but then came the fouettés. The first was on pointe, the second one was off. On the third, I lurched to the left, and on the fourth, I toppled to the right. I drifted upstage and I drifted downstage. While my partner executed immaculate entrechats six at midcourt, I looked as if I were inventing a new basketball cheer. With dancers roaring with laughter in the wings, I finished my number with the kettledrums instead of my partner.

Glaring with teary, accusing eyes, I passed Dolin in the wings. He merely shrugged and said, "I've been known to be wrong."

The performance that night ended at 1:30 A.M., to rousing applause. We straggled into the streets to find something to eat and to wait for the bus. Alicia Markova lay down on a pile of overcoats, her head resting on her hatbox. Close by, Jerry Robbins slept on a bed of suitcases. To pass the time, some of us, not in the mood to sleep, played Categories. We knew we were really tired when for five minutes neither Tudor, Hugh Laing, myself, nor any of the others could think of the name of any river other than the Euphrates! Less than twenty-four hours later we were dancing in Miami.

long with rehearsals with Fokine, who had joined the company to choreograph *Bluebeard*, and the hectic touring schedule, we were also working on a new ballet by Antony Tudor. I knew, of course, that Tudor was an outstanding choreographer whose talent had first been recognized through his ballets for Ballet Rambert in England. Over the years, we've become accustomed to hearing tales of Tudor's caustic wit and sometimes hurtful remarks to his dancers, but my experience was different. I had only the briefest day-to-day contact with him, so I didn't have the chance to really get to know him. But even during the creation of this one ballet, I felt that his work gave me a picture of his profoundly personal views of love, hate, and compassion. At the time, Tudor was still a young man of thirty-four, just gaining momentum as a leading force in American choreography, with little time to develop complex personal and psychological analyses with every member of his cast. Being called to rehearsal, I was more curious than nervous. I had no idea how Tudor wanted to use me, or what he had seen in my dancing that made him want to work with me. I knew nothing about the way he worked, about the ballet he was making, or about the role I would have in it.

When I entered the rehearsal hall, Tudor was standing calmly before a group of six dancers. His body was straight but strangely passive, his neat head resting on his long neck like a bird's. "Don't forget," he was saying, "you are Lovers in Innocence. You live in a small town. It's dusk and you're going to the corner to get a soda." As the three couples repeated their steps, he reminded them to be relaxed and casual in order to establish the mood of a particular time and place. Tudor seemed satisfied with the dancers' response to his evocation of the scene.

I was baffled. Totally ignorant of the period and setting of *Pillar of*

Fire, I could not understand what a corner drugstore was doing in a ballet. But as the days passed, I learned that we were in a small American town just after the turn of the century. The ballet was not about princesses or magic birds or sylphs; it was about a young woman's repressed emotions and her eventual release from frustration through reciprocated love. No one ever defined those themes in words, but no definitions were necessary. Before our eyes Hagar's torment and subsequent peace emerged slowly and inexorably from the flow of movement.

In the central role of Hagar, Nora Kaye became someone I'd never seen before, a woman who bore no relation to the funny, good-natured girl who squashed bedbugs with me on the road. The moment she heard the opening bars of the recording of Schönberg's *Verklärte Nacht* which Tudor used for many rehearsals, Nora closed herself off from all external stimuli. Sitting on the front stoop (a rehearsal-room chair), her spine rigid with tension, her feet flattened against the floor as if pushing it away, she was transformed. Slowly she raised her right hand to smooth her hair, and I shivered. In that single gesture she established her character indelibly. Deeper and deeper Nora dug into herself to help Tudor find the woman he wanted to create.

Out of her twenty-one years she drew an awesome understanding of repression, loneliness, and frustration, maintaining the many emotional levels of the character even as she performed the most difficult technical feats. At one moment, she had to arch backwards suddenly while balanced on pointe, then contract her torso sharply forward and walk ahead without jarring or stumbling. Flexing her steely spine like a whip, Nora mastered the convolutions of the choreography as smoothly as she portrayed the twists of Hagar's mental anguish.

As the Young Man from the House Opposite, Tudor cast Hugh Laing. Hugh was extravagantly handsome, with brooding dark features. He moved with supreme arrogance, his stark sexuality the foil for Nora's vulnerability. Pitting one against the other, Tudor created a pas de deux that was an explosion of sexual desire, intense and unrelenting. He molded their pas de deux into an emotional, psychologically charged dialogue. When Hugh left Nora prostrate on the floor, his walk alone spoke volumes, expressing at once his indifference to her shame and a passion devoid of tenderness. Though graphic, the artistic subtlety of this passage completely removed it from vulgarity.

Tudor welded acting so closely to dancing that the explicit eroticism of the encounter was expressed wholly in choreographic terms.

Rosella Hightower, Muriel Bentley, Miriam Golden, and I were cast as Lovers in Experience, partnered by Jerome Robbins, Donald Saddler, and Frank Hobi. At times I split away from the group and danced with Hugh. The unrestrained, sensuous movements Tudor gave us emphasized Hugh's lasciviousness and lust.

In some way, each character was itself and a whole world as well. The wary movements Tudor conceived for Lucia as Hagar's Eldest Sister revealed a conformist, subject to the social pressures that so ruthlessly motivate human behavior. Lucia was beautiful in this part, the embodiment of sober elegance. Moving with the dignity befitting the responsible eldest in the family, she was at once a prisoner of conventional morality and its staunchest advocate.

As the Youngest Sister, Annabelle Lyon epitomized the libidinous adolescent, rubbing her hand across her open mouth whenever a man approached, then tossing her dark hair flirtatiously. Cruel to Hagar in a casually frivolous way, Annabelle, with an unforgettable mastery of nuance, etched the bold outlines of the heartless, mature woman the Youngest Sister would become.

Tudor worked very slowly. He would often stand for a long time lost in thought and gazing into the air, one finger on his lips. When a sequence did not flow exactly as he had envisioned it, he remained calm, at times accepting suggestions the dancers offered to make the steps more manageable. Having begun dancing and choreographing relatively late, he lacked the facility for composing that enabled Fokine or Massine, after years of experience, to reel off combinations of steps as quickly as they could speak, and sometimes quicker. This is not to do Tudor an injustice. He is as great an innovative genius as they, in his own way. In those silent moments of searching, Tudor was creating a dance vocabulary that had never before been used for ballet.

In order to perform the steps properly, we had to make ourselves aware of the vast assortment of physical details that defined the world in which we moved. Tudor wanted us to know the time of day, the day of the week, where we had been each time we appeared, and where we were going next. The total effect of the ballet could be greater than the sum of its individual steps if we danced every movement with a complete sense of the life from which it had emerged.

Nora, Lucia, and Annabelle, after long, searching discussions with Tudor, had identified every particular of their characters' environment —the color of the wallpaper in their living room, the hour at which they ate dinner, the furnishings of the rooms in which they each slept.

Along with his constant emphasis on building a definite physical framework for our characters, Tudor was the first choreographer I ever heard talk about the characters' psychology. I had always been told what steps to dance, and often exactly how to dance them, but never the motivation behind them. Carefully choosing his words, Tudor established a general emotional atmosphere in which we had to pinpoint the specific characteristics ourselves. Absorbing his explicit intentions, we made them specific by searching our senses for relevant experience and adjusting our bodies to mirror what we found in our memories. It was a slow, amorphous process from which Tudor, like Chekhov, distilled the very essence of human behavior.

Tudor's verbal instructions were difficult enough to realize. In addition he consistently blocked out our dances to the phrases of the music rather than its counts. He always hummed vaguely as he demonstrated, and we stumbled along just as vaguely behind him. I had never counted, except in *Les Noces*, and counting wouldn't have helped now anyway. To Tudor, Schönberg's music was more than an arbitrary structure of counts; it reinforced the shape of the movement he wanted, and I discovered that if I absorbed the musical phrasing rather than its measures, it would often lead me to the emotional substance of the steps.

I always felt he wanted the body to sing, rapturously, languorously, and longingly in turn. The problem lay in expressing these inner states while rising on pointe without jerking or straining. He characterized one of my entrances, in the doorway of the House Across the Way, as "casually wanton." The "wanton" I could easily capture by following the slow twist of the shoulders and the sensuous rubbing of my neck that he demonstrated. The "casual" aspect of the movement was the hard part. It was simple enough to say, but could only be expressed subtly, through the smallest turn of the torso or curve of the back. An inch made all the difference. One position would appear "wanton" to him. Another, different from the first by the merest fraction of an angle, would be "casually wanton." When I was finally able to move as he wished, I felt a new sense of satisfaction in my dancing.

I had always found it easy to be "dynamic," but it was a new sensation for me to be fulfilled by giving "more of less."

Pillar of Fire was scheduled to open on April 8, 1942. After re-hearsing the major part of the ballet one day, several of us remained at Goldfarb's, a narrow, dingy studio on Broadway, to see the final pas de deux, which had been choreographed in private. Nora was tired and drenched with sweat. Because her still-unfinished costume was such an integral part of the choreography, she always wore an old woolen skirt, of exactly the same length, over her tights. When we were all seated, she and Tudor, in the role of the Friend, began to move.

As a dancer, Tudor was not a formidable technician, but even in rehearsal, the emotional quality he brought to the ballet was over-whelming. Just his bearing and the simplest gestures towards each of the sisters showed how well he knew them and how varied were his feelings for each of them. Even at rest, his face and posture revealed the depths of his love for Hagar. As they moved through the final pas de deux in perfect harmony, all Hagar's tension and agony fell away. Their steps were slow, sustained, and trusting, flowing into lifts both tender and exalted. When the final chords faded, we sat motionless, tears streaming down our faces.

Opening night was a triumph. The audience remained silent after the curtain fell. Gradually the applause came, with gathering momen-tum, increasing as the entire cast took their bows and gave way to the assembled principals. Finally, Nora walked onstage alone and knelt before the audience on one knee, one hand placed humbly to her breast, head bowed. They rose as one to give her, and then Tudor, a thundering ovation. She received twenty-seven curtain calls.

After years of effort, years of classes and corps work and tiny solo roles, Nora Kaye's incomparable artistry made her a ballerina in thirty minutes. Her sublime acting in *Pillar of Fire* enlarged the possibilities of balletic expression for all time.

Listening to the cheers, I was profoundly moved to have been a part of this great work of art, and longed for Victor, who was far away at an army camp in Virginia, to be standing in the wings where he had watched so many performances since our first meeting. My letter to him that night stretched over pages, as I related the story of Nora's dazzling success. But I didn't need the excitement of the premiere of a masterpiece to make me feel Victor's absence. I wrote to him every day, hoping my letters would somehow shorten the distance between us.

In the late spring my letters turned to the subject of the company's summer tour to Mexico City, where I had not been since 1935, and where we would appear at the Palacio de Bellas Artes as guests of the Mexican government. To my surprise, I heard that Massine would be with us on that tour. After five years of exhausting work, he had finally relinquished his position as artistic director of the Monte Carlo Ballet Russe and was due to join Ballet Theatre just in time to travel to Mexico with us.

A week or so before we were to leave, I received a letter from a Mrs. Shipley of the U.S. Passport Division. Because of my Japanese ancestry, she said, I would not be allowed to leave the country. In shock, I asked myself again and again, "What does this mean? I am an *American*." It had never occurred to me that anyone as an official spokesman for the United States government would ever doubt my loyalty to my country or deprive me of my work. Yet this notification did both.

As I unpacked my bags in disbelief, a hundred thousand people of Japanese extraction, all either U.S. citizens or permanent residents, were being interned in camps like suspect criminals. None of them, nor those Japanese residing in Hawaii, had actually been identified either as unregistered agents or as participants in any form of espionage activity.

Subject without recourse to the government restrictions, I saw the company off for Mexico and settled down with Teru, without employment or income. My job and salary would be restored to me as soon as the company returned to the States, but for the time being I was stranded. Our friends chipped in to help us, and Victor sent most of his monthly paycheck from the army. As the summer dragged on, we pulled in our belts and economized drastically, limiting ourselves to a steady diet of rice and laughingly comparing the flatness of our stomachs to ward off dejection.

When our lease expired, we spent days on end trudging the east midtown area hunting for an apartment. Some days I combed the north side of the street while Teru did the same on the south side. Rooms were not too difficult to find, but most of the superintendents squinted hard at us, grumbling, "Whad'dya say your name was?" and then made some feeble excuse before turning us away. We passed several discouraging weeks going from house to house in the broiling heat. At last one of Teru's friends mentioned by chance that she was moving and offered us her basement apartment. Our spirits revived as we carried our belongings across town to East Fifty-second Street and went to work overhauling the tiny rooms. In a few days Teru had lined one wall with a construction of storage cupboards and bookcases. I took charge of painting and unpacking. With so few demands on our time, we were soon settled and relieved to be in our new home.

At midnight on August 22, 1942, Michel Fokine died. In July, during the Ballet Theatre stay in Mexico, he had developed thrombosis of his left leg while choreographing *Helen of Troy*, his eighty-first ballet. Since there was no elevator in the hall where they rehearsed, the dancers carried Fokine gently up the stairs to the studio, where he went on supervising the final rehearsals of the ballet from a chair. Finally, he was unable to continue, leaving the completion of the ballet to Lichine. Early in August, Fokine was hospitalized in New York with pleurisy, which quickly developed into double pneumonia.

When the world learned of his death, mourners thronged Campbell's Funeral Home, where he lay for three days. Deeply saddened, I joined the many dancers and personal friends who assembled to honor him at his funeral at the Russian Orthodox Church of Christ the Savior. The church was very crowded, and dense with the scent of flowers, hot wax, and incense. Fokine lay in an open casket with his beautiful hands folded across his chest. I knelt along with the entire congregation. Next to me was Lisa Koreff, Nora Kaye's mother, who had known Fokine since Nora went to study with him as a little girl. Her enormous dark eyes were filled with tears.

Holding lighted candles, we listened to the moving chants of the Russian choir. I saw Madame Fokine approach her husband's bier, but when she staggered beneath the anguish that consumed her, the sight was too heartbreaking to bear. I turned my eyes away. She and her husband had first held hands at Krasnoe Seloe, in an Imperial Russia that was no more. They were married a few months later. From the day of their wedding in 1905, through revolution, wars, and a lifetime of travel and unending work, they had rarely been separated. Madame Fokine was to survive her husband by another sixteen years and be buried beside him under a stone that reads simply "Fokine-Fokina."

The company's return to New York in September put an end to my "leave of absence." We began our fall season at the Met with a special all-Fokine program that was arranged by the management and John Martin. After the *Times* critic asked the audience to stand in tribute to the great choreographer, the golden curtain rose slowly on a stage empty but for the décor of *Les Sylphides*. The orchestra played Chopin's Prelude op. 28 no. 7, while many of us stood weeping in the wings. The simplicity of the memorial seemed inevitable. Around the world seventeen different ballet companies danced *Les Sylphides* as the most appropriate expression of homage to the man who strove for thirty-seven years to perfect the art he adored and had helped reform.

Leaving Teru in the apartment in New York, I set off on another long American tour with Ballet Theatre. Before we had gone very far, however, I received yet another official government notification. This time the office of General John L. De Witt informed me that I could not enter the state of California. Somewhat more familiar by then with the indiscriminate fear of everything Japanese that had gripped the country, I was more resigned to this notice than I had been to the earlier one. I found it ironic that this reflection of national paranoia was a document signed by a bureaucrat who had the same last name— Goebbels—as the Nazi Minister of Propaganda.

Stranded once again, but this time in the middle of the country, far from my little apartment, there was nothing for me to do but go home to my parents in Chicago and wait for Ballet Theatre to pick me up as it traveled back east. The chagrin I blurted out as soon as I reached home shrank to insignificance beside Mother's alarming news. Visibly disheartened but coping with the latest turn of events, she told me that Father had been interned.

No one knew how long the internment would last. He was detained, along with some Germans, in a large house that had formerly been a mansion on the South Side of the city, miles from our apartment. Mother and I could visit him, but we were never allowed to speak with him privately. An armed guard sat with us at a card table in a bleak, empty room, adding a painful strain to our conversation with his silence. Even the magazines we brought Father were thoroughly examined to determine whether they concealed any weapon. I knew the precautions humiliated Father, as they did me, but he never displayed any anger or resentment. Each time we left him, I was filled with terrible sadness. Father always smiled as he said goodbye, but the smile was hollow and forced, identical to the one I had seen masking his sorrow the day I left to dance with the ballet. The hurt and bewilderment that lay in his eyes haunted me for months.

My correspondence with Victor kept me from being totally distraught. Years later, through the Freedom of Information Act, I found out that our letters, filled with the most intimate thoughts and emotions, had been passed through the hands of Army Intelligence and the FBI, searching for traces of espionage activity. Fortunately, as a further distraction at the time, I had work to do. Ruth Page, First Lady of Dance in Chicago and a personal friend of the family, had heard of my predicament and generously offered me a teaching job at her studio. I had never been anything but a student myself, and finding many of the pupils my own age or slightly younger forced me into a strange and disconcerting role of "adult" as well as "teacher." Unsure of the best way to proceed, I concentrated on their arms, drawing heavily on Fokine's instructions as teaching guidelines. The students responded so well that I became a bit more confident and added something to the class that I hoped might interest them. Each day after I had taken them through all the exercises at the barre and in the center, I would choreograph several bars of music, until I had composed a short dance. I then asked each pupil to perform it on pointe, which gave the girls a chance to express themselves individually.

Except for the time I spent teaching, I had nothing to do but worry both about Father and about Victor, who was hospitalized with most of his unit with acute jaundice at Fort Belvoir. When he recovered, the army gave him a medical discharge and, as soon as I returned to New York with the company, he moved in with Teru and me.

During my absence from Ballet Theatre, Tudor had started work on his new ballet, *Romeo and Juliet*. Markova and Laing were cast as the lovers. Tudor chose Orloff as Mercutio, Jerome Robbins as Benvolio, and Lucia as Juliet's Nurse. Tudor himself would dance as Tybalt, Dimitri Romanoff as Friar Laurence, and Borislav Runanine and John Taras as the feuding heads of the Montagues and Capulets. When the company came back to Chicago on the last leg of the tour, I was added to the cast as Rosaline.

Since Dali's original set designs did not satisfy Tudor, he asked Eugene Berman to design the décor instead. Berman created a beautiful unit set in the style of the early Renaissance, consisting of a two-tiered colonnade enclosing the stage on three sides. The elegant architectural décor and the imaginative use of curtains allowed the scenes to flow from one to another uninterrupted. Two cherubic pages closed and opened the curtains, punctuating the beginning and ending of certain episodes and denoting the passage of time between others.

The ballet's score, consisting of several pieces by the English composer Frederick Delius, took time to develop. Because of the war, it was impossible to obtain from England either full orchestral scores or the various instrumental parts for any of the pieces. After listening for hours to recordings, Antal Dorati sat down and wrote out the music for every instrument in the piece, transcribing each recorded note to paper. He also wrote and orchestrated musical bridges between the separate pieces, all in the style of Delius. The results both pleased and impressed the composer's friend and champion, Sir Thomas Beecham, whom Hurok engaged to conduct several of our performances. When he heard the orchestra rehearse Dorati's painstaking transcriptions, Beecham exclaimed, "Astounding! Perfectly astounding! It is precisely as written by my late friend."

In the forty-five minutes Tudor took to unfold the well-known story, he blended pantomime and pageantry with passages of pure dancing. For the scenes of open conflict between the Capulets and Montagues, he eliminated the traditional use of swords and daggers, and set the male dancers leaping on and at one another. Their unusual wrestling faintly resembled the positions of judo or Oriental boxing and gave the moments of violence a distinctive power.

Like Fokine, Tudor demonstrated so brilliantly that no dancer seemed to reproduce his movements with equal clarity. He worked with Lucia one afternoon on a single instant of the Nurse's part, showing her how to evoke the sticky heat of the day by rising and gesturing with her arms as if to pluck her heavy skirts from her buttocks. He did not want her actually to move the costume away from her body, but to isolate the familiar act of doing so by combining the sensations of heat, clothing, and damp skin in her gesture. Lucia eventually captured the essence of the moment, but she never looked quite so hot or sticky as Tudor had.

Ideally suited to the role of Juliet, Alicia Markova was small, slim, and light as silk, with darting feet that barely touched the floor. Markova's body was, for classical dancing, almost a miracle of construction and illusion. I would say the most characteristic element of that marvel was her line, which was always smooth, soft, and delicately controlled. Whether deliberately or unconsciously, she never strained to achieve her line or aimed for the kind of exaggeration so typical of other dancers. Hers was a style of effortless ease.

Her particular physical attributes, literally from the top of her head to the tips of her toes, enhanced the illusion of her dancing. Markova had a small head, black hair, a long white neck, sloping shoulders, and a romantically serene torso that seemed drawn into life from a nineteenth-century lithograph. Her arms were long, beautiful, and delicate. Her hands, so tiny that they must have been three-quarters the width of even the smallest woman's hand I had ever seen, seemed fragile but were deceptively strong. Like her arms, her legs were also long, beautiful, and delicate. Their most unusual aspect was the fact that her knees, unlike most people's, were so flat that they became almost concave when she straightened her legs, giving her, in arabesque, an even longer, flowing, uninterrupted line. Markova's narrow, tiny feet had high, beautiful arches. When I saw her feet naked, I was amazed to see that her last four toes were so much smaller than her first, that in pointe shoes, she literally danced on one toe! I wondered how she could get on pointe at all. But seeing her dance on pointe, knowing that she danced on only two toes, was like hearing a concert pianist whose hands were physically capable of spanning only three notes playing arpeggios with the virtuosity of a Horowitz.

Her perfectionism ranged from inordinate concern over musical tempi in lengthy discussions with conductors Dorati or Max Goberman to meticulous order in the dressing room. She would methodically lay out seven silver hairpins, each intended for a specific place to secure her white Princess Aurora wig, while most dancers had a bagful and shoved them in anywhere.

In performance her illusion of lightness was fulfilled. In pirouettes she would not "spot" in one place as most dancers do, but flicked her head one or two extra times, giving her an extra fluttering, birdlike quality. Of course, Markova is famous for being so devoted to her image of lightness that she adamantly refused to plié before being lifted by her partner. The effect was beautiful to behold but must have been murder on Dolin's back!

In every ballet Markova had a way of making the movement her own. I particularly realized this during rehearsals for *Romeo and Juliet*. At one point Tudor asked me to work with him on the bedroom scene, since Alicia was unavailable. In that rehearsal he created a beautiful moment for Juliet in which he had me sit on the edge of the bed, in profile, with my feet flat on the floor, side by side, pointing out. My left arm crossed my breast with my flattened hand touching my right shoulder. The right arm crossed my abdomen, with the flat hand on my hip. In one moment the body turned towards the audience into another two-dimensional Giottoesque position, with my legs in a wide, turned-out second position. My elbows bent in to the torso, with hands upraised, the flattened palms turned outwards. The head tilted to the left, eyes downcast. It was an arresting passage. Later, when I saw Markova do it, she had crossed her feet in ballerina fashion and rounded her arms and hands. The position was lovely but became a nineteenth-century classical pose rather than the haunting quattrocento image Tudor had intended.

But Alicia's Juliet was beautiful. In the early scenes she danced with grave shyness and grew increasingly passionate in her pas de deux with Laing. Hugh was a splendid Romeo. His impetuous, ardent performance seemed to evolve as naturally out of his own personality as had the cruel Young Man from the House Opposite in *Pillar*. Once again Tudor drew upon his and his dancers' deepest imaginative resources to create characters and evoke a style of a historical period far beyond our immediate experience.

I specifically remember one day when Tudor called the cast together and asked us, "What was the Renaissance all about? What were the key elements of that society? What was life like? How did they move?" As dancers, we could not give immediate intellectual responses to his questions. There was an almost embarrassing silence. But when we heard the music and fused it with Tudor's choreographic design, we moved contrary to every position of classical ballet, keeping our knees slightly bent, our pelvises tilted forward, and our necks curved to suggest the passive demeanor of women in Renaissance paintings. In contrast, the men stood very erect, strutted more than they walked, and imbued every gesture with the fierce masculine pride of fifteenth-century courtiers.

When Tudor called me to rehearsal, I hadn't the vaguest idea of who Rosaline was or what she was all about. Tudor spoke very little, but by demonstrating my first entrance, he immediately established the core of Rosaline's character. Romeo gestured to a black velvet curtain. In silence, I emerged in profile, with arms held stiffly to the side, a pose reminiscent of a Giotto painting. Demurely I rose on half-pointe, slowly rotating my thrust-forward pelvis, with a breathlike shift of my arms across my abdomen and breast to face Romeo. As he reached for me, I lowered my glance to the floor, rose again, and suggestively rotated my stomach away from him, priggishly smoothing my hair with flattened hands. There was an elegant but sensuous rhythm to the movement, based not on counts but on the elusive musical atmosphere. With minimal gestures my character revealed a propriety that thinly veiled a tantalizing wanton.

Hurok had set April 6, 1943, five days after the opening of the season, for the ballet's premiere at the Metropolitan Opera House, but as the date approached, we realized that it would not be finished in time. Despite the failure of Tudor's attempts to complete the last two scenes on schedule, Hurok insisted that the premiere take place as planned. Having advertised a new work for that date, he did not want to disappoint the audience by postponing it.

Hurok's insistence that the premiere go, ready or not, made us all terribly nervous. With Mme. Karinska still at work on Berman's costumes, the unusually tense dress rehearsal began without a dress in the house. Dorati repeatedly stopped the orchestra to correct both dancers and musicians. Each time the stagehands bolted down another piece of the set, we had to readjust our spacing. Every light had to be focused and gelled. We stood in one spot for what seemed like hours as the stage manager and chief electrician wrote their final cues.

As usual the beauty and fine workmanship of the costumes Karinska finally delivered justified our waiting. One of mine was cut from a bolt of heavy magenta silk that Karinska had brought with her from Paris before the war. The other, for the ballroom scene that immediately followed my first entrance, was wine-red silk velvet. They were both magnificent and fit perfectly, but wearing them in place of my rehearsal clothes posed an unforeseen problem. How could I change from the first gown, with its slight train, into an equally elaborate ballgown with only seconds between my two scenes?

While I tried to figure a way to make the quick change, I discovered that I was the only dancer without a headpiece to complete my court costume. No one had time to concern himself with such a small detail, so finding a solution was left to me. When I returned to the theatre several hours later after a late-afternoon lunch, no headpiece had yet materialized for the ballroom scene. I improvised as best I could and hoped Berman would approve. To give my hair body and contour, I puffed it out over each ear with bunches of false hair, and then rummaged in my jewelry box for some suitable decoration to complement the gown. Finding two bracelets I had last worn as an odalisque in *Schéhérazade*, I linked them together and laid them across my brow, securing them tightly to my "Renaissance" hairdo. Rushing to the stage, I passed Berman, who said, "Good. That's all right," and I nervously took my place with Hugh behind the small curtain for our first entrance.

Already costumed and made up as Tybalt, Tudor was behind the curtain too, appearing quite composed. Before Dorati took his place in the pit, Tudor slipped through the gold stage curtain to inform the audience that they were about to see an unfinished ballet. The stir caused by his unexpected announcement died down quickly with the first notes of the music. Considering the strain under which we performed, the ballet progressed smoothly through the scene in which Juliet is arrayed in a golden gown for her arranged marriage to Paris.

Then, with Markova radiantly garbed center stage, the curtain fell. We held our breaths.

At first there was total silence, then a burst of thunderous applause. Tudor stepped out again to thank the audience and offer his apologies for such an unusual opening.

A few days later, Tudor finished the ballet. I watched its moving final moments from the wings. Laing's body lay outstretched on a raised tomb in the Capulet vault. Turning her back to the audience, Markova let a small sudden spasm of her abdomen convey the act of stabbing herself. She extended one arm longingly to grasp her lover's hand, took a step forward, and then gently slid to the floor, poignantly marking their death scene with the simplicity that often characterizes Tudor's intensely dramatic moments.

Following the success of *Romeo and Juliet*, we were scheduled to start another long tour. But the thought of being separated from Victor for any length of time was more than I was willing to endure. The war-torn world made future plans impossible. Anything you wanted to do had to be done today, since there was no guarantee for tomorrow. Nothing counted but the present, and I didn't want any life without Victor. Dancing had always been the one thing I lived for, but over the past year I had discovered that it meant infinitely less to me than my love for him.

Sadly, I resigned from Ballet Theatre right after the opening of *Romeo and Juliet*. My sorrow at leaving dancing so abruptly was tempered by the listing of my name on John Martin's annual Honor Roll in the *Times*. "One of the most delightful things in Antony Tudor's *Romeo and Juliet*," he wrote, "was Sono Osato as Rosaline. Though she had no more than two scenes . . . she made from one of them one of the best realized characters in the whole work. Too bad indeed that Miss Osato has turned her back upon the ballet in favor of domestic life. It is a serious loss to the field."

had no second thoughts about my decision. The future Victor and I wanted had to begin now, if it were to exist at all. I wanted nothing but to be with Victor.

One day we decided to drive to Brooklyn to tell his parents we planned to marry. I waited in the car for what seemed like hours. When he came back to the car, Victor, visibly unnerved but in control, told me that his father, in a fit of anger, had showed him the door. Astonished, I listened as Victor told me that his parents' religious beliefs made them both fiercely opposed to our marriage. I had felt my share of racial prejudice, but religious prejudice was new to me, since religion had never played any part in my life. We were distraught over his parents' rejection, but we wouldn't allow our minds to be changed.

I would have loved to be married in my parents' home in Chicago, but Father was still interned and, war conditions being what they were, it was easier for Mother to come to New York than for Victor, Teru, and me to go to Chicago. Tim wasn't able to leave school, so Mother made the trip alone. She wasn't totally enamored of the idea of our getting married, since Victor was still recovering from the effects of jaundice, was broke and out of work, and seemed the most unlikely choice as a provider. Yet, true to her paradoxical nature, Mother came to my side when I needed her.

Not wanting to break totally with tradition, I grabbed something old (my strapped, black suede shoes), swept into a wholesale trimmings outlet for something new (a clump of white artificial flowers and a tiny veil for my headpiece), was thrilled with what I borrowed (Nora's silver-fox jacket), and got more than I bargained for in blue (a $4.98 outfit at S. Klein's that through age had faded at the hem into several shades of blue).

Early on the morning of April 24, 1943, just three weeks after the opening of *Romeo and Juliet*, Victor and I were married. At times I thought his tense clutching would crush my hand as we stood in a judge's chambers at City Hall. Mother and Teru were our witnesses, and a solitary pot of Easter lilies provided the meager decoration. As the judge raced through the ceremony, a long line of uniformed men and women sat just outside the door, waiting to be married before the war would pull their lives apart again. Forty-five minutes later, as husband and wife, Victor and I celebrated at the old Lafayette Hotel with a champagne breakfast.

To make up for the hasty ceremony that morning, we had a happy little celebration back at our apartment that evening. Nora, Muriel Bentley, Annabelle Lyon, Merce Cunningham, John Taras, Teru, and Mother were there, and Victor and I were glad to be able to laugh with them. Whatever burdens we all might have had, collectively or individually, were made light for a while by Johnnie Taras's hilarious distortions of famous ballet libretti. The beckoning hand gestures in the entrance of the Lovers in Innocence in *Pillar of Fire*, for instance, became three Brownie Scouts saying, "The cookies aren't ready yet."

My life changed overnight. After eight years I no longer leapt out of bed to rush to class or rehearsal first thing in the morning. Now I had time for leisurely breakfasts with Victor before he went off to look for a job. Teru had moved out to live with Mother around the corner so that the little rooms she had helped me arrange could become a home for Victor and me. Every morning, as we drank coffee at our table in front of the window, watching the assortment of legs walking by, Victor would tune the radio to WQXR, the classical music station of *The New York Times*, hoping to find some Mozart or Bach.

"I can't *take* Bach at eight in the morning," I'd complain. "Too much tziga-tziga-tziga." Victor would laugh and then slowly explain the structure of the complicated musical inventions. I listened and learned and grew to love the music because I was discovering it through the man I loved.

When Victor left the house, I had my work cut out for me. Being on street level, the apartment got dirty very easily. So I applied myself to dusting and scrubbing with the same concentration I had always given to morning pliés. Our old straw rug was beginning to dry out and peel; to keep it firm, I lovingly watered it every morning. I became almost subconsciously adept at squashing cockroaches. The ground-floor apartment was so accessible to the sidewalk that one night we woke up to the sound of a drunken stranger relieving himself through the venetian blinds of our bedroom window!

But nothing bothered us. Victor and I were madly in love. For a while we needed nothing else, since Victor had found work for forty dollars a week in the architectural-design firm of Norman Bel Geddes, who also designed for the theatre. But being a junior draftsman meant he could be fired without notice, which he very shortly was. May, June, and July crept by, and even second-run movies became too costly. Love was wonderful, but something had to be done about our finances, and fast!

Marriage had so consumed my time and attention that I hadn't given a thought to dancing since I'd left Ballet Theatre. I knew I had to find work but had no idea where to look. Thinking that Nora would know more about what was going on in the dance world than I did, I told her my story. She listened sympathetically and then had a suggestion. "I hear Agnes de Mille's doing a musical. Why don't you write to her and find out if she can use you in it?"

I had only met Agnes once, but I wrote to her immediately, asking if there was a place for me in her new show, specifying "but *not* in the chorus." Within a matter of days, Agnes answered that there was. A new bride like myself, Agnes soon arrived in New York, and we met to discuss the show. She offered us the use of her family's country home for a holiday before rehearsals began. Victor and I jumped at the chance and spent two weeks deep in the woods a few hours from New York, honeymooning in isolated tranquillity, far from the city's blistering heat.

In August we began work on the dances for *One Touch of Venus* at the School of American Ballet. I met our production team for the first time. Cheryl Crawford, our producer, Elia Kazan, the director (his first musical), and the writers Ogden Nash and S. J. Perelman (also their first musical) were quite unknown to me, but I had heard of the composer, Kurt Weill. The only person I knew even slightly was Agnes, but working with strangers didn't bother me much anymore; de Basil, Grigoriev, and Lucia had once been strangers too. All I needed to know was that I was being paid to dance. All that mattered were the job and the choreography. And I knew the choreography would be expert, since I had seen the hilarious *Three Virgins and a Devil* that Agnes had done for Ballet Theatre, and her rousing *Rodeo* for the Monte Carlo Ballet Russe.

For years my own performing schedule had left little time for me to see plays or musicals. *Oklahoma!*, in which Agnes had integrated the dances into the narrative of the show so triumphantly, was one of the two exceptions. *Pal Joey*, which starred Vivienne Segal and Gene Kelly and featured a loose-limbed Van Johnson in the chorus and the resounding belches of June Havoc, was the other. I turned myself over to Agnes in this unfamiliar territory and hoped for the best.

Agnes and I spoke the same language. We communicated easily in the universal shorthand of French, English, counts, grunts, and sign language so common to all dance rehearsals. She was an exuberant performer, demonstrating with an enthusiasm that swept me along in its wake. I was soon snapping my fingers and my body as smartly as a veteran hoofer.

Agnes always arrived promptly at rehearsal and worked quickly, blocking out dances between chalk marks to indicate the approximate amount of floor space we would later have onstage. Throughout the sweltering August afternoons, she drank endless cups of hot tea from a Thermos that never left her side but was often hidden by the full skirt and starched lace petticoats she wore for rehearsal clothes. As we worked through the day, her initially neat appearance deteriorated in the whirl of activity. Her blouse flew out of her waistband, petticoats were mussed and rumpled as she lifted them to demonstrate, and strands of damp hair fell in her face. Her invention and energy seemed limitless. By the end of the first week, Agnes had blocked out two whole ballets.

When he wasn't revising the score or rehearsing the songs elsewhere, Kurt Weill would occasionally come to watch us sweating over the dances. He would observe us silently through his thick glasses and then confer with Agnes or with Trude Rittman, our wonderful accompanist. I had never heard of Trude before I started work on the show, but her extraordinary abilities were evident from the first rehearsal. A gifted artist in her own right, she had worked with Agnes for years. Inexhaustibly patient, she could play and count for us simultaneously and offer both musical and choreographic suggestions, never losing her place in the music, never faltering in her attention. She was simply Agnes's irreplaceable right hand.

Agnes had assembled a bevy of talented, beautiful girls for the dance ensemble. There were the titian-haired Allyn Ann McLerie and Diana Adams, both still in their teens and, like me, trained solely in classical ballet. Allyn Ann later starred in Broadway musicals, and the dark and lyrical Diana Adams became a superb ballerina with the New York City Ballet. Nelle Fisher and Pearl Lang were also accomplished in ballet, as well as having acquired a strong modern-dance technique through their work with Martha Graham. We quickly became friends as Agnes culled the strengths of our diverse experience and fused them into a lively, unified style.

For some reason I couldn't fathom, Agnes decided that I could be funny and highlighted the opening dance number, "Forty Minutes to Lunch," with several comical passages for me. Amidst the bustle of lunch hour, Venus would transform me from a frantic New Yorker to a relaxed one, smitten by the cocky charm of a French sailor. I learned the steps quickly, but as the dance took shape, I realized that its humor was not in the steps. Since no one had ever asked me to be funny before, I'd never tried to figure out how it was done. I was simply not accustomed to making people laugh. Never gay as a child, I had spent my adolescence in the ballet using my body to express themes that were far from humorous. Madness, death, seduction, grief, magic, guilt, and the fate of man were the subjects I was most used to being a part of. The exceptions—ballets like *Union Pacific, Beau Danube, Graduation Ball,* and *Peter and the Wolf*—were few and far between, and none of them had given me a major role to portray.

Through the years I had learned that a dancer has a certain amount of leeway in a dramatic role. The overall impression of a ballet or a single performance can be so moving that even sloppy dancing can sometimes pass unnoticed. But as Agnes hammered out "Forty Minutes to Lunch," I realized that any sloppiness, such as unfinished gestures or hesitancy of attack, would not only blur the shape of a witty dance but completely destroy its humor. Timing was the key to comedy, in movement no less than in speech. Having located a vein of humor in me that had been undetected by everyone else (including myself), Agnes patiently coaxed it to the surface. As my timing got sharper, the dance became funnier. Agnes's grin measured the success of my effort. The more she chuckled, the more I understood how to move.

After we had been rehearsing for several weeks, our star, Mary Martin, arrived to rehearse the first ballet. Chic and lovely, Mary had recently come from Hollywood and was from head to toe the color of a fresh peach. Shedding her stylish clothes for a rehearsal tunic that revealed her slim, tanned legs and lithe body, she threw herself into her work. Venus was her first starring role in a Broadway musical, and we could tell she was very nervous by the way she tended to talk her way through rehearsals and continually patted down her hair.

Later in rehearsals, I noticed that working in movies had trained Mary to stand with one knee cocked provocatively next to the other. In that same pose Betty Grable graced foxholes, airplanes, and submarines all over the world. That stance cheered our fighting men, but it was certainly not a commanding posture for the Goddess of Love. Both Agnes and I knew it had to be changed. I summoned up all my nerve and offered myself to Mary as a coach. Rather than being offended, she accepted the offer and joined me during rehearsal breaks in a corner of the studio to practice walking and standing. I began by demonstrating exactly what was wrong, mimicking the limp wrists, mincing walk, and concave chest that Hollywood considered so alluring. Then I dropped the glamour-girl pose, stood up straight, threw back my shoulders, and showed Mary how a dancer's posture would lend more power to her characterization.

Among her many talents, Mary is an incredibly quick study, receptive and grateful for both advice and suggestions. Copying my raised chest and wide-open arms, she tucked in her bottom, swelled her torso, and was soon striding across the stage with Olympian grandeur. Purposefully halting her commanding stride, she planted both feet firmly on the ground to belt out Weill's "I'm a Stranger Here Myself," summing up Venus's bewilderment at being among ordinary mortals.

Once Mary had been comfortably fitted into the dances and had learned her songs and dialogue, we were more or less ready for our first run-through. The actors and singers had been rehearsing elsewhere during the weeks we had devoted to the dances. We had never heard their lines or their songs; we didn't know what characters they played. When we finally joined forces in a theatre in New York, we were total strangers. I had still learned almost nothing about the show except that it was getting a hard-working "goddess" as its star.

The entire production team gathered in the dim, cool theatre: Crawford, Kazan, Weill, Perelman, and Nash. Someone had invited Moss Hart, Weill's collaborator on the hit show *Lady in the Dark*, to give his opinion. Maurice Abravanel, our conductor, and Agnes completed the audience. Bit by bit the dialogue, songs, and dances came together in their running sequence. For the first time we could see what there was in the way of a show.

I thought the bits and snatches I saw and heard when I wasn't onstage delightful. The slight plot concerned an antique marble statue of Venus that comes to life in the suburbs of New York and falls in love with a barber. In rapid succession, Venus encounters a whole spectrum of mortals, including an art dealer, some crooks, the barber's fiancée, and the art dealer's secretary, humorously portrayed by Paula Laurence. I began to notice some of the differences between the worlds of ballet and musical comedy. To begin with, I had never worked on any ballet where separate sections of the cast were totally isolated from each other for weeks. Agnes created our dances in a vacuum, without giving us reference to the show as a whole. In addition, the theatrical jargon was a new language for me. That afternoon I heard the phrases "double take," "in one," and "take it from the top" for the first time. With the actors' lines, Kazan's directions, and comments from the producers and creators, there seemed to be more talk and confusion during a few hours than in the entire ten-day rehearsal period for the restaging of *Les Noces!*

It was altogether different from the ballet. Talk became action. Show business, it seemed, was as involved with paring things away as with building them up. One afternoon, a beautiful dance for Diana Adams was cut from the show, and both Diana and Agnes were completely unable to keep it in. Management said the dance did not further the plot, so it had to come out. I was amazed. I saw then that there was seldom room in a musical for the kind of creative exploration that thrives in ballet. Time and money were the crucial factors in deciding the validity or worth of any contribution to the whole.

A short time later, over coffee at the Hotel Edison, Agnes and Kazan asked me what I thought about having a "spot in one." I assumed they meant a solo, but long experience in the ballet had taught me to be wary of such offers, remembering how Lichine's promise to let me dance the opening night of *Prodigal* in London had failed to materialize. "That would be nice," I responded noncommittally. I decided to wait without expectation and see what would happen.

Almost before I knew it, we were heading for Boston for the out-of-town tryout. With my salary coming in and the promise of a New York architectural license in the offing for Victor, we reluctantly parted in New York, but with more security than we had had since our marriage.

I n Boston the staff of *One Touch of Venus* and its stars, Mary Martin, John Boles, and Kenny Baker, went to the Ritz. The rest of us in the cast took rooms in a small hotel close to the Shubert Theatre.

We had our first look at the setting at the Shubert the day after we arrived. I couldn't believe my eyes. I had envisioned an airy, pastel setting, but instead of playing our light, comic dances against such a background, we had grim, battleship-gray velvet curtains draped over a masking frame and several arches above the stage—curtains that were raised and lowered mechanically for the scene changes. It looked like the tomb scene from *Romeo and Juliet*.

When we saw the costumes for "Forty Minutes to Lunch," I knew we were in trouble. The dance began with the dancers in jittery clusters of working-class New Yorkers. We were expected to dance it in short, tight-fitting velvet dresses in somber shades of rust, henna, and dark red. Paul du Pont, the designer, had filled the plunging décolleté necklines with some kind of transparent chiffon, which looked ridiculous rather than sexy. Our eyes rolled back in their sockets when we were each handed matching long velvet gloves that had cost forty dollars a pair! They would have looked terrific in a fashion show, but why would he design velvet gloves for a dance that had finger-snapping as an integral part of the choreography? As we stood in our groups, jittering at the opening of "Forty Minutes," the ridiculous things fell from the elbows over the hands. Our head-shaking disbelief turned to near guffawing as our finger-snapping produced only a velvet-rubbing muffle. Dressed in velvet, surrounded by velvet, we looked more like refugees from a Buckingham Palace tea party than harassed New Yorkers rushing about Radio City.

No one uttered another word about my solo "spot in one"; Agnes was swamped with much more pressing problems relating to Mary and the full company. Since everyone thought the show ran too long, she cut and fiddled and arranged, trying to keep the choreography intact while paring away a minute here and another minute there. Underlying her professional responsibilities, Agnes was, I knew, also worried about her husband, Walter Prude, who was stationed in New Mexico. The moment I was not rehearsing, I began to miss Victor very much, wondering how he was doing all alone. At least I had the chaos around me for distraction, but what was filling his time and thoughts? I looked forward to the opening more for seeing Victor than for the reaction to the show. There would be at least one truly sympathetic person in the audience.

With the disastrous rehearsal still dragging on, I decided to finish the costume designer's work, as I'd had to do in *Romeo and Juliet*. Let the others be stuck in those dreary things, but I had no intention of dancing in the costume they gave me. In full makeup, I dashed over to a local department store and bought a few yards of bright, rose-colored velvet, a white short-sleeved sweater, two silk roses, some red ribbon, and a box of pink Tintex. Back at the theatre I rushed up to Cheryl, who was sitting calmly in the second row scrutinizing her investment, and whispered, "Here—I'll wear this." She simply nodded assent.

While someone dyed the sweater rose-pink and hung it up to dry near the stove of a restaurant next to the theatre, the wardrobe mistress ran up a circular skirt from the velvet. I was satisfied that on my body, at least, Agnes's choreography for the opening number would be clearly visible to the audience.

Mary looked beautiful and elegant, a rare quality in musical comedy, in superb clothes created by the great couturier Mainbocher. (Cheryl Crawford may have paid more for Mary's costumes than anyone had ever before paid for costumes in a musical. They cost between fifteen and twenty thousand dollars, and there were fourteen complete costume changes.) For the closing ballet, a bacchanal entitled "Venus in Ozone Heights," he dressed her in skin-colored chiffon. I remember the thunderous applause that greeted her entrance—in a long black satin halter-necked gown, slit to the knee and bare to the waist in back—escorted by John Boles. The *pièce de résistance* was a lace peignoir, the color and weight of a cobweb, in which Mary sang Weill's haunting song, "That's Him."

The opening-night audience was not particularly responsive. I was too concerned with giving a good performance to register the reaction, but backstage after the show Victor told me the audience response had been lukewarm at best. The notices were no more enthusiastic than the audience, I recall, so the following day, a Sunday, the real work began. After a fourteen-hour conference at the Ritz, the production team and creative staff decided that drastic measures were needed immediately. They ordered major scenic changes from Howard Bay, who was already exhausted from working on several productions besides ours. But the gray velvet hangings had to go.

Mainbocher tactfully offered suggestions to improve the rest of the costumes for "Forty Minutes to Lunch." My own improvisation had been accepted and remained as I designed it for the run of the show. Casual skirts and sweaters in bright primary colors soon replaced the crushed-velvet dresses. Next, he calmly slashed away at Kermit Love's costumes for the bacchanal, which looked like bad renditions of Bakst's Kikimoras from *Firebird*. He replaced their lumpy bulges with graceful, flowing folds of silk jersey over revealing leotards. I expected everyone to be as pleased as we dancers were with the improvements, but Mainbocher's alterations irritated du Pont and Love, and hasty words turned to heated arguments.

We thought the sense of the bacchanal was quite clear, but management insisted that certain passages were perplexing. So Agnes pulled those out and invented new ones on the spot, which we patched together with whatever remained of the original number. For days we cut and added and rearranged, dancing a different sequence of bits at each night's performance. The strain of keeping up with all this was all but debilitating to the dancers. Working under musical-comedy conditions for the first time, I began to realize how nondancers are ignorant of the fact that mental exhaustion can weaken a dancer faster than physical fatigue.

For several more performances Paula Laurence was doing her song "in one." "I'm doing that number where your solo is supposed to be. When is it going in?" she'd ask with irritation, passing me in the wings.

"When Agnes is ready, that's when," I'd shrug with annoyance. "She's the choreographer, not me."

One morning a few days later I was warming up backstage, wondering how long the second version of the bacchanal would stay in, when Agnes rushed into the theatre. "I think I've got it," she snapped. "How's this for your solo?" Tossing her coat, pencils, and notepad to the floor, she began to dance. She took what looked like one step of a slow-motion running stride, punctuated by two quick upward flicks of the hands toward the breasts, then a step with a cute, naughty leer backwards over the shoulder, with two snaps of the fingers, then repeated it.

"That's good, Agnes," I said.

She stopped as suddenly as she had started, gathered up her things and, without a pause, bustled off to rehearse the second version of the bacchanal, calling back over her shoulder, "And after *that*, I'll think of something else."

"That's *really* good," I thought delightedly to myself, and followed her into rehearsal.

Again we performed the final ballet for the staff and again they were not satisfied. As a dancer I began to get more and more annoyed at what seemed to be their constant assault on Agnes's work. It seemed to me that the book was in as much, if not more, trouble as the choreography. During the performances, many lines were not getting the belly laughs the writers had counted on, but it seemed always to be the dances that became the scapegoat for the show's weaknesses.

We started a third version of the bacchanal. By then I didn't much care what I did. With each new version, we became more worn out. My knees hurt, dancers were getting ill, and Trude's fingers were aching from pounding the piano all day. Agnes was exhausted and discouraged too, but not defeated. One evening, she invited me to spend the night and talk things over at her room at the Ritz. Along with her concerns about the show, she had been unable to locate Walter for nearly a week. After our long discussion about the conflicts of career and marriage, I had my first look at a choreographer's pre-rehearsal search for a dance conception.

Curled up in a tired heap on my bed, I saw Agnes kick off her shoes and sit down at the desk. Straddling the chair, with her beautifully arched stockinged feet on demi-pointe, she stared straight ahead at the blank wall. As soon as an idea came to mind, she'd scribble it down and then, jumping from her chair, transfer the scrawled thought into motion. She must have worked far into the night, long after I fell asleep, for the next day she arrived at rehearsal fully armed with yet a fourth version of the closing ballet.

This one concluded with Mary, looking quite nude in her gauzy shift, borne aloft, presumably back to Olympus, on the shoulders of Robert Pageant. Behind them, in solemn procession, were me, as the head nymph, Peter Birch, Duncan Noble, and the rest of the nymphs and satyrs. As the lights slowly dimmed, Kenny Baker stood forlorn and alone, center stage, holding a wilted bouquet as the only memento of his lost love. I thought this ending was both moving and quite logical, but now Mary was not satisfied. Agnes breathed a quiet, exasperated sigh, scrapped her notes, and stoically began a fifth version. In random moments between those rehearsals, she started in earnest to teach me my new solo.

I loved it from the start. With keen insight, Agnes zeroed in on all the things I did best and most enjoyed doing. Each move and pause looked right when she showed them to me and felt right when I danced them myself. In fact it turned out to be one of the best demi-caractère dances I had seen in a long time.

Late in the afternoon, we left the theatre to the actors and went back to the hotel to rehearse. We were brought to an empty dining room where a large luncheon had just concluded. We cleared space among the still-littered tables and started work, going over and over the dance, trying to come up with the right, upbeat ending. We tried some jumps, then a long string of turns, but we kept getting stuck in the same spot. After a time, Kurt Weill poked his head in to take a look at Agnes's latest creation. Her eyes lit up when she saw him.

"We need something here, Kurt. A sea chanty would be perfect." I suggested "Volga Boatmen," the only sea song I knew (and that was about a river), but Agnes waved it aside. Pushing her hair out of her eyes, she sang short, rowdy bits of one chanty after another, as Weill stood and listened, nodding thoughtfully without saying a word. When she came up with "What Shall We Do with a Drunken Sailor?" the elated grin on her face showed that she had finally hit on it.

"Now I understand," she crowed. "Now the whole dance will work. An American sailor will saunter in. He'll lean on the proscenium and ogle you. He'll stop you dead in your tracks. You'll go balmy over him, he'll go balmy over you and offer his arm. You'll stare at the audience thumping your foot, thinking it over. Then bolt straight up, slap your skirts, hitch your bosom, tweak your roses, and perk your head in his direction. He'll stride over to you. You give him the eye, he gives you the eye. Take his arm, bend over, do some snappy little foot patter towards the wings, and then, just before you go, lurch back with one quick take at the audience and strut off! That'll get 'em!'"

Weill looked very pleased with Agnes's inspiration and went off to interpolate the old chanty into his score. Amid coffee cups and soiled napkins, Agnes, as the swaggering sailor, and I translated her thoughts into action with genuine fun and enthusiasm. We slipped it into the show the following night, and for once everyone seemed delighted. Soon after, the bacchanal received its stamp of approval. It now ended with Kenny offstage as Mary was swept back to Olympus. The cast, management, and audience seemed pleased. It was "set."

Yet the show was still not right. No one wanted it to finish with the bacchanal, since that ending left Kenny alone and heartbroken without Venus. Again Agnes came to the rescue. As a lighter, more cheerful ending, she suggested a short scene in which Kenny would meet his "new" love—Mary again, but this time as an ordinary girl carrying a straw suitcase, who would tell him she comes from Ozone Heights. The barber would have his "Venus" back, and the audience would go home happy.

The idea worked like a charm. Brief and to the point, it required some new dialogue but no new songs or dances to burden Weill, Agnes, or the production budget. It was clear to me by this time that money was a primary determining factor behind musical comedy. Because of the unions' pay scales, which required musicians and stagehands to receive a higher hourly wage after a certain time of night, the show had to run by the clock. In ballet no one ever cared if *Le Beau Danube* took four minutes longer to dance one night than another. But then no one had had to deal with unions until the last season I danced in New York with the de Basil company.

In addition, I realized that the theatrical producer staked enormous sums on a single production. Cheryl Crawford, who spent $115,000 on *One Touch of Venus*, stood to make a great deal if the show was a smash hit or lose everything if it was a flop. To my knowledge, successful creation in ballet had nothing to do with money, in the sense that success was gauged by the beauty and endurance of the end result, not by its cost or anyone's profit. The best possible work was often done with virtually no budget. Diaghilev's Ballets Russes existed that way for years.

I had always lived like everyone in the ballet, only concerning myself peripherally with money. At one point in the thirties, the colonel had refused to give me a ten-dollar raise, asking cheerfully, "Vat does a little girl like you need vit money?" Instead he surprised me with the gift of an elegantly fitted traveling case that I lost somewhere between Albuquerque and Detroit. In the end I had neither the gift nor the money, but the profit I cleared for the season could be measured in professional achievement and personal satisfaction. Now I was making more money than I had ever dreamed of, over one hundred dollars a week. Management was urging me to sign a run-of-the-play contract at that amount, but Agnes took me aside just before we left Boston and urged me to hold out for something better. "Wait for your notices," she cautioned. After years of experience in the theatre, Agnes knew much more than I about its financial and legal aspects. I didn't fully understand her advice, but I trusted her judgment and did as she suggested.

One Touch of Venus opened in New York at the Imperial Theatre on October 7, 1943. To say simply that I was nervous before my Broadway debut would be a gross understatement. But knowing that Victor, Mother, and Teru were all in the audience that night gave me the extra boost of confidence I needed to get through it. An hour before the curtain rose, I sat at my dressing table making up, with intermittent glances at Victor's flowers, when someone handed me a handwritten note from Jerome Robbins. His good wishes came as a complete surprise, since we had been only casual friends at Ballet Theatre. I had no idea what he was doing now. His thoughtfulness in remembering my opening night touched me deeply.

The months of preparation boiled down to a few hours of buoyant fantasy. Once again the deep concentration on the physical effort required to perform, and the nervous anxiety that precedes it, was so intense that at the end of the performance, I felt numb, disembodied, almost suspended beyond reality. Emerging from this semiconscious state, I found it difficult to be aware of exactly what happened that night. Besides, there is no way to see yourself as a dancer and to judge exactly what it is you have done to elicit enthusiasm from an audience. The judgment comes from the people out front. And from their response on the opening night of *Venus*, we all must have done something right. The applause was overwhelming. Well-wishers crowded backstage to congratulate us on our fabulous success. Mother, Victor, and Teru worked their way through the crowd to hug me. "You were lovely, dear," Mother said quietly, "and it was so good to see you off your toes."

The next morning, Victor gently woke me from a deep, sound sleep. "Sono," he whispered, "someone from Paramount Pictures is on the phone." My eyes creaked open, with Victor's words only faintly registering.

"What . . . who . . . ?" I mumbled.

"Paramount . . . for you!" He handed me the phone.

"Miss Osato, we saw your sensational performance last night, and would very much like for you to meet with one of our representatives," said the voice on the phone. I was still too exhausted to take in much more, so I thanked him, made an appointment, hung up, and crawled back to bed.

A few days later at Paramount's New York offices, I told them as politely as possible that I wanted to remain with my first love, the theatre. Although I was very flattered by a Hollywood offer, I had no illusions about myself. "As long as the war lasts," I said to Victor, "what on earth could I do in Hollywood with my looks? Sit around the back lot waiting to play a Japanese spy?"

The greatest reward was reading my notices. The review that gave me the most joy was by Wolcott Gibbs in *The New Yorker*: "I can only . . . pay my deep respects to Sono Osato, a marvelously limber girl of cryptic nationality, who led the dancers and alarmed and fascinated me almost unbearably." I had apparently become "an overnight hit." But that "night" had been nine years long and had ended only because of Agnes de Mille's expert use of me.

Later in the run the entire company was honored with the presentation of the first annual Donaldson Awards for achievement in the theatre. These were voted by all the members of the theatrical community: managers, directors, performers, stagehands, and box-office personnel. *Venus* swept the field:

Venus	Best Musical Play of the Season, Second Place [*Carmen Jones* was first]
Elia Kazan	Best Musical Direction
Mary Martin	Best Lead Performance in a Musical (female)
Kenny Baker	Best Supporting Performance in a Musical (male)
Sono Osato	Best Dancer in a Musical (female)
Agnes de Mille	Best Choreography
Howard Bay	Best Scenic Design
Paula Laurence	Best Supporting Performance in a Musical (female)
Ogden Nash	Best Lyrics for a Musical, Second Place
S. J. Perelman	Best Book for a Musical, Second Place
Kurt Weill	Best Musical Score

The success of the show was enormously gratifying. Servicemen packed the theatre each night, and their enthusiastic applause was as valuable as any review, reminding us that for a few hours our work offered them laughter as a brief distraction from war.

Whenever I saw the authors or Cheryl, their faces were all smiles. *Variety* reported that we played to "capacity clean-up; gets $35,600 weekly right along." Amazing when you realize that in those days the top price for a seat was $4.40. Confident that the laughs would come where we expected them and that the show would flow smoothly, the cast relaxed. We settled in for a long run, and with a new contract, my salary soared from one hundred to three hundred and fifty dollars a week.

My favorite moment in the show was Mary's solo "spot." She was not "in one," but alone in a full set, exquisitely dressed in her cobweb peignoir. After carrying a golden chair to the front of the stage, she held the audience spellbound as she sat quietly singing of intimate gestures between lovers. Her warmth and tenderness set Weill's "That's Him" aglow every night.

For my own part, I discovered that Agnes's assessment of me as a comedienne gave me a new source of strength and theatrical power. Every night the comic inflection of my movements drew hundreds of chuckles. After years of subduing my private self to the choreography, I was now happy as an individual artist, proud of the pleasure I gave to others. Inspired by the public's warm response, I tried to make each performance as fresh and spontaneous as the first one. It was harder than I had expected, for I'd never before repeated the same steps to the same music at the same time every night. The size of the ballet repertory guarantees variety for audience and dancers alike; rushing among ballets by Fokine, Massine, and Tudor, I had never had to worry about "going stale." I couldn't count on Agnes to give me notes if my performances began to sag, for as soon as *Venus* opened, she returned to Ballet Theatre to choreograph a new work, *Tally Ho!* So keeping my performances fresh became my own responsibility. The glowing reviews I had received were a marvelous boost to my ego, but after all the raves and applause and laughter, hard work still remained.

However, personal thoughts began to distract me from my work. For the first time in my life, I was thinking about having children. Mary was the only woman I knew in the theatre who seemed capable of successfully combining career and family. Hoping she would help me sort out my thoughts, I went to her dressing room during several intermissions to discuss the pros and cons of motherhood. Despite her obvious love for her two children, Mary's advice was firm. "Keep working," she said. "You're too young to think about giving up this kind of personal success." Not at all convinced that I could handle the dual role of mother and performer, I decided she was probably right. I put aside my half-formed dream of a family for another time, went back to work, and gave my undivided attention to dancing.

The war news that came with the spring made us more conscious than ever of our isolated lives onstage. The Allies had landed at Anzio several months earlier but were still trapped on its beachheads. My brother Tim was training at Camp Shelby, Missouri, with the 442nd Infantry Division, made up solely of Japanese-Americans.

As a contribution to the war effort, Agnes organized groups of dancers from *Oklahoma!* and *Venus* to perform at army camps, hospitals, and embarkation centers, which were known officially as "staging areas." She prepared some of her concert solos, asked me to dance my *Venus* solo, and rehearsed the other dancers in rowdy hoe-downs and intimate duets. For security reasons, the soldiers waiting to leave for combat were isolated, not even allowed to communicate with their families. It was anyone's guess how they would react to "show dancing" at this most crucial time of their lives. Our bus pulled up to the gates of a camp, and uniformed guards waved us past. How ironic that the same military and governmental red tape that had forbidden me entrance into California was now passing me without a glance into a highly restricted area. The magic of the theatre!

The immense hall was filled to the rafters. It was clear from the outset that Mary's tender singing of "That's Him" would be the high spot of every performance. Seeing the young men's unlined faces look-ing up at her so wistfully, I felt that she must have embodied all the girls they were leaving behind. The soldiers liked our dances, I'm sure, but their reactions seemed a little confused at times. Surely, most of them had never even seen an arabesque before, so they were either quiet and reserved when they should have laughed and applauded, or they hooted during the most moving pas de deux. I was glad the laughs and catcalls I got for my dance were both genuine and appropriate.

Actually, the only important thing was that we entertained them and made them happy even for a short time.

Between numbers I squeezed among them out front. "What do you think of the show, soldier? Do you like the dances?" I asked a few boys. "Yes, ma'am," was always the polite reply. How strange it seemed to me that they were so shy with me, in view of what they were about to face!

At one hospital we tossed our skirts and kicked up our heels for dozens of men who might never walk again. It took a lot of acting to suppress the distress we all felt seeing those young men so terribly and irreparably damaged. They never took their eyes off us, and we never stopped smiling at them.

Back in town, Agnes's newest piece for Ballet Theatre, *Tally Ho!*, was scheduled to open at the Met in April. Listening to her worry aloud one night about the role she herself would be dancing, I started to think about something I could do to help. "I know more about makeup than you do, Agnes," I finally said bluntly. "Let me do it for you." She looked startled for a minute, and then agreed.

The opening night of *Tally Ho!*, I fixed my own hair and makeup for *Venus*, and then taxied over to the Met. Agnes and Lucia were in the same dressing room that Baronova, Toumanova, and their mothers had shared in 1936. Although icons no longer held their places of honor on the dressing table, that same familiar opening-night tension filled the room. Nervous and exhausted, Agnes sat there in a daze. She had such a case of the jitters that her eyelids couldn't stop quivering long enough for me to glue on her false eyelashes. In less than half an hour, Agnes was dressed, made up, and looking lovely. Forty-five minutes later she was radiant as the curtain fell on another success.

Venus continued to play to standing-room-only crowds night after night, while beyond the walls that contained dancing and laughter, men fell, dying, in strange jungles and on sandy beaches.

The temperature climbed so fast in May that the tar in the streets began to soften. Management installed a wonderful new contraption called an air conditioner in Mary's dressing room, but the rest of us simply threw open the windows and hoped for an occasional breeze. I was sharing a dressing room several flights above the stage with two other girls, and we spent a good part of every performance racing up and down the stairs. When we began to droop from the heat and the long climb, I put in a request to the company manager for an electric fan. I remembered dancing in the heat of Australia as I pulled on my sweater for "Forty Minutes to Lunch" one evening and realized that it hadn't dried yet from the matinee. I had to wear that sweater for two scenes at every performance, so to avoid dancing in a wet costume every matinee day, I also asked for a second sweater. Neither request was costly or unreasonable, but I never heard a word in response. I think the company manager had a grudge against me. After the opening he had pestered me daily to sign a run-of-the-play contract for the same salary I had been receiving out of town. But I ignored his pressure as Agnes had suggested I should, and finally signed a new contract for twice the original amount. Turning a deaf ear to my requests seemed like deliberate retaliation on his part.

In any case, the anger that was brewing in the back of my mind erupted on June 6, 1944, D-Day, when I happened to arrive at the theatre earlier than usual. One of the actresses told me that all the Broadway shows were making special plans for that night to honor the countless anonymous heroes of the invasion. Before the curtain rose in each theatre, some member of the cast was to step before the audience and read the prayer President Roosevelt had written that day as the Allied troops were landing in Normandy. It was up to the company manager to make the necessary arrangements, but with only an hour and a half before curtain, no one in our cast had been asked to read the prayer. Dumbfounded by his silence, we phoned Cheryl to get her permission for the brief ceremony, but couldn't reach her either at home or at her office. "My God," I kept saying, "we'll be the only show on Broadway that does nothing!" Angry and ashamed, we decided to take matters into our own hands. John Boles volunteered on the spot to read the President's prayer.

Before the overture began, Boles stepped onstage in the dressing gown he wore for the first act, adjusted his eyeglasses, and read. His solemn voice rang over the bowed heads of the audience. The prayer ended, "Help us to conquer the apostles of greed and racial arrogancies. Lead us to the saving of our country and with our sister nations into a world unity that will spell a sure peace—a peace invulnerable to the scheming of unworthy men. And a peace that will let all men live in freedom, reaping the just rewards of their honest toil. Thy will be done, Almighty God, Amen."

By the time Boles finished reading, four thousand ships and one hundred fifty thousand men had reached the shores of Normandy in the first wave, and thousands had died.

The callousness of the company manager left me in a cold rage. I was also totally exhausted. Except for one month's vacation out of every twelve, I had been dancing for ten solid years, and the crisis at the theatre aggravated my fatigue past remedy. Motivated by my fury, I gave notice that I would leave the show. Since the first days of *Venus*, Cheryl Crawford and I had always been comfortable together, so we spoke freely. I took the opportunity of a meeting with her to criticize the company manager's irresponsibility. By the end of our talk, we were both close to tears, but nothing she could say swayed me from my decision to leave. I didn't bother to enumerate the accumulated reasons for my decision: the heat, the fan, the stairs, the sweater, the fatigue. My mind was made up.

So in the summer of 1944 I was again at liberty. Fortunately, Victor had a job. Having opened an office in midtown with Sidney Katz, an experienced architect, he was working enthusiastically, even though commissions were scarce since the bulk of building materials was directed towards the war effort.

During the ten months of dancing in *Venus*, I'd been too tired to take class. But now that my time and energy were totally my own, I resumed dance lessons, this time with Edward Caton at the Ballet Arts Studio at Carnegie Hall. Caton had studied in Moscow with Nelidova and in St. Petersburg with Vaganova, and had later danced with the Pavlova and Mordkin companies and with Ballet Theatre. His instructions were accompanied by a duet for voice and piano—he sang, loudly and off-key, as he taught. His passionate style of teaching was entertaining as well as instructive, and I felt a renewed sense of vitality.

Just as I became a student again, a friend asked me if I would like to become a teacher. He wanted me to teach ballet at the American Theatre Wing Youth Association in Harlem, where a newly organized canteen provided the neighborhood teen-agers with facilities for after-school recreation. When many of them expressed interest in more constructive pastimes, forum discussions on art, music, and drama were arranged. Stimulated by the discussions, the youngsters began to talk about producing their own show.

Having enjoyed my brief teaching stint in Chicago, despite the conditions that made it necessary, I was eager to take part in the new venture. A room had been set aside for my classes, but when I arrived to meet the twenty-five energetic youngsters, I found that there was neither a barre nor a mirror to work with. Someone had donated an old piano that seriously needed tuning. With the students' help I located two unused Ping-Pong tables, which the older boys set up in the makeshift studio. I placed the children around the tables, grabbed a thin edge myself, and started to explain the use of the barre. I showed them the five basic ballet positions and some simple exercises, and many picked them up immediately. For some time I taught weekly, somewhat disorganized classes, never dreaming that nearly twenty-five years later, Arthur Mitchell would establish the internationally acclaimed Dance Theatre of Harlem and a permanent school with students such as these. We never got around to staging a full production, but the children worked hard and made visible progress, and we were all proud of our work.

A few months later I left the Youth Association because someone presented Victor and me with an outline for a new show in which they suggested I play the leading role. We were immediately taken with the idea of a musical based on the romance between Solomon and the Queen of Sheba, and decided to try producing it ourselves. Before raising any money, we asked both Tudor and our friend the scenic designer and painter Boris Aronson if they would like to get involved with it too. Tudor's reaction was rather vague, but Boris was very interested. Victor continued to work and I continued to take class, but we both devoted more and more of our time to realizing our new project.

Around this time I realized that Victor and I had never had the chance to share much more than our home and our love since I'd begun work on *Venus*. As long as I had danced in the show, we had maintained a rotating schedule that was far from ideal. Just as he'd come home from work, I'd leave for the theatre, so we had had little time together except a few hours after the performance. Understandably, he preferred to spend his evenings at home rather than standing around at the theatre. How many times could he watch *One Touch of Venus*? But he never complained, as he had every right to do; instead, he offered continual support. While I was earning most of our money, nightly applause, and lavish newspaper coverage, Victor was still struggling. At twenty-five he had found the work he wanted to do, but for a young, unknown architect, the road was constantly rough. Many marriages have floundered in far less trying circumstances. Yet without resentment, Victor quietly buried the loneliness he must have felt much of the time. Not with a single word or gesture did he even imply that my career gave him anything but the greatest happiness.

When I left the show, we discovered that we both had the time and some money to do things together. And first we started going to the theatre and to the ballet, which we had badly missed. Jerry Robbins's first ballet had premiered at Ballet Theatre that April, and we put seeing it at the top of our list.

Though Jerry and I had never been close friends during my two years in Ballet Theatre, I'd always liked him and enjoyed dancing with him. He was an excellent partner in *Pillar of Fire* and an ardent suitor in *Romeo and Juliet*, in which we caressed each other's palms and gazed into each other's eyes for several minutes. Offstage he was reserved and seemed rather melancholy, particularly on tour. But his audacious sense of humor shone on stage, most brilliantly in Agnes's *Three Virgins and a Devil*. In one passage Jerry walked jauntily to center stage and paused to admire one of the virgins, while twirling a flower nonchalantly in his hand. He gave the chaste girl a knowing nod, tipped his hat, and sauntered offstage again with a bobbing gait. With just those few gestures he never failed to make an audience chuckle or titter with glee. His talent as a performer was obvious, but I didn't know that he wanted to choreograph.

When we saw *Fancy Free*, the combination of the work itself and Jerry's performance in it convinced me that his extraordinary talent would someday raise him to the ranks of the few great male choreographers of our century who had also been exceptional dancers—Nijinsky, Massine, and Fokine. As one of the three sailors celebrating their shore leave in New York with a few drinks and a few girls, Jerry was agile, graceful, and poignant, insinuating a spirit into the rhumba-dancing sailor that I have never seen equalled. This irresistible ballet catapulted Jerry Robbins to instant fame, being one of the first American ballets to be, in show-business terms, a "smash."

Several weeks after we saw *Fancy Free*, Jerry introduced us to its young composer, Leonard Bernstein. Although *Fancy Free* was his first ballet score, Bernstein was far from unknown. In November 1943 he had blazed into America's musical life by replacing the ailing Bruno Walter, on extremely short notice, as conductor of the New York Philharmonic's weekly Sunday-afternoon concert, which was broadcast throughout the United States and Canada. The next day *The New York Times* praised his extraordinary musical talent in a front-page review and an editorial devoted solely to him.

The score of *Fancy Free* established Bernstein's reputation at once. He was so engaging and outgoing that shortly after we first met him, I asked whether he would like to compose the music for our Solomon and Sheba show. Lenny was immediately interested in the idea of a musical that would take place in Israel during Biblical times and said he was "born to do this show." We asked him to dinner to discuss the project in earnest, and he spent much of the evening doing bizarre imitations of the unusual instruments he wanted to use for the score. We were delighted. But although Boris and Lenny, two extraordinary artists, showed interest, there was still an enormous problem —we had no script. Most of the established playwrights were at war or working for the government, and the others we approached lacked either the time, the experience, or the interest to take part. Nevertheless we were confident that a writer would turn up sometime, somewhere.

In all the years I had been onstage, I had never uttered a sound. So I began to take speech lessons in preparation for the role of the Queen of Sheba. My voice teacher was a large, lively woman named Susan Steell, who started me on a set of vocal exercises that consisted primarily of open vowel sounds. For weeks on end I diligently repeated "oh," "ah," and "oooh," both in class and at home, even while taking a bath. Susan encouraged me as if a Metropolitan Opera debut lay in the balance, and finally decided it was time to stop making noises and prepare a speech.

I memorized a passage from the Prologue of *Henry V*, but on the day she said, "Now, entertain me," I was so nervous that I took off my shoes and clutched the side of her grand piano for support. "Oh, for a

Muse of fire that would ascend / The brightest heaven of invention," I whimpered. My teacher's face made it all too clear that I was still far from entertaining her, or *anybody*. So I continued vocalizing daily, and tried to concentrate on relaxing and strengthening my chest and throat, the parts of my body with which I was least familiar. Progress was painfully slow, but there wasn't a time limit as far as I could see. Our musical still had no script. Then one night at dinner Lenny said, "Look, you have nothing to do until this show gets written. Why don't you do the one I'm working on right now with some friends?"

"What's it about?" I asked casually.

"It's an expanded *Fancy Free*—the ballet with a script, songs, the works."

He told us that Betty Comden and Adolph Green would star and write the book and lyrics. They had recently appeared at the Village Vanguard with Judy Holliday as "The Revuers," and had won such a following for the act that it subsequently moved both uptown and upstairs to the Rainbow Room at Rockefeller Center. *Fancy Free*'s scenic designer, Oliver Smith, would design the sets and co-produce the show as well, with Paul Feigay. And Jerry Robbins would choreograph the dances.

At the rate things were going, it looked as if *Solomon and Sheba* wouldn't get together before Judgment Day. Lenny's sudden offer and briefing on the show tempted me; the idea of joining the group of talent already committed to his show was too good to resist. By the time he left us that night, I had agreed to join the cast of *On the Town*.

By then I had a professional handling my legal and business affairs. Herman Levin, later famous as the producer of *My Fair Lady*, had added my name to a short list of theatrical clients for whom he served as both agent and lawyer. His gift for wry humor assured me that even the most difficult negotiations wouldn't rattle him. Thanks to his efforts, the contract he drew for me with Oliver Smith more than doubled the $350 weekly salary I had eventually received for *Venus*.

Nervous, excited, and still amazed at the suddenness of joining the show, I set out for the theatre to meet the company. Most of the staff and cast were still in their twenties, but our director was a man with experience in the theatre for more years than some of us had been able to walk. George Abbott—Mr. Abbott, as he was always called— towered above us, a pillar of calm among anxious, youthful beginners. The incomparable Nancy Walker was probably the most experienced veteran of Broadway in the cast, with the musical hit *Best Foot Forward* to her credit.

Once everyone had arrived, Mr. Abbott asked us to sit in a semi-circle around him and to read straight through the play. As we drew up on chairs, even Nancy seemed nervous. But she laid her script flat on the floor, leaned forward over her crossed legs, and read her lines with a brilliant sense of comedic timing, as if she'd been saying them for months.

I didn't share her aplomb. I could move on cue, but speaking on cue confused me, and I read haltingly. In the story, Nancy was a brash New York cabbie with a deep-down tender heart, Betty was a dignified lady anthropologist who succumbs to the zany exuberance of a sailor, and I was Ivy Smith, an all-American girl who is so ambitious that she performs hootchy-kootchy dances at Coney Island every night in order to pay for her daily singing and ballet lessons. Ivy's claim to fame is that out of thousands of New Yorkers, she is chosen as Miss Turnstiles for June. Adolph, Cris Alexander, and John Battles were Ozzie, Chip, and Gabey, three navy buddies on twenty-four-hour leave in New York City. On the Times Square Express, Gabey is smitten with the picture of Miss Turnstiles, tears it from the subway car, and vows to find her. The rest of the show brings the sailors together with Nancy and Betty as they comb New York for the elusive Ivy Smith.

Mr. Abbott listened to us without interruption while we stumbled through the script. When we disbanded for the day, he called me aside, kindly pointing out, "Sono, you'll have to speak up." Knowing I had difficulties other than mere volume with the words, I was glad to be let off so lightly.

Dance rehearsals will be different, I told myself. At least there I knew what I was supposed to do. I expected to work with Jerry as I had with Agnes, experimenting with steps until we found movement that was just right for the character and situation. But when I got to the first rehearsal, I found instead that Jerry had already completed the first ballet, "Miss Turnstiles," without me! He danced through my part, showing me exactly how Ivy and her movements were to be comically defined in the choreography.

Jerry's choreography gave me a much better grasp of my character than the script did, simply because I found movement easier than words. I picked up the steps quickly, with much greater confidence than I'd felt reading my lines. Jerry had thought the dance through so well that after I stepped into it, the number needed no major modifications to fit neatly into the show. It was a relief that I would make my first appearance by dancing, since I needed all the reassurance I could get before braving the unfamiliar terrain of acting.

Rehearsing the dialogue scenes made me more self-conscious than I'd been since my first classes with the de Basil company. Singing was even more exasperating. One scene originally included me, Betty, Adolph, John Battles, and Cris Alexander. We rehearsed it one day with Lenny at the piano. After belting out a few bars, he turned to me and said, "You sing this phrase, Sono." I tried to repeat it as he picked out each note, but when I aimed for the highest note and missed it by a mile, Lenny decided right there that it would be much better if I remained mute and amorous in John's arms.

Before the scene was cut, I tried to placate Betty and Adolph by telling them that I was taking speech classes with Susan Steell. They were encouraged to hear I was working on my own, but more important, they were so amused by my struggles with Susan that they wrote a scene into the show caricaturing my lessons. Susan's hilarious audition for the role of Mme. Maude P. Dilly, a vocal coach prone to hitting the bottle during her classes, had just the screwy quality they wanted and won her the part hands down.

Rehearsals became increasingly frenetic as Jerry plunged into one dance after another. He devised a beautiful lyrical pas de deux for Nelle Fisher and Dick d'Arcy, following the song "Lonely Town." I remember that during rehearsals, Nelle's only complaint was that her new contact lenses made it harder for her to see Dick than her own weak vision.

Next Jerry taught me the solo he wanted me to do. As pleased as I was to have it, I became uneasy during rehearsals when I saw that it had none of the clever and humorous structure of "Miss Turnstiles" or the tender sentiment of "Lonely Town." It seemed diffuse, badly in need of a sharp focus. But Jerry's responsibilities were themselves diffused, and my solo was only one small part of his enormous job. He had to mount several long ballets, stage twelve songs, and provide innumerable bits of "business." He was just twenty-six years old and grappling with what was only his second major attempt at choreography. He had no assistant, no dance captain, no one to supervise or rehearse the dancers but himself.

Inevitably, *On the Town* would be compared to *Fancy Free*. The huge success of that ballet, barely a year old at the time, was still fresh in the public's mind, and everyone would be waiting to see if Jerry could possibly top it. Knowing Agnes's struggles with *Venus*, where her responsibility was only to choreograph the dances, I could imagine how heavy the additional burdens and pressures must have weighed on Jerry. Nevertheless, he worked without a hint of anxiety. Calm, serious, and highly organized at the dance rehearsals, he neither wasted a minute nor rushed us along. He was patient and managed to blend humor with authority. He was already a professional in every inch of his lean, tired body. We respected Jerry enormously, and liked him just as much.

For the latter part of the show, he created a "dream ballet," a new convention introduced by Agnes with "Laurey Makes up Her Mind" in *Oklahoma!* Dance was used not only as a visual interlude in the script but as a vehicle to further the plot.

"Gabey in the Playground of the Rich" began realistically enough, with Adolph, John, and Cris, together with Nancy and Betty, sitting on the subway, exhausted, but on their way to Coney Island, still in search of Ivy. In less than twenty-four hours they'd been to the Brooklyn Navy Yard, the Museum of Natural History, Carnegie Hall, and three different nightclubs, whooping it up to Latin rhythms, low-down blues, and corny dance tunes. With their shore leave coming to an end, separation from their girls imminent, and Ivy still lost in the crowd, they slumped against each other, nearly asleep. I would appear suddenly and then, within seconds, disappear again through the subway doors. John would run after me, but the subway would drift off and leave him still searching for me. Because so much happened at once, Jerry had to work with the soloists and with the groups of the dream ballet in turn. Naturally, choreographing for many was more time-consuming than choreographing for one or two. So when Jerry turned his attention to the others, sometimes developing twenty-four bars or so of new group movement, I would have to stand wherever he had left me in the previous day's rehearsal. While Jerry's creative juices flowed, I stood stock still in the midst of the moving dancers for minutes at a time, until I would yell out, just in case he'd forgotten me, "Jerry, what do I do, *now?*"

"I'll think of something," he'd call back over the music. And he did.

Several days before we left for the Boston tryouts, Jerry showed up at rehearsal with a huge grin on his face and a length of red jersey in his hand. "I've *got* it!" he announced. He flipped one end of the fabric to Ray Harrison, who was my partner as the Dream Gabey, and gave me the other end. Next, with a slight shove, he set me turning into its length until I was wound into Ray's arms. It worked. Then we spent hours experimenting, winding the jersey around my waist, chest, and neck until it finally ended up as a turban on my head. Enormously pleased with his invention, Jerry said, "Now Ray will pull on one end and your hair will tumble down." I was just a little dubious, since dancing with any prop can be hazardous. What would happen if Ray couldn't find the end of the cloth tucked under my right ear and pull it on the right beat? One wrong yank and the turban would slide over my face like a flimsy muzzle. We practiced winding and unwinding, matching every turn with the music until we had it down pat.

The harder we worked, the less attentive I became to Victor. We both left our jobs at the same hour now, but I couldn't manage to leave Ivy behind at the theatre when I came home. Most nights I sat limply at dinner with my elbows propped on the table, staring into space, and muttering, "But I *have* been practicing, Mme. Dilly." Even then Victor was patient and understanding. The day we left town I was slightly frantic, clutching Victor for reassurance. He nestled me in his arms, soothed my nerves, and promised to be in Boston for the opening.

We opened at the Colonial Theatre in Boston in December 1944. Backstage, amidst the actors' last-minute reciting of lines and the dancers' warming up, Lenny, looking very handsome in his evening clothes, paced up and down, flushed with excitement. I was wondering why he was headed for the orchestra pit when someone told me that he, rather than Max Goberman, would conduct the first performance. Adding to his first-night nerves was the fact that his mentor, Serge Koussevitzky, was in the audience.

The show went well until the scene where two sections of a subway car were supposed to slide out from opposite directions and meet on-stage. At that point there was a great commotion in the wings and absolutely nothing happened. Because of the war, stagehands, like everything else, were hard to come by. The sections of the subway set stood in readiness, but no one was around to move them. So to fill what seemed like an eternity of dead time, John Battles snatched up a photograph of me and paced back and forth behind the footlights, looking yearningly at my picture and moaning to it, "Ivy, where are you?" The missing subway car finally rolled on, John worked his way back into the written dialogue, and the show sailed on as if nothing happened.

Victor was proud of me and genuinely liked the show, despite the one lapse into confusion. The next day the reviews were predominantly favorable, but we knew there was a lot more work before us if we wanted a sure-fire hit. The New York opening was only twelve days away.

Mr. Abbott spent each day trotting up and down stairs and from one corner of the theatre to another, guiding the actors through new lines that had not existed when the curtain fell the night before. Betty and Adolph stayed awake for hours after each performance, struggling to eliminate the snags. As they rewrote, I lay in bed, tossing and turning, my hands drenched with sweat, going over every word and every step of my part. By morning I'd always have it down cold, but I woke up as exhausted as I'd been the night before. At rehearsals the same greenish pallor of tryout fatigue was on everyone's face.

One thing I didn't have to worry about this time was my wardrobe. At my insistence, Herman Levin had inserted a clause into my contract giving me final costume approval. Since I had certain ideas on how I should look in the show, I worked together with Alvin Colt, our costume designer, and created three of the five outfits myself. Because Ivy was a simple working girl, she didn't need a chic wardrobe; she merely needed to be attractive and able to move freely.

In "Miss Turnstiles," I wore a modest apricot dress, lined with frothy pink and red ruffles, to add some flair when I kicked. The dream-ballet costume was a floor-length gown of heavy ivory silk, unadorned except for the sequined bracelet I wore on one bare arm. Jerry's choreography with the red jersey turban took care of my hairstyle.

Alvin and I also devised a costume for the solo. It was a cheery little yellow dress, spruced up with a few daisies threaded through the two doughnuts of my coiled hair. But the dance itself continued to elude Jerry. He had placed me in a full, dimly lit set depicting a door-lined corridor of practice studios that occupy the upper floor of Carnegie Hall. I flitted from door to door like a lost sylph, striking balletic poses as I listened to the various musicians playing behind the doors, then imitated their instruments in dance. Unlike everything else Jerry had created in the show, this solo was neither comical nor charming. Dancing it on opening night in Boston, I suffered the nightmare of all performers: I laid an egg. The applause barely covered my exit.

When I went hunting for Jerry that night to discuss it with him, I discovered that he had left the theatre, left the hotel—left Boston altogether! With one hard look at our opening performance, he realized that some of the numbers he thought were complete needed revisions. To gain better perspective on his work, he took the train back to New York. I was left holding my "egg," but I believed in Jerry and never doubted he would return with a brilliant solution. When word got around that he had left town, another choreographer was called in to replace him. Despite the momentary crisis, I resented the idea of having to work with another choreographer, but before she even set foot in the theatre, Oliver Smith apologized for the inconvenience of her trip, told her she wasn't needed, and advised her to catch the next train back to New York. Which she did.

Just a day later, after the evening's curtain fell, Jerry materialized in my dressing room like a genie. He was rested and bursting with ideas. I told him I'd work until we both dropped, so he took me back to the empty stage before I could even remove my makeup and kept me there until the wee hours of the morning. What he'd created by the time we staggered off to bed was, to say the least, a vast improvement over the original number.

He discarded the full-stage set and put the solo "in one"—that is, between the proscenium and the first wing curtain—since he wanted the "spot" to be brief and lightly impromptu. Jerry, too, saw the humor in the stories of my speech lessons, and based the number, later called "Do Do Re Do," on my struggles with the musical scale. I half-talked, half-sang the lyrics, which reminded Ivy that she "mustn't be discouraged if the going is slow." Following the song, my dance was a burlesque of all the steps that had always caused me trouble. Having been in Ballet Theatre at the time, Jerry had seen my infamous *Princess Aurora* pas de trois on the basketball court, and highlighted the number by having me do fouettés, off pointe, with knees bent and one foot pointing straight up. While turning, I did the breaststroke with my arms until the wobbles carried me clear offstage to the powerful syncopation of Lenny's swing beat.

Though I was delighted with this new number, I now felt that Lenny's orchestration might be suited to the sound of Glenn Miller's Orchestra but was inappropriate for such a light-hearted little dance. Since my role in the show had me talked about more than I was actually onstage, I wanted to make as much of an impression as possible when I did appear. During a rehearsal break I went to Lenny with a suggestion. "Lenny, you know I'm not Wagnerian in size or in looks. Don't you think the sound will overpower the dance? Maybe the number would work better against a quintet instead of the entire orchestra."

He listened politely, then looked me straight in the eye, grasped my arm affectionately, and said, "Sono, you're *marvelous* in the show."

"There goes the quintet!" I thought. The music stayed the way it

One Touch of Venus. *Mary Martin*
is surrounded by me, Diana Adams,
Pearl Lang, and Patricia Schaeffer

Rehearsing with Jerry Robbins

With Susan Steell

MEET MISS TURNSTILES

Exotic Ivy Smith   for the Month

Ivy is a home-loving type who loves to go out night-clubbing.

Her heart belongs to the Navy, but she loves the army.

She's not a Career Girl, but she's studying singing and ballet at Carnegie Hall and painting at the Museums. She is a frail and flower-like girl—who's a champion at polo, tennis and shotput.

Exotic IVY SMITH

Miss Turnstiles

ON THE TOWN

Al Hirschfeld's drawing *in* The New York Times

Performing at the Stage Door Canteen

As Cocaine Lil in Ballet Ballads, 1948.
Paul Godkin is reaching up towards me

OPPOSITE *Leonard Bernstein*
and I present the company album to
Mayor Fiorello La Guardia, 1945

With Frank Sinatra in MGM's The Kissing Bandit, *1947*

With John Garfield in Peer Gynt, *1950*

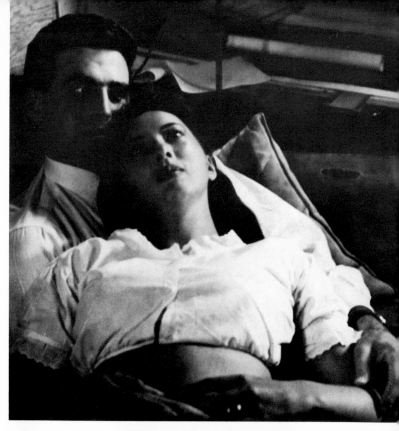

With Victor, June 1943

Niko's on top, I'm in the middle, and Tony's at the bottom, 1951

ABOVE *A get-together before the 35th American Ballet Theatre Anniversary.*
Jerome Robbins, me, Alexandra Danilova, Nora Kaye, and Maria Karnilova—
January 10, 1975
BELOW *With Hugh Laing in* Romeo and Juliet *at ABT's Anniversary Gala*

was, with the full orchestration of the musical scale forming the base of the lyrics. He packed it with wit and clever musical invention, contributing as much to the success of my number as Jerry's choreography.

We rehearsed the dances in the theatre basement near the toilets, while a few actors at a time worked onstage. In between rehearsals one day, I borrowed Adolph's newspaper and read that the German counteroffensive, which Hitler had begun on December 10, had cut fifty miles into Belgium. Appalled at the photographs of gaunt, snow-bound soldiers huddled in blankets beside their stalled tanks, my thoughts flew to Tim, who was somewhere in combat with the 442nd. Mr. Abbott cautioned us to keep our minds on our work regardless of the news, but I couldn't stop worrying. Much later Tim told me that his regiment lost over half its men in the four-day rescue of the Texas 36th Infantry Division, the "Lost Battalion."

With the war news weighing heavily in the back of our minds, and exhausted by the never-ending cycle of practice and performance, we left Boston for a few rehearsals in New York. During our very last run-through, the day before the opening, Mr. Abbott took me aside once again and said, with uncharacteristic but unmistakable impatience, "Sono, you're still too stiff. Relax. Loosen up."

I mulled over his words all night and most of the next day, trying to find the source of my wooden delivery. Once I memorized my lines, I struggled to speak them as naturally as possible, but I was still unsure about how to project; there were no microphones onstage in those days. While I sensed the effect of my body in motion, I still couldn't gauge the effort necessary for projecting my voice. Mr. Abbott had coached me tirelessly from the first day, and I'd followed his instructions to the letter.

I discovered that that was precisely the problem. Used to performing exactly as a choreographer demanded, I was speaking like an automaton, sticking to Mr. Abbott's directions without imbuing them with anything of myself. With his help, I had assembled all the ingredients of the character as written in the script but had never let them take on a life of their own.

hen we opened in New York at the Adelphi Theatre on December 28, 1944, I'm sure all of us in *On the Town* were much more concerned with our individual performances or contributions to the show than with guessing at what kind of success it would have. Of course we all wanted it to be a hit, though there were too many elements to deal with at every moment before the final curtain to give it much thought. But it seems that the audience was set up to expect a smash from the very beginning. The curtain rose on Oliver Smith's set of a sleepy Brooklyn Navy Yard at dawn. A deep bass voice, backed by a male chorus, sang a slow, adult lullaby, dominating the silence. The second stanza flowed into lyrical three-quarter time, and the third stanza, finishing at the stroke of 6:00 A.M., was shattered by a percussive, brassy burst of music. Workers swung onstage and sailors raced down the gangplank, among them the three small-town heroes, Ozzie, Chip, and Gabey, who broke out into their paean of syncopated song and patter, "New York, New York," a song that made swing almost classical.

The audience had just minutes to recover from the impact of the opening's startling energy, when strings and a brass fanfare announced "Miss Turnstiles for June." An announcer's voice enumerated the qualifications of this "typical New Yorker." My first entrance was among a long line of subway-riding girls, backs to the audience, fannies wiggling, feet close together side-shuffling across the stage to the musical rhythm of racing subway wheels. Selected from the masses by a spotlight resting on my fanny ("Who, me?" "Yes, you. Ivy Smith."), I emerged to perform the Miss Turnstiles variations. This music-and-dance portrait of the All-American Girl was one of the most innovative of its kind ever seen on the Broadway stage. Lenny's music was brash, bold, frantic, and funny, capturing the pulse of New York life. It was symphonic, jazzy, atonal, and operatic. It was low-down, honky-tonk, and "hot." It was something only Leonard Bernstein could have written. Every instrument in the orchestra seemed to have its own statement, just as Jerry's dance for me captured perfectly every facet of the frenetic pace of wartime New York. I liked sailors, soldiers, and poets. I loved home and high society. I danced lyrically and comically. I did acrobatics and athletics. I was acclaimed, photographed, and raised to fame on the shoulders of my male admirers. But at the end of every month, a new Miss Turnstiles would be chosen. I was lowered slowly from my pinnacle to the floor, turned my back, walked forlornly to the shuffling line of female commuters, and shuffled off with a last, longing glance back over my shoulder at my fleeting moment of instant fame.

The audience chuckled and laughed at the hilarious misadventures created by Comden and Green that followed—Chip and Hildy in the taxi ("Come Up to My Place"), Ozzie and Claire at the Museum ("I Get Carried Away"), and Gabey meeting me at Mme. Maude P. Dilly's studio in Carnegie Hall. I can't remember whose idea it was to have me demonstrate Mme. Dilly's "vocalizing position no. 8," but Gabey's first glimpse of me in person was standing on my head, feet propped against Mme. Dilly's upright piano, struggling to project my voice up and down the scale. With Dilly out in search of another snort, Gabey and I fell in love at first sight and made a date to meet at Nedick's Times Square at eleven o'clock. Dilly's return had me back to my practicing with a warning not to mix sex and art—and a reminder that I owed her fifty-six dollars' worth of bumps and grinds at "Rajah Bimmy's Night in a Harem." The scene ended with "Do Do Re Do." Jerry's inspiration was right on target. The audience loved it.

More hilarity followed, including Nancy's inimitable delivery of the rollicking, suggestive patter of "I Can Cook Too." My next speaking scene was at the Times Square Nedick's. Through Mme. Dilly's interference, Gabey and I never kept our date. Ozzie and Chip, with their girls, consoled Gabey by promising him a date with the "mysterious" Lucy Schmeeler, a lovable, runny-nosed loser, touchingly portrayed by Alice Peerce. Following their exit came the "Times Square Ballet," which closed Act One. Lenny wrote a pastiche of the pulsating rhythms that give New York its unique energy. Jerry's choreography was a carousel of racing, meandering, meeting, and parting of the throbbing, never-ending crowds of a New York that never sleeps. One thing I particularly remember about this number was that the lights were placed low in the wings. Crowds of dancers appeared to be rushing about in a kaleidoscope of nocturnal dimness, illuminated by the headlights of passing cars and taxis in Times Square traffic. The effect was like a shot of adrenaline.

Standing in the wings to watch the three hilarious nightclub scenes that opened Act Two, I sensed we just might have a hit from the sound of the audience's roars of laughter. In those scenes even the rhumba-beat of "Ya Got Me" failed to cheer Gabey. Meeting a very drunken Mme. Dilly in the last nightclub, the Slam Bang, Gabey finally found out where to find Ivy—Coney Island, "the playground of the rich." On the subway to Coney Island with his pals and the girls, Gabey drifted off to sleep and dreamed himself to be "Gabey the Great Lover," the beginning of the dream ballet with the red jersey turban. At the end of that very sensual, bluesy pas de deux, which became a sort of prizefight, I was hoisted slowly into the air by male dancers, with my hands clasped high over my head, acknowledging that I was the victor in this symbolic battle of the sexes.

After my favorite song in the show, "Some Other Time," sung by all the principals *except* me, the weary group arrived at Coney Island. They found me at Rajah Bimmy's bumping and grinding and picking up a handkerchief with my teeth. After last-minute confusion, complicated by the coming together of minor plots that ran through the show, there was a last-minute resolution. The boys ran back to the ship, with their girls waving goodbye, just in time for the next group of sailors to rush down the gangplank for *their* twenty-four-hour leave, and a rousing reprise of "New York, New York."

The final curtain fell, and we stood bowing to an ecstatic crowd. Their applause took on the sound of a force of nature, like the steady beat of falling rain. Still in my post-performance daze, I noticed nothing more than the dour face of Billy Rose, who sat in the second row throughout the ovation with his hands folded in his lap. A friend who sat with Victor in the gallery later told me that throughout the performance, Victor had been too nervous to sit still and continually elbowed him, whispering "She's coming on now," "Here comes her solo," "Wait till you see this!" At the end he sprang to his feet, cheering along with many other members of the audience.

Looking back at the experience of *On the Town* now, I realize more than I did at the time how original a creation it was. First of all, it was amazing to me that, at the height of a world war fought over the most vital political, moral, and racial issues, a Broadway musical should feature, and have audiences unquestionably accept, a half-Japanese as an All-American Girl. This is probably the most indelible impression I have had of the magic of the theatre. I could never have been accepted as Ivy Smith in films or, later, on television. Only the power of illusion created between performers and audiences across the footlights can transcend political preference, moral attitudes, and racial prejudice.

Second, it was a show that featured women who were independent. Hildy the cab driver, Claire the anthropologist, and Ivy the kootch dancer working her way "to the top" were drawn to their sailors on the basis of mutual (if sometimes unusual) attraction rather than desperate need. Their independence was typical of women in wartime, and the show was original in presenting a humorous and affectionate view of our own reality without the veil of glamour.

I also think that *On the Town* was a first in the way it grew organically from a balletic concept. A choreographer creates a ballet with the resources of dance talent available to him in mind. Rarely does he create the ballet and then look for dancers from the outside to "plug in" to the roles. *On the Town* was created almost like a ballet. Jerry, Lenny, Betty, and Adolph worked together as one, "choreographing" words, songs, *and* dance into a work of art, with particular talents and personalities in mind. It is hard to imagine Betty and Adolph creating the role of Hildy for anyone other than Nancy Walker, or the comic situation in Mme. Dilly's studio had I not studied voice with Susan Steell. Beyond that, Betty and Adolph were able not only to create the story, the hilarious lines, and the lyrics but also to inject their own performing qualities—Adolph's warmth and zaniness, and Betty's wry humor and dignity—into two unforgettable characters onstage.

Without the value of hindsight, John Mason Brown in the *Saturday Review* immediately responded to the originality of the show. "It is exciting to see so many young people possessed of such manifest talent, assembled on one stage, saying a fresh thing freshly. It is exciting to observe the bounce, intelligence, gaiety and style of the production as a whole. . . . It is exciting to realize that you are faced with something new, young, and vital; something which dares to turn its back upon the conventional; something that is intelligent without being highbrow, and artful but not arty. . . . It is one of those notable offerings which our show shops make from time to time, and in which the theatre shifts its gears and goes into high."

Other critics were equally enthusiastic, and *On the Town* brought me the most lavish reviews of my career, with many critics referring to my success in *Venus*. "Once again," said Brown, "she proves herself to be an extraordinary performer. She manages to combine the cool beauty of Sorine's 'Pavlova' [a Russian artist's painting of the great ballerina] with a sense of humor subtler than Fanny Brice's, but Brice-like in its contagious qualities. Miss Osato is a genuine addition to our musical comedy stage. She is a young person, arresting and brilliantly endowed, who is already a personage." Et cetera, et cetera. As far as the public was concerned, I was a new star. But the "star" had still not fully mastered the technique of speaking from the diaphragm instead of the throat. Shortly after the opening, I lost my voice. For several performances Nelle Fisher spoke Ivy while I danced her. But the alternating appearances of tiny, blue-eyed, blonde Nelle and myself must have baffled audiences. Fortunately it didn't last long. When my voice returned, I once again had to face speaking and dancing Ivy for eight performances a week. I gradually discovered what my greatest difficulty in acting was.

Repeating the same dances day after day gave me no trouble, for no matter how tired I felt, I danced. Occasionally I forgot steps, but years of experience enabled me to keep dancing, even if I had to make something up. But I had no automatic mechanism to govern my voice. After months in the show, I began to suffer lapses of memory just before going on. As the run went on longer and longer, I developed a strange reaction to the repetition of lines. On matinee days, I would often stand in the wings waiting for an entrance when, suddenly, in near panic, I would begin to wonder: "Do I say those lines now, or did I already say them? Did I say them this afternoon or in the last scene? Or haven't I said them since yesterday?" As far as I know, my internal backstage dramas weren't visible onstage, and audiences responded to my performances warmly.

The acclaim given to a Broadway "star," except for the financial rewards, did nothing to change my private life. I never set foot in the Stork Club or the Rainbow Room. I was tired after performances and preferred entertaining at home to going out on the town. Theatre friends would drop in after their shows with their dates or wives and their own bottles of liquor. Gene Kelly was stationed in Washington with the navy but frequently showed up on leave. Many times he entertained us with soft-shoe routines squeezed into the tiny space between our kitchen and the living-room couch. Another regular guest was Maureen Stapleton, who was to make her Broadway debut in *The Playboy of the Western World* the following year. She would pour theatrical passion into our games of charades. Her equally fierce competitors were Nancy Walker, Adolph Green, Stanley Donen, Zero Mostel, and his new wife, charming Kate Harkin, a Rockette who had formerly danced with the Catherine Littlefield Ballet.

These boisterous games were our way of winding down, and often lasted through the night. Victor, who had to be at the office every morning, would grab an occasional catnap in a corner during our games, but would wake up in time to stroll over to Reuben's with us for an enormous breakfast at dawn.

By now the war had pushed into nearly every part of the world. Even the streets of Manhattan bore painful reminders of its horrors. We saw more and more crippled and mutilated young men, some without arms or legs, some with faces transformed by surgery into plastic masks. It was to me a sobering irony that I should achieve my greatest personal success at a time when my country and my father's were attempting to annihilate each other. My photographs and publicity clearly stressed my Japanese heritage, yet many soldiers wrote to me from the Pacific battle zones, asking for my autographed picture in letters that carried their loneliness right into my dressing room. One sergeant wrote to me for a younger buddy who was too shy to ask for my picture. The letter was so personal and moving that I found myself worrying about the safety of those two GIs. My heart leapt when I heard from them again several months later. How ironic that in the same letter he told me that after his unit had finished "mopping up" a small island somewhere in the Pacific, the mail call had brought the battered photo I had sent to his buddy, which was thereafter kept guarded in the company safe.

Tim wrote to me from Italy, where his unit was part of the U.S. 5th Army, which, along with the British 8th, launched a counteroffensive against the Gothic Line. Allied troops entered Mantua, Verona, Genoa, and Milan. On April 12, 1945, President Roosevelt died in Warm Springs, Georgia. It was almost impossible to conceive of what life would be like without the ever-present image and voice of the great man who had guided the country through some of its most terrible times with such valor and strength of spirit. I had grown up during his twelve years as president and, like millions of others, couldn't believe that we were now deprived of the warmth and security of his paternal guidance.

V-E Day, May 8, lit up a sunny matinee day. Between scenes we rejoiced quietly in our dressing rooms, while through the windows of the Martin Beck Theatre, our new home, we saw crowds of men and women, in uniform and out, crying, hugging, dancing, and shouting. That day the reality outside in the streets blended gloriously with our glimpse onstage of the preciousness of our todays in the face of our unknown tomorrows. Joy and tearful relief engulfed the theatre and the city.

I was nearly overcome with personal happiness. The war in Europe was over, and I had Victor, success, and good news of my family. Tim had survived three years of almost continual combat. Teru had married a naval lieutenant, Vincent Meier, and was living in Newport News, Virginia. And Father finally came to see me perform in *On the Town*. Shortly after his release from the humiliation of ten months' internment, Father had suffered a stroke that shattered his hopes of being with us on opening night. He was thinner, smaller, and so feeble he walked with a cane when he came to New York many months later. But when he entered my dressing room, he was so filled with love and pride that his gentle smile and teary eyes, brighter than I had ever seen them, erased every sign of his physical pain. For the first time in many years, his face hid nothing from me. We came together in silence and embraced. Welling up inside me I could feel what it must have meant to him to see that, instead of imprisonment, I had applause.

Victor and I had celebrated our third anniversary in April. As the months passed and the show continued to draw capacity audiences, my thoughts kept returning to my talks with Mary Martin about having children. The more I examined my position as a Broadway "star," the more clearly I saw how lucky I had been. Though Mary had said I was too young to give up success, I knew life in the theatre was precarious at best. I might be in other shows, but what guarantee did I have of a triumph greater than the one I already had? I felt a stronger, deeper need than the continual pursuit of success.

At twenty-six I was suddenly conscious of the passage of time. Victor and I wanted children. If things went on as they were, years might go by until we suddenly realized it was too late for me to have a child. I was unwilling to wait any longer. All at once, being a mother was all I wanted to do.

On the Town had played for nine months when I took my last bows in September 1945. With eyes filled with tears, I hugged Nancy Walker with all my strength. The curtain fell and the applause faded. For once, my departure from the stage was based neither on anger nor exhaustion but on a firm decision to have what I wanted most in the world.

More than keeping up with the habitual round of dance classes, my main concern was to get pregnant. I became deliriously domestic and concerned with my marriage. But beneath my domestic bliss was a growing tension with Mother. She was designing and making clothes, and lived alone one block away from Victor and me. For quite some time, visits had been strained and unpleasant because of her treatment of Victor. It was difficult to be with her when she aimed jabbing sarcasm at Victor, who refused to make an issue of it. I couldn't bear being in the middle of the situation any longer. I wanted Victor to bring an end to the tension of these so-called family get-togethers but realized I would have to take a stand on my own. Facing Mother about something so unpleasant would be especially difficult since I had never confronted her with my true feelings about anything. I drew on unused sources of strength and planned to have it out with her.

Mixed with my resentment of Mother's treatment of Victor was my feeling about what she had done to Father. After his internment, he was living for the day that he would rejoin her. He had even sent his photographic equipment ahead to New York in expectation of starting a new life. His pain and humiliation must have been greatly magnified when Mother wrote to him saying she could not live with him any longer. Already stripped of his pride, he was now deprived of the comfort of a family.

Involved in my own marriage, I felt helpless to alter their long history of unhappiness. Yet to me, this was the last straw. Mother had hurt Father more deeply than ever at a time when he had never been more vulnerable, and I was helpless to do anything about it. Nevertheless, despite my anger, I had ambivalent feelings of pity and even some kind of sympathy for her, having known since my childhood how terribly unhappy she had been.

With all this in mind, I went to her apartment to "clear the air," telling her that, in all honesty, I couldn't continue this farce, this game of playing at being an intimate family. I told her how unfair she was to treat Victor so badly when he had never done anything to deserve it, and that I would not stand idly by and see him mistreated. I said everything I had to say calmly and objectively. "You don't have to *love* Victor, Mother," I finally said. "I love him and respect him and admire him, and that's all I need. But I can't abide your uncalled-for treatment of him anymore. I've had it."

"I marvel at your patience," was all I remember her saying as she wept.

Suddenly I realized this had been a sort of game, a test to see how much I could endure before I would stand up to her. I finished by telling her that all this was too painful, too difficult, and too unfair. If I had to choose between her and Victor, I would choose Victor even if it meant giving up our "family life." I walked out the door, and outside that little house on Fifty-first Street I could still hear her sobbing.

I didn't see Mother for quite a while after that. Sometimes I would catch a glimpse of her on Third Avenue and would choke back sobs, thinking of her alone, struggling and unhappy. But I would not give in. The period of separation lasted months, until one day she arrived at our apartment with a terrible expression on her face. She told me that Teru had cancer. At her home in Newport News, Teru had had an exploratory operation on her leg that revealed a malignant tumor. It was unthinkable, but it was true.

Shortly before the operation, Teru had given birth to a beautiful boy named Vincent, after his father. With her husband still in the service, she brought her baby back to New York and found a small apartment in Brooklyn. There, as sick as she was, Teru used her still-strong talents to create a beautiful, serene, all-white room draped in unbleached muslin to brighten the days of her young son. When I visited her, I would bring her baby to her as she lay on a couch, too weak to move much of the itme.

Even when Teru finally had to be taken to a hospital, her ability to endure was awesome. I never saw her break down or give in to such an unbearably unfair fate. I was pregnant by that time, and the unmitigated joy I had hoped to feel was diminished by a breaking heart. To avoid showing Teru my grief, I spent my time with her in the hospital dwelling on mundane matters and trivialities. I would turn on the radio, discuss morning sickness, or give her manicures—anything to give a semblance of normality to the ghastly reality. I still marvel at how bravely Teru bore the presence of an oxygen tent. I stood it as long as I could, but in the last days, I couldn't bear to see my sister die. I wasn't there when she succumbed on her twenty-sixth birthday in October 1946.

The hard injustice of Teru's death was eased by the immense joy I felt at carrying a new life, and slowly the sense of loss was dulled. I grew larger and larger, going from 117 pounds to 156, and loved every pound of it. I was so big that I had to wear low heels to keep my balance. Even then there were mishaps. One day, on the corner of Fifty-second Street and Fifth Avenue, I lost my balance and fell, but slowly, like drifting, onto all fours. All I saw were hundreds of shoes walking at me. Finally, with the help of a stranger, I rose like a small elephant, gave a tug to my little fur jacket, and, with as much dignity as possible, sailed off into the sunset of a lovely fall day.

For some reason, losing the trimness I had always had as a dancer didn't bother me. In fact I luxuriated in my bigness. I think I even felt a strange sort of pride in growing so big that, whenever I turned around too quickly in our narrow little kitchen, I would knock pots and pans onto the floor!

Winter came, and it was terribly cold. On the night of January 29, 1947, after a tremendous snowstorm, Victor and I decided to go for diversion to Loew's Lexington to see Larry Parks in *The Jolson Story*. Just as Parks sank to his knees to belt out "Mammy," I felt a large contraction. I nudged Victor, "It's time." We walked home through the snow, and when we got into the apartment, I started to undress. "Dear, what are you doing?" he said, rather curious. "Don't you think we ought to pack and get ready to go?" He called the doctor, who said that if the contractions came every five minutes, it was time. They came every five minutes. We left for the hospital.

Seated in the elevator on the way up to my room, I experienced pain to a degree that all my years of dancing had never prepared me for. Aching muscles, bones, and joints were nothing compared to this pain. It was so great it was almost unreal, an abstraction. But this magnificent mystery produced by the union of two people is an experience so unique and separate that the pain can almost be thrilling. The feelings I experienced in childbirth were immense, ancient, primitive. Rather than retreating from the enigma, I gave myself to it, knowing that my surrender would produce a child.

Coming out of the anesthesia, I remember Victor saying, "Dear, it's a boy!" I was flooded with joy but was a bit surprised, because Teru had said I would have a girl. They brought my baby to me, and he was the most perfect little being I had ever seen. Looking at him all wrapped up in his blanket, my first words to him were "Hello, Sassafras!" I don't know why. I felt totally serene, fulfilled, and in wonder that this gorgeous child had come from me.

While waiting for my baby to be born, I had begun, like all mothers, to think of names. At the time I had been reading *Theodora of Byzantium*. In the book there were descriptions of the turmoil in those days between the peoples of the land and sea. In those passages crowds kept yelling "Nike! Nike!" for victory. Since I was so convinced I would have the girl Teru had predicted, I decided to name my daughter Nika. When Victor said it was a boy, I stayed as close to the original intent as possible and named our son Niko.

In the months that followed Niko's birth, we couldn't bear to be separated from him, even for a few hours, so we took him with us in a picnic basket whenever we went to visit friends. But like most new parents, our lives revolved around our baby, and we stayed home much of the time. During those cold winter months Victor would gently wake me in the middle of the night, saying, "Dear, Niko's hungry.'" I would put on Victor's athletic socks and sweaters, brace my feet up on the bottom dresser drawer to keep them off the cold floor, and breast-feed my baby until he fell asleep.

The routine went on for several months, until Stanley Donen called from California and asked me to appear in an MGM musical, *The Kissing Bandit*, starring Frank Sinatra and Kathryn Grayson. At first I didn't know what to think. My thoughts had never been further from dancing, and even if I had fleeting moments of missing it, I had certainly never considered working while Niko was so young. But when Herman Levin told me that he had arranged a contract that would pay me $1000 a week, I saw this as the means to a particular end.

Victor's architecture office was not doing terribly well, and his father had recently asked him to join the import-export firm that he ran with some members of the family and friends. A muddle of unanswered questions brewed in Victor's mind. Should he stay in architecture, which he loved and for which he was specially trained, or should he strike out in a new direction, where prospects seemed better?

If my work could support us for a time, he would have the opportunity to examine his own situation at a distance. He could leave his business in the hands of his partner, Sidney Katz, and go with Niko and me to California. Thirteen weeks would give him time to think, free from other obligations. We also wanted to do what was best for Niko. Getting out of the city for a few months of grass, sunshine, and fresh air was an irresistible idea, especially in contrast to summer in a two-room apartment, blocks from any park.

This was the first time I had accepted a job solely for the salary, but I couldn't think of a single reason for not doing it now. I had no idea what making a movie would be like, but after ballet and Broadway, I didn't think it could be very hard. So we left for California.

Gene Kelly and his wife, Betsy Blair, invited us to stay with them in their house in Beverly Hills, and provided a crib, a bassinet, and even an English nanny to look after Niko. Gene, under Vincente Minnelli's direction, was then filming *The Pirate* with Judy Garland and had to be on the set at the crack of dawn. The Kellys' generosity was exceptional, but I worried about Niko's hungry crying at night disturbing Gene, who must have been exhausted. However, he never said anything or showed any annoyance, or even any awareness of the nocturnal wailing in the bedroom across from his own. The Kellys made us feel comfortable and welcome every moment we stayed with them.

For the first few days I hurried to MGM at six each morning, right after Niko's second feeding, for makeup tests that would give the director an idea of how I would photograph. I had to sit absolutely still, like an object, while Sidney Guilaroff, master coiffeur, fixed my hair and assistants patted at my face with different shades of pancake, in irritating, tiny dabbing gestures that seemed interminable. In less time than it took to apply just a basic screen makeup, I could have put on two completely different stage makeups. Rather than creating an impression or a look that would reach the farthest balcony, the goal here was a kind of symmetrical perfection that would be acceptable to the brutally revealing eye of the camera. In those seconds when my eyes were free, I would stare at Ava Gardner sitting across the room. Even without makeup and sitting under a hairdryer, she was gloriously beautiful. But being peered at, dabbed at, stroked, patted, and fussed with made *me* feel frustrated, restless, confined, and helpless.

And the costume fittings bothered me even more. Several wardrobe ladies studied my body from all angles, concentrating as much attention on my measurements as Fokine had devoted to the fine points of *Les Sylphides*. In those days Hollywood was totally committed to the high bosom and wasp waist. To their horror, the women found that the distance between my nipple and my shoulderblade did not conform to the Hollywood standard. I had the distinct feeling that they wouldn't be satisfied until my breasts were shoved up under my chin. My waist had expanded with Niko's birth, so I was hardly an ideal sylph, but undaunted, the MGM ladies pulled and tugged and yanked at my muslin bodice.

"What about dancing? I have to dance!" I gasped. "I can hardly breathe!" Throwing me only the most cursory glances, never answering, they tugged even harder. The image of Scarlett O'Hara still reigned at MGM.

Time came for the screen test. As they set up the lights, I stood cinched into my costume, wondering, "What have I let myself in for?" But the test itself was painless, Later, however, when I saw myself on film, I was shocked. I didn't like what I saw at all—in my opinion I looked just plain fat and unattractive. But my opinion wasn't important. When I saw Frank Sinatra for the first time since arriving in Hollywood, he was warm and encouraging.

"Saw your test. You looked great!"

"I didn't think so," I demurred.

"I'm telling you, Sono. You looked great!"

Frank must have been right, because the screen test was accepted. I had first met Frank after a performance of *On the Town*, when he came backstage with Goddard Lieberson, who later married my old friend Vera Zorina. When Sinatra spoke to me about my screen test, he was wearing the leather flying jacket he had worn while entertaining our troops in Europe. Thin and tense, yet radiating great warmth and charm, he seemed more like just one of the boys than the idol of millions.

In *The Kissing Bandit*, I played the Mexican innkeeper's daughter. I don't even remember her name. But J. Carroll Naish played my father, and I do remember that my main function was to be sexy and to entice Frank, the Kissing Bandit.

In those first rehearsals Stanley Donen, the choreographer, told me I was going to maneuver a twelve-foot bullwhip during my dance. "Okay," I thought to myself, "a bullwhip—that's Hollywood!" But when it became clear that it was going to be a question of whether I or the bullwhip would do the manipulating, the studio hired a real cowboy to be my private tutor. I met him daily before shooting in a huge empty hall. Patient to a fault, my poker-faced teacher showed me how to snap the whip while tracing circles and figure eights in the air. I ached so badly after these rehearsals that I could hardly lift Niko when I came home at night. But in the face of imminent paralysis of my right arm, I slowly became competent, if not expert.

Completing my first task satisfactorily, I had another Donen inspiration to perform. This time he wanted me to jump to the floor from the top of a six-foot armoire.

"You must be crazy," I yelped. "You've been working with Gene Kelly too long. I've just had a baby!"

Stanley must have been disappointed to see his brainstorm rejected, but he saw my point. I think the replacement for that was a "dramatic touch." I tried at least twenty-four times to cast the whip out so that the end coiled around a beam in the ceiling. Letting go of the handle, I had to prowl around the dangling whip and "look sexy"!

Shooting began on my one scene. The director, Laszlo Benedek, was very matter-of-fact.

"Now, Sono, play the guitar, walk down the steps, and look sexy."

Fingering the instrument as I'd been shown how to, I started down the long flight of stairs. Each step was so shallow that, in order to walk, I had to turn my feet out in first position. "Gliding" down the stairs I felt like a waddling duck.

"Go back," cried Laszlo. "Do it again. Look sexy."

I went back. I picked at the guitar and dutifully waddled down the steps. This time I reached the fifth step, and Robert Surtees, the cinematographer, called out, "Wait a minute. There's a shadow on the wall. Better go back." I went back.

Somehow I reached the bottom of the steps. Then I had to dance. There seemed to be endless interruptions and interminable waiting around. Every day brought the same problems. The cameras were lined up to photograph me on certain chalk marks that I couldn't find in the glare of the lights. We stopped. We started. Waiting for the cameras to be rearranged, I wasn't permitted to sit down because my costume would wrinkle. Instead, between takes, I leaned against a contraption like an upright ironing board with arms. My muscles were stone cold from waiting.

We started again. Even my costume seemed to conspire against me. It was a bright profusion of color, with layers of real petticoats, tight sleeves with rows of tiny gold buttons, and dozens of silk ribbons fluttering from my hair. Once I began spinning, the petticoats took over and I couldn't stop. I reclined some more. When I whipped my head in the "passionate" dance, my hair caught in the buttons on the sleeves. The ribbons flew in my face. I couldn't draw a deep breath. "Look sexy!" yelled Laszlo. "Hit your chalk marks!"

At the end of the dance, Donen told me to snake the whip out so it wrapped around Frank, pinning him to his chair. After my first attempt, Laszlo excused Frank from the shot and called for his stand-in. Frank was too valuable a property to subject to target practice.

The petticoats and I spun some more. I reclined some more. People patted at my makeup every two minutes. Surtees rechecked the lights. I hunted for my chalk marks.

Finally, we got to the end of the dance. Frank sat down at a big wooden table with a branched candlebrum before him. Stanley told me to drape myself provocatively across the table and slowly pinch out each of the candles, one by one. When I did, blisters formed immediately on my bare fingertips. Makeup people came running with bits of adhesive tape and flesh-colored pancake.

"Do it again," cried Laszlo, "Not so fast! Look *sexy!*"

Hollywood was not all bullwhips, chalk marks, pinching candles, and looking sexy. Life at the Kellys' was friendly and informal, with Sunday-afternoon volleyball games in the backyard. Gene unwound from the rigors of his heavy shooting schedule by playing as fiercely as Victor, director Nicholas Ray, Peter Lawford, and Stanley Donen. I was usually done in from looking sexy, so I stretched out under an avocado tree with Niko and talked to John Garfield, sweet and unaffected as he was talented.

Late in our stay, we rented the home of composer Saul Chaplin. To show our appreciation of our friends' kind hospitality, we threw a big, inelegant "swap party," asking each guest to bring along something old but still usable to swap. Edward G. Robinson traded a china platter for Cary Grant's suede jacket, brought by producer Norman Panama. Sporting his bargain on his back, Robinson crawled under the piano to talk to Sam Jaffe for the rest of the evening. Our guests haggled over the collection of odds and ends with the cunning of Arab traders until the room had been picked clean. When nothing was left but Saul Chaplin's own furniture, he sat down at the piano with a laugh, as if to protect it. We ended the evening with a medley of tunes by Cole Porter, George Gershwin, and Harold Arlen.

Away from the studio I found much of Hollywood, except for our immediate friends, as far removed from my experience as the film set was. We went to several parties where the conversation centered around grosses and percentages and the subject of who was working and who wasn't. Those who weren't hardly spoke and seemed uncomfortable and embarrassed, as if disgraced. Even taking a stroll in Beverly Hills was unlike walking in any other town. Policemen in patrol cars would follow Victor and me for several blocks and invariably stop us to ask where we were going.

We left Hollywood in July 1947, agreeing that despite everything it had been worthwhile. Victor had decided to go into the import-export business with his father, and Niko was plump and tan. I was exhausted and relieved that it was all over. California was pleasant, with its palm trees swaying, sun shining, and balmy breezes blowing, but I felt that one day was just like the next and life there could become numbingly languorous. I returned to my beloved Manhattan, no longer ignorant of film-making. It had been a tedious, frustrating experience. Although I have enormous respect for the people who create art and entertainment through technological means, it was not the life for me.

The life that I felt *was* for me was to stay at home with my husband and baby and to go to an occasional dance class. Months passed without a hint of the urge to perform, until the following spring, when I was asked to appear in an Off-Broadway show. I jumped at the chance.

Ballet Ballads, produced and lit for ANTA's Experimental Theatre by Nat Carson, was a complete change of pace for me. The three separate works in one evening, written by John LaTouche and composer Jerome Moross, relied exclusively on music and dance to develop each section. The first, "Susanna and the Elders," was a Bible Belt revival-meeting version of the Biblical story, choreographed by, and featuring, that beautiful blonde modern dancer Katherine Litz. The third piece, considered by most critics to be the best, was Hanya Holm's "The Eccentricities of Davey Crockett." I was featured as Cocaine Lil in the second ballad, "Willie the Weeper," choreographed and danced by Paul Godkin.

Paul had to conceive and structure seven episodes of the "dreamy triumphs and desolate awakenings" in the "untidy mind" of Willie, the reefer-ridden folk-blues hero. As the low-down, seductive episode in his dreams, I tried to give what I imagined to be the slow, smoky motion of a cocaine addict. I moved deliberately, without sharpness or precision, behind the Jerome Moross music some writers referred to as a "boogie-woogie bacchanale." My costume emphasized the image of the tawdry temptress—fishnet stockings, a tight-fitting dark-greenish leotard, skimpy black tulle ruffles at the hip, a rose dangerously close to the groin, and a clump of droopy, pale-pink feathers at the shoulder. At one point I paused, posed with my hands on my hips hitched provocatively to one side, and watched as Willie reached desperately and pleadingly towards me. My answer was a blank stare and a disdainful puff of air out of the side of my mouth that set the thin, dreary feathers wafting shabbily over my shoulder.

The set, which was used in different arrangements for all three pieces, consisted almost entirely of huge units of stairs. My entrance was a slow descent down one of them towards Willie. An additional theatrical device came near the end of the number, when a large sailing-ship rigging was lowered onto the stage and Willie climbed yearningly over it to reach me. Murky lighting enhanced the drug-induced atmosphere. Though bright spotlights focused on Paul and me, the semidarkness around us altered our sense of space. It made moving in a drowsy, almost floating state even more natural, as the chorus urged us on with "Give me a little love / while my hands are still warm. / I crave affection / in a not too simple form."

Unlike a big-budget Broadway show, we opened after a short rehearsal period and no out-of-town tryouts at Maxine Elliott's Theatre on May 9, 1948. The night of the opening, and for every night of the run, I had to warm up longer than I had had to on a winter night in Butte, Montana, for three ballets. I wanted my body to be so limber that I could move almost like glue.

Coming at the end of what was considered a poor Broadway season, critics came prepared for the worst. But despite slight variations in opinion as to which of the three ballads was the most successful, the show as a whole was truly a hit. It proved so popular that we soon moved uptown to the Music Box Theatre for a Broadway run. I realized more than ever that the theatre was my first love. Despite the limited resources available for *Ballet Ballads*, it was a totally fulfilling experience for me. This struck me even more sharply several months later when I read the reviews of *The Kissing Bandit*, which opened that November.

In the *New York Herald Tribune*, Otis L. Guernsey called *The Kissing Bandit* a "grand technicolored vacuum" that "falls as flat as a bad joke with a big build-up." Crowther in the *Times* said the film was "a bleak and barren burlesque" with nothing wrong with it that Gilbert and Sullivan couldn't have cured. Although I had found film-making unrewarding and frustrating, I must admit that there was a certain satisfaction in reading that the dance sequences (which included Ann Miller, Cyd Charisse, and Ricardo Montalban) were called "the best footage in the show" by Guernsey, and Crowther said, "Sono Osato comes through with the spirited Spanish dance ['Look *sexy!*'] in the one opportunity she has."

Victor was now firmly established in the import-export business with his father and several relatives and friends, and he found out at this time that he had to go abroad on business. The trip would take several months, and I had no intention of staying behind. I gave my notice and left *Ballet Ballads*.

We drove, with an overpacked car, slowly from Le Havre to Paris, where we stayed at the Hotel Brighton. Outside Lyons we reached a crisis in space and finally sent some luggage on to Morocco by air. In Barcelona we stayed at the Hotel Oriente on the Ramblas, which was less grand than I remembered it from my Ballet Russe days, and I saw Los Caracoles again, this time with Victor. Surrounded by oppressive poverty and incessant heat, with intermittent battles with bedbugs, we made it through Spain and finally reached Morocco. Our months there were highlighted by watching Niko stand transfixed as he stared through the gates of our rented villa at passing camels, a near life-and-death struggle between our Arab cook and gardener over a bicycle, and a remarkable belly dancer, whose movements reminded me of Fokine's choreography in *Prince Igor*.

In November we returned to Paris and spent many evenings in the company of friends like Robert Capa, David Seymour, Irwin and Marian Shaw, John Huston, Yul Brynner, and Claude Dauphin. To keep warm and physically conditioned that winter, I started taking ballet classes at the Salle Wacker, close to the Boulevard de Clichy and the hotels where I had lived as a teen-ager. Class was harder for me than it had ever been. For a fleeting moment, I feared its cause was not the cold but a slipping away of years of acquired technique. But propped against the barre and breathing hard halfway through class, I paid more attention to the other students than to myself. Alexandre Kalioujny, premier danseur of the Paris Opera, displayed incredible elevation but seemed to be having a great deal of trouble with his double air turns to the left. The more he practiced them, the less he accomplished and the more frustrated he became. I thought of my double pirouettes as the Lilac Fairy, knowing too well what insurmountable difficulties the mind can impose on the body.

I glanced from Ludmilla Tcherina, the dark beauty who spent as much time admiring herself in the mirror as working on combinations, to the dancer who interested me the most. She was a small, striking girl with long, shapely legs, who wore her hair cropped like a boy's. Unlike Tcherina, Zizi was totally absorbed in her work. I later saw her in Roland Petit's *Carmen*, which put her name, Renée Jeanmaire, on the lips of every ballet-goer who had seen her incredible performance.

It was wonderful to be back in Paris after so long, but the winter was bitterly cold and Niko was constantly sick. When his temperature shot up to 105 degrees, the only remedy the French doctor would recommend was cupping, the medieval practice of applying heated glass cups, *"les ventouses,"* to the skin. We tracked down a more modern doctor, and by the time Niko's health had improved, spring had come, and Victor and I had decided to go home.

t had never been our intention to have just one child, so Victor and I were thrilled when I became pregnant a few months after we returned to New York. I was so excited about becoming a mother for the second time that I dispensed altogether with ballet classes and started instruction in the then-new concept of natural childbirth. But I never experienced the joy I anticipated from having a natural birth, because late in my pregnancy complications developed.

Early in the eighth month of pregnancy, I was in the middle of dinner with some friends when I began to hemorrhage so badly that I became frightened. My doctor, Norman Pleshette, diagnosed the condition almost on the spot as *placenta previa*, and I was rushed to the hospital, where I had to remain completely at rest under observation for almost ten days. And after that I had to stay in the house, absolutely still. About a week later, despite the rest, I began to hemorrhage again. This time Dr. Pleshette decided it would be dangerous to wait any longer. He prescribed a Cesarean section, and on the beautiful warm afternoon of June 15, 1950, at 4:35 P.M., I heard the first cry of our second son, Tony, as he was lifted into the world.

Tony was as beautiful as Niko but plumper and infinitely more energetic. Ever since his birth, Niko had been calm and self-possessed. But we soon saw that Tony couldn't bear any kind of confinement. Once he could walk, he'd scramble out of the sandpile in Central Park and strike out alone for his favorite spot, the seal pond.

There was suddenly a great deal of scattered activity in my life, between the grocer and the laundry, the teething and the roseola, the dancing and the acting—so much activity that, looking back, I find the specific sequence of events blurred in my mind. Subconsciously, I had become very greedy. I wanted everything—to be the loving, devoted wife and the perfect mother, and to continue a successful and rewarding career in the theatre. I overestimated my own strength and ability to juggle all the elements of my life. But that was not immediately clear to me. What *had* become clear was that, at thirty, I found my body no longer the flexible instrument it had been, largely because daily practice had long since been out of the question. Because I was unwilling to give up performing, I turned more and more to acting, which, for me, required less physical discipline.

That was why, surprisingly soon after Tony's birth, in the winter of 1950, I accepted an offer to appear as Anitra in the ANTA production of Henrik Ibsen's *Peer Gynt*, produced by Cheryl Crawford, with John Garfield in the title role. In addition to John, the production had a large cast of extraordinarily talented and dedicated actors—Mildred Dunnock, Ray Gordon, Pearl Lang, Karl Malden, and Nehemiah Persoff—theatrical choreography by Valerie Bettis, and the promise of brilliant direction from Lee Strasberg.

My initial enthusiasm for the venture dwindled rapidly at the first gathering of the cast. Reputedly at the forefront of the intellectual vanguard of the American theatre, Strasberg, with the model of Donald Oenslager's exciting set design at his side, gave such a long-winded and esoteric dissertation on the play that after a while I didn't understand a word he was saying. The rest of the cast, being experienced in Method acting, seemed to hang on his every word. I think I was the only non-Method actor in the production, including Sheree Britton, the famous stripper, who was not a Strasberg disciple but obviously had her own "method."

Valerie Bettis, the choreographer, gave us lively directions much easier to respond to. The scene in which I appeared took place outside the tent of an Arab sheik in an oasis and came in Act Four. Pillows came hurtling onstage as the scene began. Two men carried a litter on which I sat, eating grapes and spitting out the seeds. "Remember you're desert rats," Valerie would say to us. The image was perfect for the mangy characterizations called for in this version. I swirled around in a few enticing steps, then threw myself on the floor at Garfield's feet. To the accompaniment of two Israeli musicians, Hillel and Aviva, in the seduction scene, I rolled around with John on the floor until I landed on top of him, laughing.

John Garfield brought his own warm, unaffected directness to his acting. I loved him as a person and admired his courage in returning to the legitimate theatre in such a difficult classic role, especially after having established himself in a great screen career as, more times than not, a "down-to-earth" guy.

We opened in January 1951 to predictably mixed reviews. The consensus was that Oenslager's sets and John Garfield's performance were the dominant virtues of the production. The other actors were given passing credit for helping to bring the production to life. "Some other good actors have worked hard to find the genius of Ibsen's drama," said Brooks Atkinson in *The New York Times*, and on his list was "Sono Osato who has found a place in the desert for a brief dance."

Perhaps *Peer Gynt* is an "unproducible" play. Even the producer, Cheryl Crawford, considered it as such in retrospect. However, it was a noble experiment in quality nonprofit theatre, one of the last produced by ANTA in the early fifties. We closed after thirty-two performances.

Although I was more at ease in the dancing part of my role in *Peer Gynt* than in the acting, I realized that family obligations would continue to prevent me from a rigorous schedule of dance classes to maintain the necessary physical shape. I also knew that I would certainly never again be a member of a ballet company. Still, I felt I could keep up the roles of wife and mother and performer in the theatre. I was still self-conscious as an actress, but because I felt it was the direction my career should take, I began to take acting classes.

I studied briefly with Uta Hagen, whose intense yet open enthusiasm almost forced you to come out of yourself. Rehearsing at home for a scene in Uta's acting class, I would often be interrupted by Niko wandering into the room and saying, "Mom, why are you talking so loud?"

Daniel Mann, the director, asked me to participate in classes at the Actors' Studio, the mecca of the American Theatre. The Actors' Studio was supposed to be a place in which to experiment, to free yourself, to fall on your face; but I had rarely witnessed such a total group inhibition, a fear best exemplified in my memory by a class where the students were asked to feel "wanting each other." The men on one side, women on the other, seemed so terrified that they could only raise their outstretched arms in front of them and march towards each other like zombies.

I sat intimidated for many weeks along with my friend Elliot Reid, neither of us feeling ready for Shakespeare or Clifford Odets. Finally we felt there was no sense continuing on as voyeurs, so we decided to dig up the nerve to plunge in. Elliot wrote a sketch for us in which a great ballerina is dressed down by her less talented partner for failing an important audition. Elliot, a master of several languages and a brilliant creator of character, wrote the scene in Russian and broken English. Time came for our scene. We got on the little Actors' Studio stage before the critical eyes of our fellow students, and I got such stage fright that I didn't recognize Elliot when he made his entrance.

Confused at first by the Russian language, the observers began to chuckle a bit when the scene lapsed into the heavily accented English. There was mild applause at the end, but, being a dancer, I was unaccustomed to being judged by my peers. I welcomed the criticism of a choreographer or a director but felt fellow actors could not be impartial and view another's performance without being subjective. The tense aura of the place was just too uncomfortable for me to learn how to easily "fall on my face."

I looked for classes that were smaller and more relaxed. I found them with Martin Ritt. In my classes with him were John Baragrey, John Newland, Robert Webber, and Felicia Bernstein, known to American audiences as Felicia Montealegre, one of the most gifted actresses in the early years of live television drama.

Ritt's classes began with physical exercise, limbering up to lessen tension. We were asked to choose and become animals we felt we resembled. I remember John Baragrey prancing around the room as a horse, while I was a squirrel busy storing nuts for the winter. After warming up, we were given situations for improvisation. Ritt asked Felicia and me to be rival actresses after the same job. Before I knew what was happening, Felicia launched into an impassioned attack, insinuating that I would get the role because of my relationship with the director. "There's no use hiding it," she said with great dignity in her low, musical voice. "You'll get this part because you're *sleeping* with him!"

I was so awed by the power of this delicate, cameolike beauty that

I became totally convinced. All I could muster up in self-defense was a weak "That's not *true!*"

"Sono," Ritt interjected, "you're letting Felicia run away with this scene. What are you *doing?*" But I admired Felicia's skill so much that it hampered my own ability to enter fully into the exercise.

In his classes Martin Ritt created an atmosphere of consideration and workmanship. The intimacy of the group and Ritt's direct, positive criticism, aimed never at the personality but at the work at hand, provided the kind of support needed for me, at least, to feel ready to free myself in acting.

After a while a friend who knew I was concentrating on a dramatic career submitted my name to a major network to be considered for a role in a television drama. The prospect of breaking into TV was really tempting, considering the caliber of live video presentations in the early fifties. Of course that time also saw the United States, so soon after the disaster of World War II, dragged into another war in Korea. The fear of Fascism had been exchanged for the fear of Communism. Nationwide paranoia, focused by McCarthyism, pervaded every corner of society, and the theatre was certainly not left unscathed.

Aware as everyone was of the climate of fright and suspicion, few people, I think, felt it would ever touch them personally. The forties and early fifties were a time of "causes," and because I believed in alleviating human suffering, I lent my name and support to a number of them. Mixed in with discussions of liberal humanistic views were rampant leftist opinions, especially in intellectual and artistic circles, but public declarations of Communist affiliation were unheard of. Everyone moved in a kind of haze with the facts veiled, leaving anyone suspect. My friend in television called me one day. "Your name has come back with a line through it." Like many, many others in the theatre, I was blacklisted. I was just another one of the thousands, labeled by unseen forces, who had no recourse from possible and probable damage to their personal and professional reputations. This was the second time that I had been personally affected by the fear of Communism, and times had definitely changed for the worse.

In the forties theatre people were continually asked to sign petitions, perform at benefits, and speak in favor of humanitarian causes, especially those dedicated to fighting Fascism. One of the greatest causes at the time was the Spanish Refugee Appeal. Fleeing Franco's Spain to France, two hundred thousand refugees had remained there in destitution throughout the war. The deprivation was so great that most were left in rags and had to wrap their babies in newspapers. The appeal was for immediate and much-needed aid from the American public.

A large rally for the Spanish Refugee Appeal was held at Madison Square Garden in September 1945, and I, along with four other performers in Broadway shows, was asked to appear. Margo (A Bell for Adano), Jean Darling (Carousel), David Brooks (Bloomer Girl), Luba Malina (Marinka), and I (On the Town) all said a few words of support, then left for our respective shows at eight. Only later did we learn that more than an hour later a speech by Professor Harold J. Laski, a British Labour Party leader, referring critically to the role of the Catholic Church and the Vatican in Spain, was piped into the meeting.

Two days later an interview by Howard Rushmore with Frank Fay of Harvey appeared in the Journal-American. In the piece Fay called for a full-scale inquiry into our rights to appear at a "Communist-backed rally." I was walking to the theatre that day when someone I knew stopped me, saying, "Did you see what Frank Fay said about you in the Journal-American?"

"What are you talking about?"

"That you're a Communist!"

I was shocked. Similar confrontations to Margo, David Brooks, and the others made it clear that the situation was untenable. We appealed for a hearing at Actors Equity. Before the meeting of the Equity Council took place a month later, the five of us experienced unbelievable repercussions. Margo was accosted on Fifth Avenue and spat on; anonymous phone callers to Jean Darling and her mother threatened to cut their throats; Luba Malina was called a "dirty Russian Spanish Communist," was punched in the ribs, and had her life threatened; and David Brooks received menacing mail. Anonymous phone calls late at night had me terribly frightened. I received letters such as, "I understand you're part Japanese. Does that yellow streak account for your anti-Catholicism? Jap or no Jap, you're distinctly un-American." These things and pickets at the various theatres unnerved me so much that I missed two performances of *On the Town*. All of our shows were threatened with boycotts, and for several weeks we needed bodyguards to escort us from our homes to our dressing rooms and back.

Before the final meeting of the Equity membership, which, after great internal furor, censured Frank Fay by a vote of 470 to 72, we were subjected to such harassment that all of our performances began to show visible strain. However, the support of the Equity membership proved that we had recourse through democratic means.

The blacklist of the fifties was another story. Unable to alter judgment on their professional desirability, many performers, I among them, found work Off-Broadway. Because Off-Broadway was primarily the place where independent individuals presented experimental productions, with the artists receiving little and sometimes practically no pay, these theatres were not subject to the same restrictions as the commercial ones on Broadway.

Therese Hayden had assembled a fine repertory group of wonderful talents such as Patricia Neal, Eli Wallach, Kay Medford, Frank Corsaro, Richard Waring, Mark Rydell, and Susan Strasberg, and she asked me to join them. Terry's idea was to present four different plays in four weeks at the Theatre de Lys in Greenwich Village. I appeared in the first play, *Maya*, and the last, *The Little Clay Cart*.

Maya, by Simon Gantillon, was a series of vignettes about a Marseille prostitute, featuring Helen Craig, Martin Ritt, Leo Penn, and the thirteen-year-old Susan Strasberg. I was Ida, the "self-centered hoyden" (according to Walter Kerr). I remember little of the play itself, but I have vivid memories of rehearsing lines in the alley and jamming into tiny dressing rooms with walls so thin that, if you spoke up, you could be heard in the back row of the audience. Costume budgets were small, to say the least, so I wore a pair of Moroccan slippers I had bought for myself in Casablanca. For me, there was a vague semblance of being back in the ballet, where the variety of the repertoire had actors rushing from rehearsing major to minor roles on the same day.

"Ascribed to King Shidraka" and translated by Arthur William Ryder, *The Little Clay Cart* was an ancient Hindu fantasy about a poverty-stricken prince, a courtesan, a burglar, a jewel theft, a rainstorm, mistaken identity, and a last-minute rescue. In the short time we had to rehearse, we aimed at a serene mixture of pantomimed gesture, such as opening imaginary doors, and refined, stylized speech. Again, the tiny production budget called for a wealth of imagination, and, from cut-out beer-can tops fluttering from suspended coat-hangers, William and Jean Eckart created one of the most enchanting evocations of a forest that I had ever seen.

Opening-night jitters over yet another performing experience were magnified for me by a broken-down air-conditioning system in the theatre on the last, steaming night of June 1953. Facing the audience seated in the blackness and fanning themselves furiously with rustling programs, I felt as if I were playing to a dark house of frantically flying seagulls.

Perhaps the rest of the cast was as disconcerted as I, for many critics felt that the play, though charming, lacked a certain vitality. But Brooks Atkinson praised Richard Waring for his performance and was very appreciative of mine as Vasantesena: "Sono Osato is extraordinarily beautiful; and from the way in which she moves about the stage, you know how all the other actors should walk and dance. Everybody should be an accomplished dancer for a play of this sort. Gorgeously caparisoned in Eastern dress, Miss Osato gives a perfectly designed performance." Still, he reminded me of the same fault I had exhibited since my first speaking role in On the Town. "It is deficient only in speech, which is casual and unfinished," he continued, and then, with remarkable gentleness for a critic, went on, "Speak up, Sono, dear. You've got something very special in your performance."

Special or not, my performances at the Theatre de Lys were over by July, and I was left with finding yet another project. In what I initially thought would be an interim period between shows, I had time to weigh my situation more carefully than before. Unlike many other performers whose careers were seriously and sometimes tragically crippled by the loathsome political spirit of the times, I fortunately had my husband and family and was not dependent on the theatre to live. Besides, I still thought of my real self as the dancer, not the actress, and it was obvious that dancing had passed me by. I began to realize that it was impossible to have everything and saw that Victor, Niko, now six, and Tony, three, would suffer if I continued to have one foot in the theatre and the other at home. On my way out the door to *Clay Cart* rehearsals, I would look at my two boys and ask myself, "How important can what I'm doing be?" Possibly some women can deal with the visceral guilt in leaving at home those who love and need them and whom they love and need, but I couldn't. I decided my family would be the center of my life.

Watching Niko and Tony grow gave me a new kind of joy. But at the same time I became slowly aware of how completely cut off I was from other people. Life in dancing and the theatre had been almost communal, an environment of constant activity, stimulation, and companionship. There was no denying that, by comparison, the repetition of household chores became confining and boring.

I used to bathe the boys together just before their dinner. One day I felt a strange tingling in my body, like a wave of infinitesimal tremors. It passed quickly as I dried the boys, sat them down to eat, and watched—fascinated by their healthy appetites and boundless energy. But the next night the sensation, like a rustling of leaves under my skin, returned. It wasn't an unpleasant feeling, just unsettling. For months it returned every night, just as I soaped their firm, smooth bodies and watched them splashing and giggling with their rubber ducks in the tub.

Finally I understood. It was five o'clock pre-performance anticipation, the last holdover from twenty years of habit—my body was reminding me that I should soon be leaving for the theatre. As long as it persisted, I thought less of the fun I associated with bath time and more and more of the world outside. But the love I felt for Victor and the boys was irresistible, and I willingly stuck by my decision to live in a new kind of world. Without the stimulation of theatrical life and an outlet for self-expression, I tried to channel my frustrations into activities Tony and Niko would enjoy. I had no time to take class, but when the urge to dance became overpowering, I danced with the boys. Tony loved to sit on my hip as I waltzed him around the living room. Niko begged me to whirl faster and faster, and made himself dizzy with floppy imitations of my tours en l'air.

For several years Mother had been living in Greenwich, Connecticut, earning her living by making and designing clothes. With her innate artistry and knack for making something beautiful out of relatively little, she had created an ambiance of elegance in her apartment with a few Japanese screens, some plants, and simple furniture. Once a month I would take the boys to visit their grandmother. Under the appearance of enjoying ourselves on picnics or at pony rides with the children, I realized that after all these years, I still felt physically and emotionally uncomfortable with Mother. Yet at the same time I admired the kind of pride and courage it took for her to decide to live alone in such meager circumstances without making any demands for assistance on her children.

About this time, I found out that Mother was seriously ill. She too had developed cancer. As with Teru, I was overcome by Mother's stoicism, completely undone by her ability to face the terror of her illness. Listening to her tell, with characteristic candor, the details of the many depersonalizing treatments she was undergoing for possible cures, I was horrified and blocked out much of what I heard. By the time she had to be hospitalized, it was early spring 1954. Every day as I drove up to the hospital to see her, I resented the fact that the sun was shining and the grass was growing while my mother was dying. I was so terrified of facing that fact that, as a protection, I convinced myself I should let her spend her last hours with Tim, with whom she shared a very special love. I sat in a daze watching Montgomery Clift and Maureen Stapleton in Chekhov's *The Sea Gull* when Mother died in May.

Tim surely felt great anguish at Mother's death, but I hope his pain was alleviated somewhat by an important opportunity in his already impressive career. Since the end of the war, Tim had graduated magna cum laude from Yale, married, received a master's degree from Columbia, served for a year in three major capacities with the 3rd Infantry Division in the Korean conflict, received a master of public administration degree from Harvard, and been appointed Assistant Professor of Social Sciences in Modern European, Far Eastern, and Southeast Asian History at West Point. Less than a week after Mother died, Tim was selected for temporary duty with the Department of State as an observer with General Van Fleet's SEATO mission in Southeast Asia. I had always been proud of Tim's remarkable intellectual and military achievements. Now I was very grateful that they could occupy his time and thoughts during a time of painful adjustment.

Early in Mother's illness I had begun to have severe headaches. They persisted after her death, and intensified when we learned that now Father was ill in Chicago. I went to see him in the Salvation Army hospital there several times. On one of those visits I rented a room in the same hospital. For the first time in my life I was surrounded by devastating age, loneliness, and senility. Through the night I was awakened by a man yelling, somewhere in the darkness, "Oh, my God! Oh, my God!" The next morning, on my way to see Father, I saw an old woman strapped to a wheelchair, chanting, "I want to go home. I want to go home."

"Nurse, that lady wants to go home," I said, edging towards the desk.

"Ignore it, miss. She's got no place to go," she said, tapping her temple knowingly.

Father's spirit had been shattered by the separation from Mother, his incarceration, and two strokes. Although I had spent most of the past twenty years away from my home and parents, I had always felt a closeness and special empathy for my father. I knew with Father, as I had never felt with Mother, that he was proud of me. I also identified with his being a nonverbal person who guarded his innermost feelings. Now I was so riddled with confusion over what I could do to ease his pain that I could hardly focus on what it was that was causing his final illness. On one of my visits to him, Father wept. It was the strongest external sign of emotion I had ever seen from him.

We talked about Mother and, amazingly, there was not a hint of reproach or bitterness about their tortured relationship. He never explained, nor do I even now understand, what it was that kept them "together" all that time. Perhaps it was some inexplicable kind of commitment to a decision once made, whatever the consequences; or it may simply have been the most simple explanation, yet the most difficult bond to describe—love between two people.

Father survived Mother by nearly a year. Once again in the spring, I lost a parent.

My headaches, the result of suppressed grief, guilt, stress, and rage, continued. Although I didn't dare articulate it, even to myself, for fear of feeling guilty towards Victor and my boys, deep inside me I yearned to be an adolescent in the corps de ballet again. There, hard physical work, with no other responsibilities, resulted in applause. But there was no applause for raising children, keeping a house, or watching your parents die. You don't get applause for living your life. Eventually I had to face this *and* the fact that I couldn't have both loves, my family and the theatre, and still function. But before I could come to any firm resolve, I was asked to appear in not one, but two Off-Broadway revues at the same time. I had to decide between the Phoenix Theatre production of *Phoenix '55*, starring my dear friend Nancy Walker, and an offer to work with Zero Mostel and Jack Gilford. I accepted Stanley Prager's offer to be featured with Mostel and Gilford. This revue was not your heaviest piece of theatre. In fact, it was so light it had to be called *Once Over Lightly*.

During the rehearsal period it became evident that there was very little material to work with. Without a book or score to cling to, the various elements of a revue—songs, dances, skits—have to be carefully balanced. We worked very hard with the material at hand and tried our own improvisations and inventions as well. Jack Gilford worked on a hilarious skit about a wine-making monk who gets stinking drunk. The three of us tried, unsuccessfully, to present a lopsided view of the classic film *Rashomon*. And I had, for my "big moment," a dance choreographed by Lee Becker to some experimental atonal music suited to a recital at the New School for Social Research. After one rehearsal with that music, I almost had convulsions. "No, no, no, *no!*" I said, shaking my head. "I will not *do* that!" The artistic moment was o-u-t.

Something had to replace the dance. Soon Marshall Barer and Dean Fuller, two young contributors to the show, came up with the idea of my doing a version of *Peter Pan* Kabuki-style, with me switching character from Peter, to Wendy, to Captain Hook. As usual I came up with my own costume. I thought a slight touch of the Oriental theatre was needed, so I wore a brightly flowered short kimono, black tights, and black sneakers. Lee devised a delightful number. I loved manipulating fans and doing mincing little pigeon-toed steps as Wendy, bouncing and cock-a-doodle-do-ing around as Peter, and jutting out my chin, crossing my eyes, and stomping all over the stage as Captain Hook.

Meanwhile Zero was stomping around in rehearsals as a petulant child in a miniature operetta about the making of Kreplach, or practicing a ballad by the great Alec Wilder. But the true *pièce de résistance* was a skit for all three of us written by Melvin Brooks, who was then a little less known than he is now. The one hit of the show, it was a zany but touching vignette. In it I played an alley cat whose mother had just been run over by a Chock Full O' Nuts truck and was now hopelessly enamored of an obstreperous stray dog, howled, growled, whoofed, panted, and ogled by Zero. Jack was a gentle squirrel, stoically bearing near-starvation because people in Central Park wouldn't feed him nuts. The philosopher of the piece, Jack tried to explain to us why our love was doomed. Despite all his explanations and warnings about an affair between a cat and a dog, we refused to relinquish our love. "All right," declared Zero, my canine lover, at the close of the skit, "if they won't have us here, we can go to France to live!"

This was something we felt we could really sink our teeth into, throwing ourselves with abandon into rehearsals, and sure that this skit would strengthen the show—until the day the author came to see what was happening to his creation. After an especially energetic rehearsal in one of the lobbies of the Barbizon Plaza, where the show would run, we stood like self-satisfied children waiting for Daddy's approval. Melvin turned to our director, "Stash" Prager (a gifted comedian in his own right), and announced, "He's shit, she's shit, and he's shit!"

"How *dare* you say that about my actors!" yelled Stash into Melvin's face. The two stood chin to chin, screaming in rage, Stash's elbows twitching up and down like pistons. The three of us sat blankly, like spectators at a fierce Ping-Pong match, until Jack's eyelids began to quiver, I sank back in my seat, and Zero's huge eyeballs bulged. Just as it seemed that Mel and Stash were coming to blows, we began to titter and finally howl with laughter over the absurdity of the whole scene.

Although we never achieved the Actors' Studio interpretation the author had in mind, we continued rehearsing. The day of the opening we had our last long, strenuous run-through, but without feeling much optimism. Mel was there again, and this time, without warning us, he launched into an extemporaneous one-man operetta version of *Anna Karenina*, complete with howling wolves chasing Anna in her troika across the frozen steppes of Russia. He reduced the entire cast to hysterics.

"Mel," I said, laughing, with tears in my eyes, "*you* go on. You'll be a bigger hit than we ever will."

We opened without *Anna* à la Brooks in March 1955. Every review was as kind as possible, crediting the cast for at least trying very hard. It was summed up by Walter Kerr in the *Herald Tribune*. In a long review that seemed funnier in spots than some of the material we had to work with, he concluded: "What hurts *Once Over Lightly* is the fact that it comes from the trunk—and the moths have been there first."

Sometimes the audiences were so small, scattered aimlessly throughout the little theatre, that I felt like stopping and saying, "Folks, would you all mind sitting together so we can play to one group?" Not foreseeing a long run, I felt I should have the boys see me onstage, now that they were old enough (eight and five). At the last curtain call I bowed only to them. Niko looked shyly down at his lap in embarrassment. Tony, however, poked his neighbor in the ribs and announced in a loud voice, "That's my Mom!"

Those were the last moments I spent on the stage for twenty years.

T hat last statement was true in terms of my own reality, which, until I had married, had been the ballet and the theatre. Then, for over ten years, I led a double life of two realities, the theatre and my family, and each satisfied me. But after *Once Over Lightly*, the professional engagements came farther apart, and the few television and summer-stock jobs I got were far less rewarding and real to me than my earlier career on the stage had been. Frankly, I thought even less of television work than I had of film-making, and I undoubtedly felt this way to a certain extent because my physical appearance, scrutinized by the closeness of the television camera, limited the types of roles I could play in a way that the theatre, with its ability to create illusion, never had.

But even on the stage in summer stock, I still felt less an actress than a dancer. I might have pursued acting more, but it was a medium in which I was far less secure than dancing, and in my late thirties the drive to train myself as an actress with the same ardor and passion with which I had become a dancer just wasn't there. Also by that time, handling my private life while pursuing a career had sapped me of the energy I might otherwise have had.

Even greater than the question of having enough energy was the question of having enough confidence. Confidence comes from practice, from constant performing night after night. You instinctively learn and make discoveries about performing *while* performing. If you don't continually practice your skill, you not only get rusty, you begin to lose confidence. So as time passed, with whatever small things I did do professionally, the doubts and fears became far greater than the rewards. But as late as the 1960's, Harvey Orkin, my agent, *and* a great fan of mine, was eager to revive my "career." He had heard that the producers of *Camelot* were looking for someone to play the as yet undefined role of Morgan le Fay. He thought I would be perfect for the part and said I should audition for the show.

I had never really auditioned for anything in my career on the stage. Three minutes of dancing backstage for the colonel had started my professional life at fourteen. I had gone from the Ballet Russe to Ballet Theatre to Broadway without the kind of auditioning that thousands of actresses have to endure as a way of life. Being a member of a ballet company, a dancer does not get used to failure. There is a certain security in ballet that is unknown in theatre. If a ballet fails, there will be a new ballet, and you continue to work on your craft by dancing in the classical repertoire. But in the theatre it is difficult to perfect your skill if there is no work, and even when there is, you must compete against anything from a few to hundreds of other performers trying to convince the producers that each one alone is right for one role. Few theatre people have the good fortune that I had had in stepping from one hit into another with *Venus* and *On the Town*. So it was not in my experience to audition, and at this point in my life it was nearly unbearable.

But I went to the Adelphi Theatre to audition for *Camelot*—and waited in the very dressing room I had had in *On the Town*! The irony was almost too much, and the idea of having to audition unnerved me even more. As I walked onto the stage, I realized that I had lost so much confidence that I felt more terrified than I had as a child when I forgot my Shepherd's dance in Milwaukee's Pabst Theatre. Moss Hart and Hanya Holm sat alone in the orchestra and asked me if I could sing. Petrified, I sat down under a work light, stared out into the semi-dark cavern of the theatre, closed my eyes, and sang "Au Claire de la Lune" in French. "Thank you very much," they said, and I didn't get the part.

After that experience, the idea of having to prove my talent again and again became so distressing that I was absolutely unable to audition. My pride simply could not bear the process of selection that might lead to humiliating rejection. I think now that if I had had only to dance, I might have done anything gladly. But for acting I lacked the inherent love I had for dance. Gradually the erosion of both my confidence and my energy made me accept the painful reality that I could no longer sustain a career.

C O D A

Lucia Chase and Oliver Smith
Invite You to Celebrate
American Ballet Theatre's 35th Anniversary
January 11, 1975, at 8 P.M.

The invitation announced that Lucia, Agnes de Mille, André Eglevsky, Maria Karnilova, Nora Kaye, John Kriza, Hugh Laing, Jerome Robbins, and Antony Tudor would appear, among other stars, in the gala. Donald Saddler, who had been my regular cavalier in *Princess Aurora*, would direct the program.

Moved at the idea of what promised to be an extraordinary evening, I wrote away at once for tickets for Victor and myself and Tony and Niko. Early one morning several days later, I answered the phone. After all these years, it was Tudor. Just a brief exchange— "Hello. How are you?"—and he came right to the point. He asked me to add my "casually wanton" entrance in *Pillar of Fire* to the gala.

"I'm too old to be a young Lover in Experience." I laughed.

"Then how about doing your entrance with Hugh in *Romeo and Juliet?*" he persisted. We were now talking about a passage in the ballet that lasted only a minute and a half.

"I think I can handle that," I said, delighted.

"Good. You remember it of course," Tudor went on offhandedly, certain that there was no chance I might have forgotten a step after thirty-two years. "But we'll have an hour to rehearse just to make sure."

I think I was more thrilled at the thought of seeing many of my old friends again than of performing. I was especially anxious to see Irina Baronova, with whom I'd corresponded for years. Irina had left Ballet Theatre in 1943. After a month of what she called "slavery," dancing at Radio City Music Hall, she took up acting in a summer-stock production of *Dark Eyes*, whose cast also included Genia Delarova. While appearing on Broadway as the Ballerina in the musical *Follow the Girls* with Jackie Gleason, Irina's marriage to Gerry Sevastianov came to an end. She then went to South America as a guest artist of the Monte Carlo Ballet Russe. Later, she toured as a guest with de Basil's company in Cuba. After the war Irina appeared in England as an actress again in *Dark Eyes* on the stage and in the films *A Bullet in the Ballet* and *Train of Events*. She retired in 1949 when she married Cecil Tennant, a distinguished English producer, and had three children, two daughters and a son. Tennant was killed in an automobile accident in 1967, and three years later, Irina resumed her life with Gerry, who had lost his second wife.

We had last seen them in April 1974, in a clinic in Montreux where Gerry was a patient. He was alarmingly weak and pale, but he reminisced with us, laughing and joking about the old days, trouping across America with the Ballet Russe. Late in June, Irina cabled us that he had died.

Lucia and Tudor knew that an appearance by Irina would add a special excitement to the anniversary gala. She agreed to appear, but wrote insisting that she didn't feel able to cope with any social engagements during her four-day stay with us. Feeling that her spirits could use a boost, I decided to ignore her request for privacy and began to invite Ballet Theatre veterans to a party in her honor.

On January 6, 1975, I walked into the American Ballet Theatre school to rehearse, feeling as much at home in the large studio as if I'd never been away. Laing, Tudor, and I hugged each other affectionately, then got down to business. The music drew out the memory in our bodies. In minutes steps that had lain dormant for years resurfaced. Within the hour we rehearsed the nuances and timing of our short entrance to our satisfaction.

Just as we finished working, Natalia Makarova entered the studio, carrying an enormous bag bulging with pointe shoes. Enrique Martinez, one of the company's regisseurs, introduced us, and I sat down to watch her rehearse the *Don Quixote* pas de deux with Fernando Bujones. Makarova's dancing took my breath away. She worked full out with fiery intensity, yet so silently that at times I doubted her feet were touching the floor. Her technique was superb. Even when she bounded in fast leaps, her wrists and the muscles of her neck remained totally relaxed. Bujones devoured the whole space in the studio in three magnificent jetés and, at one point, lifted Makarova into a pose over his head, supporting her whole body, in midair, with just one hand.

The moment they paused for a rest, Makarova lit a cigarette. "You're smoking so much," I couldn't help saying after she lit her third in a row.

"I do all time," she said with a puff and a little shrug. "Tobacco here better dan Russia."

Wandering in again, Tudor took one look at me and said, with some surprise, "What, are you still here?"

"I'm not leaving unless I'm thrown out," I answered. "I haven't seen dancing like this for years."

I followed Tudor to another studio where he, Martine van Hamel, and Michael Denard rehearsed *Jardin aux Lilas*. Watching Martine and Michael as the desperate, repressed lovers having to separate because of conventional Edwardian morality, I realized how Tudor's masterful ballet retains, after forty years, an indelible poignancy.

After the *Jardin aux Lilas* rehearsal, Roland Petit, who had just arrived from Paris, took over the studio to work on *Le Jeune Homme et la Mort*. As the bed, chair, and table of the ballet's set were being placed, Mikhail Baryshnikov walked in. I had never seen this Russian, considered the greatest male dancer in the world, and I tried not to stare as he sat silently waiting. He was wearing tan jeans, and his arms were folded over his pale, bare chest, the expression on his face almost melancholy. But when Bach's *Passacaglia* began, his entire being changed. Catapulted into space by the music, he leaped to the top of the table, landing perfectly on one foot. Without effort or preparation, seconds later he fused classical steps with fantastic acrobatic ones, one minute jumping on the back of the chair and tilting it with his feet to the floor by only shifting his weight, and, moments later, circling the room in huge jumps with his head bent to his powerful chest, his legs folded sharply under his soaring body. He was the greatest dancer *I* had ever seen. When not dancing, his manner was humble and restrained as he listened intently to every word Petit had to say.

I had not laid eyes on Pat Dolin for years, but when he walked in to coach Makarova in his *Pas de Quatre*, we greeted with great hugs and kisses. "Come and watch," he said, and I didn't have to be asked twice. I followed him into a smaller studio. By then, Makarova had been rehearsing on pointe for nearly four hours. But without a hint of fatigue, she held the many long balances in arabesque of the Taglioni variation as securely as if a partner were supporting her. If even the most minute angle of a position did not satisfy her, she would stop. "I do again," she'd say quietly to the pianist. For a full hour, she and Dolin worked patiently, lapsing into Russian now and then, until she felt close to her ideal.

It was dark when I finally left the school. On my way home in a taxi, my mind swarmed with impressions of what I had seen and with thoughts of the great progress ballet had made since my dancing days. So many things had changed.

Dancers now live a relatively organized life. They have unions and many have agents and business managers. Thirty years before, we had consoled ourselves with spiritual or artistic rather than financial reward. At last the scales are coming into balance. After they buy their tights, dancers have something to offer their landlords besides a winning smile. Wages are fairer. First-year corps dancers now receive $225 per week for rehearsal and performance—a far cry from my starting salary of $25 per week—and second-year corps dancers, $275 weekly, more than ten times what I had earned. Ironically, with much more money than we ever had to spend on food, they seem to eat less, since they are generally much, much thinner than we ever were.

They do not tour night after night, town after town, as we did, but jet lag from guest appearances has replaced our bus and train fatigue. Since jet planes make foreign engagements readily accessible, the dancers, by necessity, are more highly conscious of the strain that air travel places on their bodies. Dancing more often at home, as with the New York City Ballet's three-month winter season and two-month spring season at the New York State Theatre, gives them the chance we never had to conserve energy—and consequently to develop a fundamental strength and more of an artistic and emotional security than we had known.

America's dancers are members of a large, well-established dance community that links Australia to London, New York to Tokyo. Even though the great Russian émigrés of today have permanent homes, they fly off to dance wherever they are invited. They are first-class citizens of the world. Yet they are goaded by an almost tangible awareness of the brevity of their performing lives, a thought that had rarely entered our minds. In eleven months of touring, dancing sometimes seven days a week, we had little time to think about whether we would still be dancing in twenty years. Besides, in de Basil's company, nearly half of our dancers were almost a generation older than the others, giving us a sense of continuity. Finally, there were roles in most of the ballets in the repertoire for all of them. Today it seems the performers are much closer in age, and character roles, which suited older dancers, are given much less attention. Consequently, the feeling must be that a company holds little for dancers after a certain age, and they must dance as much as they can, while they can.

When I was with the Ballet Russe and Ballet Theatre, dancers just never thought of *not* dancing a performance, unless a bone was broken or a fever reached 102. We were far less aware of the strain of *dancing* than we were of the strain of *touring*. Now the technical demands of the ballet repertoire are so great that dancers must take the greatest possible care of their bodies. And those bodies perform technically as ours had never done. They are immeasurably stronger. That afternoon I saw Baryshnikov jump in the air in positions that my generation wouldn't have dreamed of.

Perhaps because of an ever greater emphasis on technique, there are now more abstract ballets, where a dancer is asked to enter into the music and choreography but not into a specific character. In abstract ballets the body and the motion are all. It is possible that the rise of impressionism and abstract-expressionism in painting has altered all the arts, including the dance, and there is less need for variety and elaborateness in the décor and librettos.

Yet, for me, something is lost if a dancer is not required to identify with specific types of characters in specific places and times. A tradition that came down to de Basil's company from Diaghilev's was our habitual visits to the museums of the cities we danced in. There, viewing masterworks of arts, we could assimilate qualities of color and movement, visual clues to a feeling, a desired appearance for ballets such as *L'Après-midi d'un Faune*, *Scuolo di Ballo*, *Francesca da Rimini*, or *Le Tricorne*. In performance, hearing the music, bearing in mind the images we had absorbed together with the choreographer's intent, we could blend motion with emotion—and enter into the atmosphere of sensuality and violence in an Oriental harem, or the baroque gaiety of a carnival in Venice. With repeated performances dancers developed a sense of belonging to a special place and time with every fiber of their being.

With fewer and fewer story ballets in the current repertoire, that sense of emotional involvement has become more and more elusive. The recent mood in society and in all the arts seems to be a creeping cynicism; expression is less rhapsodic, ecstatic, and passionate—except in great dancing. Yet, even in dance, amidst all the exuberance, dynamism, and lyricism, a certain kind of joy is missing. In de Basil's company the Russians especially conveyed a tangible sense of pleasure in dancing. You could see *and* feel that they adored not so much the fact that they were performing but the fact that they were *dancing*. They were unabashedly sentimental about their art.

But today, with notable exceptions, sentiment seems to be out, which makes dancing somehow less joyous, often missing a certain kind of *life*. This is apparent in dramatic or story ballets, where most dancers *cannot* pantomime. They relate most readily to technique, and, unless they are protected by an almost slavish dedication to the music and the choreography, they become self-conscious almost to the point of embarrassment. They cannot convey their inner, personal romanticism. Their bodies seem unable to say "I love you."

This growing disparity between a technical and an emotional approach to the art can have many sources. The technique, once acquired, is merely the tool. Perhaps a lack of direction is responsible for not shaking young dancers from their self-consciousness. In crowd scenes, for example, most dancers instinctively form a semicircle around the periphery of the stage, freeze, and gape at the central action. There is, I suppose, little or no time to compose scenes the way Fokine did, making movement true to character, providing a sense of environment. I am not sure if this is because the dancers are not told what to do, or because they simply cannot enter into the spirit of the work, which requires total belief.

I do know that there is less rehearsal time for imbuing dancers with the aura of a work, because every hour the atmosphere is shattered by the announcement that union regulations dictate a ten-minute break. After the break the dancers, to say nothing of the choreographer, must recapture the concentration and the creative mood necessary to produce great work. Without even noticing, we often worked long past lunchtime in a surge of Fokine's or Massine's creativity. Ironically, the very thing that was meant to lessen certain hardships in a dancer's life has robbed it of a great deal of the spontaneity, the deep involvement, the spirit, that produces art.

But watching Baryshnikov in rehearsal, I was thrilled to see that these two elements of dance, passionate belief and technique, could be brilliantly merged—which brought to mind the similar quality of being possessed by ecstatic joy in the dancing of such great dancers as Natalia Makarova, Patricia McBride, Gelsey Kirkland, Martine van Hamel, and Maya Plisetskaya.

Yet, for all the differences between then and now, the work is the same. Today's dancers take daily classes and rehearse and practice, watch and learn with the same silent dedication we developed. They dress in blue jeans instead of Lerner dresses; they warm up in plastic or rubber sweatpants as well as woolen legwarmers. Outside the classroom, neighborhoods in which I had once lived are now wholly unrecognizable. But in the studio there are the barre and the mirror. The process of learning and the daily sweat and effort will never change.

Several weeks earlier, our friend Shirley Bernstein, who represents Gelsey Kirkland, had asked me to help the young ballerina with her makeup. Gelsey and I met in her dressing room at the City Center, a small room overflowing as ever with practice clothes, damp sweaters, tutus, and satin slippers, but minus mothers. She was in exactly the same predicament I had been in forty years earlier. No one had taught her how to make up. Holding her small, lovely head between my hands, I showed her how shadow, smoothed on in a particular way, could diminish the childlike contours of her cheeks and delineate the shape of her nose. She was surprised when I painted a dot of moist rouge in the inside corner of each eye. Leaning closer to the mirror to examine what I had done, she asked, "What does *that* do?"

"It makes your eyes look brighter," I told her.

I found her curiosity touching and was struck once again by the marvelous continuity of ballet tradition. What I had learned in the dressing room from someone who had learned it from Tchernicheva, I now showed to Gelsey. I saw that my place as part of a long chain of dancers had been a wonderful accident. Chance had forged many links of my career. The chance to see the Diaghilev ballet in Monte Carlo had led to Bertelin, to Toumanova at the Trocadéro, to Bolm, and to Berenice. Berenice directed me to the colonel, where I met Gerry Sevastianov. Gerry took me into Ballet Theatre, where I met Nora. Nora led me to Agnes; *Venus* to *On the Town*. Perhaps chance had also brought Gelsey and me together in her dressing room. As we sat side by side, gazing into her makeup mirror, I felt as if a timeless tradition merged in our two faces.

The past again caught up to the present less than twenty-four hours before the orchestra rehearsal for the gala, when Victor and I went to meet Irina at the airport. She was elegant and radiant as ever; only the expression in her eyes revealed the cares she had borne in recent years. We chattered like schoolgirls all the way home and far into the night. But the long flight and her great excitement at being back in New York after twenty-three years was tiring her. In spite of her protests we ordered her to bed.

The rehearsal had already begun when we entered the darkened City Center auditorium the following afternoon. Oliver Smith sat directing light cues, but when he saw Irina for the first time since 1945, he rushed through the orchestra seats to embrace her. We turned and welcomed Nora, who had just arrived from Hollywood with her husband, Herbert Ross, and then spread our arms wider to include John Kriza, who hurried to us from the back of the theatre.

Onstage, Agnes as the Fanatical One and Yurek Lazowsky as the Devil rehearsed *Three Virgins and a Devil*. Sharing the scene were Sallie Wilson, who would take on the dancing part for Agnes, Ruth Mayer in Maria Karnilova's role, Hilda Morales in Annabelle Lyon's, and William Carter in Jerry Robbins's. I had not seen Lazowsky in thirty-five years, and there he was, leering wickedly at the virgins, exactly as I remembered him.

As quickly as possible after my rehearsal with Hugh, I introduced Irina to Makarova, and they immediately began to whisper in Russian. Leaving them to get acquainted, I turned back to the stage and saw my first crush, André Eglevsky, Igor Youskevitch, Scott Douglas, and Gayle Young partnering Cynthia Gregory in the Rose Adagio from *The Sleeping Beauty*. With a turn of my head, I could see Irina, a regal and joyous Princess Aurora from three decades earlier. Looking back, there was the statuesque Gregory, bringing the role to life as if it were being danced for the first time.

We whispered hellos to Harold Lang, also fresh off the plane from California, and then gathered in the foyer to record a message to Alicia Alonso, who unfortunately could not make the trip from Cuba. My party for Irina was due to start in a few hours, but the jazzy blare signalling the opening of Bernstein's *Fancy Free* was irresistible, and we dashed back into the theatre, where Terry Orr, Buddy Balough, and Bujones were romping exuberantly across the stage.

Irina and I had just enough time to powder our noses at home before the guests began to arrive from the theatre. Many were still in rehearsal clothes. Irina reminisced in a corner with Delarova and Danilova, proudly showing pictures of her three grown children and a granddaughter whom her Russian friends had never seen. Agnes and Tudor curled up in an intense tête-à-tête by the fireplace. Hugh, Miriam Golden, David Nillo, and Johnny Kriza shouted warm hellos to Nora and Herb Ross as they walked in the door. Rushing in some time later, with his arms tangled in his overcoat as he tried to take it off, Jerry Robbins simply demanded, "Where *is* she?" I took him straight to Irina. They held each other closely, barely able to speak.

Amidst the babble of news and recollections among Lucia, Eugene Loring, Scott Douglas, Dolin, John Taras, Youskevitch, and the others came the loud announcement that dinner was ready. True to form, the dancers lunged for the food. Sprawled on the floor, we ate and talked. Between bites we laughed at Laing's impromptu imitation of a ballerina dancing serenely, oblivious to her partner's wig caught accidentally on the back of her tutu. Niko and Tony sat back and watched with bemusement at what was, essentially, excited children at play.

What emerged, in the more serious moments, was the fact that through the years we had all gone different ways. Many of us had stopped dancing altogether. Maria Karnilova is now a Tony Award–winning actress. Youskevitch, Lazowsky, and Loring head dance departments at universities. Danilova is a direct link between the Maryinsky School tradition of her youth and the students at the School of American Ballet. In 1960, while driving through Europe with her new husband, Herb Ross, Nora had thrown all her pointe shoes out a car window into the Black Forest and never danced again. Now she is a film producer, with perhaps her most famous contribution to the dance world being the unforgettable *The Turning Point*. Of course Jerry went on, after *Fancy Free* and *On the Town*, to more ballets, more musicals, and films, and is indisputably one of the greatest choreographers in the world. Great distances and different livelihoods may separate us, but the warmth of affection and a common past bind us together.

Around midnight the crowd began to thin out. There were lots of hugs and kisses and shouts of "See you onstage!" Before going to bed, we reminisced a bit more and, in her lace-trimmed nightgown, Irina danced the Prelude from *Les Sylphides* exactly as Fokine had taught it to her. Despite the years her long, beautiful, lyrical line was still there. As she moved, I could see Fokine dancing, too, in his rumpled clothes. I could hear him telling us never even to move in that ballet until we were inspired by some image of nature. Irina's slim body could itself have been that kind of breathing natural beauty he had envisioned.

On January 11, the night of the gala, I climbed the stairs to the gallery of City Center with Victor, the boys, and their girlfriends. I wore an apricot silk evening gown and a short-sleeved brown velvet coat trimmed in fur, which I hoped would evoke the Renaissance style of *Romeo*. There was an aura of electric anticipation throughout the crowded theatre. Lucia and Oliver Smith walked down the aisle to their seats. The audience rose as one to give them a rousing ovation.

The evening began with the Nocturne from *Les Sylphides*, danced by Karena Brock, Hilda Morales, Marianna Tcherkassky and John Prinz, followed by Eleanor d'Antuono and Ted Kivitt in the *Don Quixote* pas de deux.

Next, the three sailors in *Fancy Free* bounded onstage. Each in his turn swaggered to the wings and held out his hand to bring out the originator of his role, Harold Lang, Johnny Kriza, and Jerry Robbins, all looking fit and trim in their evening clothes. Beaming, they bowed to their young successors and acknowledged the deafening hurrahs and cheers that welcomed them. Cynthia Gregory came next, with her retinue of famous cavaliers in the Rose Adagio, then de Mille's *Three Virgins and a Devil*, followed by Makarova and Ivan Nagy, hypnotically serene in the pas de deux from Kenneth MacMillan's *Concerto*. One of ABT's most popular hits, Alvin Ailey's *The River*, with the great Duke Ellington's jazz score, brought the first half of the program to a close.

During the intermission I pushed my way through the packed lobby to get backstage. Heaps of flowers filled the narrow passageway near the stage. Dancers were everywhere, in the corridors and in the wings, some in evening clothes, others in costume or their dressing gowns. The young ones jumped and stretched in front of a large mirror, while their older colleagues stood out of the way, against the walls, whispering excitedly. The performers ran for a last step in the rosin box, while they strained to hear what Agnes de Mille was saying in front of the curtain.

She spoke with emotion, and with her famous wit, about the company's long history. Lucia gratefully accepted New York City's highest cultural award, the Handel Medallion, from Angier Biddle Duke, just before the dancing resumed.

The opening of *Etudes* began the second half of the program. Knowing that Hugh and I were next as I watched a radiant Marianna Tcherkassky and Fernando Bujones in the *Nutcracker* pas de deux, I began to feel that inevitable surge of stage fright. I'd feel better, I thought, if I knew my feet could touch the floor, so I stooped over to take off my high-heeled shoes. "I'll hold them for you," said a young dancer. Grateful for the offer, I handed them to her with a smile and felt less nervous already.

In my stockinged feet I took my place with Hugh behind a small curtain. Tudor was waiting there calmly to give the stagehands the same directions he had first uttered at the premiere of *Romeo and Juliet* in 1943. Another wave of stage fright swept through me in the darkness, but when I heard the familiar Delius music, I lost my fear. For a few short minutes Laing and I danced. Time had stopped. I couldn't believe that thirty-two years had passed since I first looked into his eyes in that brief pas de deux.

Retreating back to the present through the curtain after we danced, I saw Erik Bruhn warming up in the shadows. Impulsively we embraced, though we barely knew each other. Thunderous applause greeted the swift, clean jumps and electrifying turns with which he began *Miss Julie*. His dancing with Sallie Wilson and Cynthia Gregory so inflamed the audience that he was literally pushed onstage to take several unplanned solo bows.

The whirlwind pace never let up. Though the dancers tripped over electrical cables and the veterans filled the narrow space near the wings, Jerry Rice, ABT's stage manager, remained calm throughout the confusion. While Bruhn, the great classical dancer of one generation, received his ovation, Baryshnikov, the rising star of another generation, pranced and bent and jumped in his plastic practice pants. Even with this almost grotesque addition to his costume for *Le Corsaire*, every position he took, on the ground or in the air, was perfect. Minutes later, his perfection was matched by Gelsey Kirkland's flawless performance, as together they dazzled the audience with their pas de deux.

While cries of "Bravo!" filled the house, Jerry Robbins directed the stagehands in positioning the front stoop for *Pillar of Fire*. Nora took her place, and the opening bars of Schönberg's *Verklärte Nacht* stilled the prolonged applause. Jerry and I held each other tightly as we watched Nora perform the same eloquent gestures that had moved us to tears in 1942. Lucia made her stately entrance as the Eldest Sister with the young Elizabeth Ashton at her side as the flirtatious adolescent. Then Hugh entered, glanced at Nora lasciviously, and started to remove his coat. His look and gesture sent a current of tension through the audience. Spellbound, we watched Tudor and Nora run towards each other with outstretched arms, only to be separated by a callous gesture from the Youngest Sister. Four minutes later, the curtain fell on the haunting image of Nora, seated again, moving her head slowly, despairingly, from side to side. Leonard Bernstein rushed backstage, unable to speak, to lay his head on Nora's breast.

Nagy and Makarova returned to knock out the audience with the *Spring Waters* pas de deux, and the program ended with the entire company in an explosive performance of the Finale of Harald Lander's *Etudes*.

Before the final curtain we veterans had agreed that, after bowing ourselves and at a signal from Tudor, we would lead the young dancers to the front of the stage and retire to the rear. But after the "historic cortege" including Robbins, Lang, Kriza, Bernstein, Chase, de Mille, Dolin, Baronova, Tudor, Kaye, Laing, myself, Karen Conrad, Leon Danielian, Lazowsky, Youskevitch, Don Saddler, Eugene Loring, Scott Douglas, Miriam Golden, Michael Lland and David Nillo, the general excitement of the evening erupted into a kind of frenzy. As we and the young dancers took our bows, the plan and form vanished. The generations embraced. The audience stood.

After my bow with Lazowsky, I stood to the side with Irina for a while. Trembling with joy, I was in that rare state when powerful elements of the past and present merge. Wherever I looked onstage, there were those with whom I had shared so much—youth, energy, ambition. But above all there was the work, devotion to the hard, precious work that aims always towards perfection.

INDEX

A NOTE ON THE TYPE

The text of this book was set on the Linotype in Fairfield, the
first typeface from the hand of the distinguished American
artist and engraver Rudolph Ruzicka. In its structure Fairfield
displays the sober and sane qualities of a master craftsman
whose talent was long dedicated to clarity. It is this trait that
accounts for the trim grace and virility, the spirited design, and
sensitive balance of this original face, first issued in 1940.
Rudolph Ruzicka was born in Bohemia in 1883 and came
to America in 1894. He set up his own shop devoted to wood
engraving and printing in New York in 1913, after a varied
career as a wood engraver, in photo-engraving and bank-note
printing plants, as an art director and a freelance artist. Mr.
Ruzicka died at Hanover, New Hampshire, in 1978. He had
designed and illustrated many books and had created a
considerable list of individual prints—wood engravings, line
engravings on copper, aquatints.

"Sono," the display face used on the title page and for each
chapter opening, was created especially for this book by
Margaret Wagner, who named it in honor of the author.

Composed by
Maryland Linotype Composition Co., Inc.,
Baltimore, Maryland.
Printed and bound by
American Book–Stratford Press,
Saddle Brook, New Jersey.
Book design by Margaret Wagner